Donated by
The Public Interest Institute
to The Heartland Institute
2016

THE DELICATE BALANCE
FEDERALISM, INTERSTATE COMMERCE, AND ECONOMIC FREEDOM IN THE TECHNOLOGICAL AGE

By
Adam D. Thierer

PROPERTY OF
PUBLIC INTEREST
INSTITUTE

JAN 2 2 1999

Cover photos copyright © 1998 by PhotoDisc, Inc.

ISBN 0–89195–074–5
Copyright © 1999 by The Heritage Foundation
214 Massachusetts Avenue, N.E.
Washington, D.C. 20002
1-202-546-4400
www.heritage.org

"Every journey to a forbidden end begins with the first step; and the danger of such a step by the federal government in the direction of taking over the powers of the states is that the end of the journey may find the states so despoiled of their powers, or—what may amount to the same thing—so relieved of the responsibilities which possession of the powers necessarily enjoins, as to reduce them to little more than geographical subdivisions of the national domain. It is safe to say that if, when the Constitution was under consideration, it had been thought that any such danger lurked behind its plain words, it would never have been ratified."

Justice George Sutherland, 1936
in *Carter v. Carter Coal Co.*

TABLE OF CONTENTS

FOREWORD vii

PREFACE AND ACKNOWLEDGMENTS ix

CHAPTER 1
Commercial Federalism
at the Dawn of the 21st Century 1
    A Conflict of Federalism Visions 2
    The Textualist Divide 5
    Steps Toward a Federalism Revival 13

CHAPTER 2
The Founders' Vision of
Constitutional Federalism 15
    Why the Founders Abandoned the
        Articles of Confederation 15
    The Framers' Constitutional Framework 21

CHAPTER 3
The Jurisprudence of American
Commercial Federalism 25
    The 19th Century Supreme Court
        and the Commerce Power 25
    Reconstruction, the Fourteenth
        Amendment, and Substantive Due Process 28
    The Corrupting Influence of the New Deal 34
    The Beginnings of a Federalism Backlash 40

CHAPTER 4
Competing Theories of Federalism 47
    The Broad Constructionist Vision 48
    The Textualist Vision 51
    State Sovereignty Textualism 54
    Libertarian Textualism 63
    Synthesizing the Textualist Schools of Thought 76

CHAPTER 5
New Federalism Tensions and a Framework
for the Future 81
   A Framework for Dealing with Federalism
      Disputes Involving Interstate Commerce
      and Economic Liberty 84
   Tier 1 Test: Strict Textual Analysis 85
   Tier 2 Test: Practical Interpretory
      Considerations Regarding Interstate Commerce 98
   What Constitutes Interstate Commerce
      in the Technological Age? 105

CHAPTER 6
Practical Steps Toward a Revival of Federalism . . . 119
   Restoring the Founders' Vision:
      Is a Constitutional Convention Necessary? 120
   Other Ways to Help Determine Jurisdictional
      Responsibility or Ease Federalism Tensions 125

CHAPTER 7
Federalism's Future 145

APPENDIX I
The Articles of Confederation. 149

APPENDIX II
The Constitution of the United States. 157

APPENDIX III
Chronology and Summary of Important
Supreme Court Cases Dealing with Federalism,
Interstate Commerce, and Economic Liberty 179

APPENDIX IV
Executive Order 12612 on "Federalism" 203

APPENDIX V
Executive Order 13083 on "Federalism" 209

SELECTED BIBLIOGRAPHY 215

INDEX 227

FOREWORD

BY THE HONORABLE GEORGE ALLEN
FORMER GOVERNOR, COMMONWEALTH OF VIRGINIA

Few founding principles are as important as federalism to safeguarding our birthright as Americans to liberty and self-determination. The years during which I was privileged to serve as the governor of Virginia reinforced my belief that a return to the Founding Fathers' original balance of constitutional powers is essential to protecting that freedom. While the Founders *did* intend for the national government to exercise some important powers, these powers were intentionally limited in number and scope. Most powers were intended to be reserved to the states or, more important, the American people—a vision made explicit in the Tenth Amendment.

Regrettably, however, this past century has not been kind to the Founders' original design. A long string of decisions by Congress and the courts have steadily reversed the equation and eroded our freedoms. Centralized power and one-size-fits-all solutions from distant bureaucrats contribute to the sense of powerlessness and frustration among Americans who find their lives controlled by a government that is out of reach and out of touch. At best, politicians in Washington have paid mere lip service to federalism; at worst, they have played an active role in undermining its foundations. Little thought has been given to how to reverse this equation, restore our federalist foundations, and return power to the states and the people.

The sad fact is that, since the time of the New Deal, the discussions in our nation's capital regarding the proper division of political power and responsibility have focused on how federal agencies and officials should divide power among themselves. The states, to the extent that they have been considered in the larger constitutional scheme of things at all, are viewed by Washington as mere administrative offices of the federal government, subservient to the federal government's edicts and directives on a stunning array of social, economic, and political matters.

The Founders' original framework of federalism, as constructed within the Constitution and secured by the Tenth Amendment, has fallen out of favor with Washington policymakers, federal judges, and many of the academic elites who advise them. To this crowd, the Tenth Amendment and federalism as a principle are viewed as mere relics of the nation's political past, with little or no role to play in the daily functions of our Republic as we approach the 21st century.

Adam Thierer's exciting new book, *The Delicate Balance: Federalism, Interstate Commerce, and Economic Freedom in the Technological Age*, vigorously challenges these mistaken notions. With a passion and flair not usually associated with modern volumes on the subject of federalism, Adam Thierer calls upon policymakers, jurists, and the public at large to rediscover and celebrate the Framers' "enduring work of political art" and "most important contribution to modern civilization," recognizing it as "the bulwark of liberty that it was intended to be."

Although our modern industries, means of communication, and technologies could not have been specifically envisioned at our nation's founding, Thierer argues persuasively that the Framers' original model of federalism is ideally suited to addressing the post–industrial-age policy issues that America's political leaders face today. Indeed, such was the genius of our Founders that their vision and system of governance are as appropriate, helpful, and applicable to modern America as they were to colonial America.

Those of us who believe in the Constitution and the goals and principles it embodies know that the Founders' original system of governance for the United States is still the best system for the people who live in our diverse and unique culture. Federalism stopped working in this century not because it is no longer relevant but because it was abandoned by lawmakers and jurists who chafed at its constraints. The result is a seemingly boundless, centralized government in which bureaucratic whim seems to have replaced the rule of law. Clearly, this centralization of decisions and powers was not the Framers' original intention.

It is high time our nation's political leaders rediscovered and embraced the original guiding vision of a federal republic that puts the people and their liberty first. A reinvigoration of federalism will require a concerted effort by leaders at all levels of government to work together, along with the courts, academia, the media, and the public at large, to build a new respect for and understanding of the unique role federalism was meant to play in our polity.

Adam Thierer's thoughtful book will be viewed as a catalyst of that vital movement and will provide the guideposts for this long-overdue positive revolution. While one may not agree with all prescriptions expressed by the author, his book is certain to spark a lively, healthy debate and spawn constructive ideas.

Preface and Acknowledgments

Since the New Deal, there appears to have been little political interest in revisiting and seriously debating the underlying economic, legal, philosophical, and constitutional origins and effects of America's federalist system of governance. Many politicians, interest groups, academics, legal scholars, and even judges have somewhat casually accepted the growth of the national government relative to that of the states and localities. Some even suggest that the expansion of federal authority is a natural outgrowth of an expanding, changing nation and therefore should be accepted as the norm. In other words, federalism need no longer be the subject of much serious intellectual discourse or debate.

But for a brief moment in the summer of 1998, all that changed.

It started on May 14, 1998, when President Bill Clinton signed Executive Order 13083 on "Federalism." President Clinton's proclamation on federalism began by reiterating the benefits of the Founders' federalist system of government, including checks and balances, limited national powers, and the supremacy of state and local control in most political matters. For example, E.O. 13083 noted that:

> Federalism reflects the principle that dividing power between the Federal Government and the States serves to protect individual liberty. Preserving State authority provides an essential balance to the power of the Federal Government.... Effective public policy is often achieved when there is competition among the several States.... Policies of the Federal Government should recognize the responsibility of—and should encourage opportunities for—States, local governments, private associations, neighborhoods, families, and individuals to achieve personal, social, environmental, and economic objectives through cooperative effort.[1]

But these noble sentiments proved to be little more than lip service to the Founders, since the Clinton order went on to outline a broad set of new "Federalism Policymaking Criteria." These criteria would allow, and even encourage, federal bureaucracies and regulatory agencies under the President's control to intervene in the affairs of the states or pass uniform, pre-emptive federal rules under a remarkable variety of circumstances.

For example, the Clinton executive order argued that federal action could be justified "When decentralization increases the costs of government thus imposing additional burdens on the taxpayer"; "When States would be reluctant to impose necessary regulations because of fears that regulated business activity will relocate to other states"; "When placing regulatory authority at the State or local level would undermine regulatory goals because high costs or demands for specialized expertise will effectively place the regulatory matter beyond the resources of State authorities"; or "When the matter relates to Federally owned or managed property or natural resources, trust obligations, or international obligations."[2]

Perhaps more important, the Clinton executive order proposed the revocation of an older executive order on federalism issued by President Ronald Reagan. President Reagan's Executive Order 12612, implemented in October 1987, also outlined a set of Federalism Policymaking Criteria for federal agencies. In contrast to President Clinton's effort in E.O. 13083, however, President Reagan's followed through on its promise to adhere to constitutional first principles.

Unlike the Clinton order, the Reagan order noted the importance of the Tenth Amendment in preserving the proper constitutional balance of powers and reiterated Thomas Jefferson's belief that the states are "the most competent administrations for our domestic concerns and the surest bulwarks against antirepublican tendencies."[3] Despite borrowing much of the sound language from President Reagan's earlier document, President Clinton chose to drop the quote from Jefferson, and also abandoned any mention of the Tenth Amendment's significance within the Founders' constitutional framework.

Footnotes:
1. President William J. Clinton, Executive Order No. 13083, "Federalism," May 14, 1998, *Federal Register*, Vol. 63, No. 96 (May 19, 1998), pp. 27651–27655. The text is presented in Appendix V of this volume.
2. *Ibid.*
3. Quoted in President Ronald Reagan, Executive Order No. 12612, "Federalism," October 26, 1987, *Federal Register*, Vol. 52, No. 210 (October 30, 1987), pp. 41685–41688. The text is presented in Appendix IV of this volume.

Preface and Acknowledgments

Furthermore, the Reagan order crafted very narrow grounds for federal pre-emption of the states. It demanded that maximum latitude be provided to the individual states and localities and that "Federal action limiting the policymaking discretion of the States should be taken only where constitutional authority for the action is clear and certain and the national activity is necessitated by the presence of a problem of national scope...."[4]

Thus, President Clinton's executive order on federalism stands in stark contrast to President Reagan's executive order on the same subject. Within these two documents are two distinct visions of federalism laid bare for the world to see. President Reagan's vision stressed, above all, adherence to the original intentions of the Founders and the language of the Constitution regarding limited, enumerated national powers, and a healthy respect for the benefits of state and local autonomy. President Clinton, on the other hand, argued that the Reagan vision must be revoked in favor of a new federalism paradigm that calls for greater constitutional malleability and acceptance of the frequent need for federal intervention to alleviate the nation's ills.

At first, President Clinton's federalism manifesto did not generate much media or public attention; the White House quietly released the new executive order while Clinton was out of the country. But by mid-summer of 1998, a growing number of Capitol Hill lawmakers and state and local officials and organizations had become aware of the Clinton order. Concerned about its potential effects, they began asking the Administration to explain its new thinking on federalism.

These concerns culminated in a hearing on July 28, 1998, before the House Government Reform and Oversight Committee's Subcommittee on Regulatory Affairs during which the Clinton Administration was castigated uniformly for the decision to abandon the fairly non-controversial Reagan executive order and replace it with new federalism guidelines that seemingly granted the federal government unlimited policymaking authority over the states.

Several Members of Congress condemned the President's new federalism vision, and many introduced legislation to encourage or force President Clinton to revoke his executive order. For example, a sense of the Senate resolution introduced by Senator Fred Thompson which encouraged the President to revoke his order was passed unanimously in late July. Congressional dissenters were joined by representatives of respected state and local organizations, including

Footnotes:
4. *Ibid.*

The Delicate Balance

the National Governors' Association, the National Conference of State Legislators, the United States Conference of Mayors, the National League of Cities, and the National Association of Counties.

On August 5, the White House announced it would "suspend" the proposed executive order "in order to enable full and adequate consultation with State and local elected officials, their representative organizations, and other interested parties...."[5] At least temporarily, those organizations and public officials that believed the Constitution placed firm limits on the scope of federal power had won.

What makes this entire episode so surprising, however, is that such a vociferous dissent and heated backlash against the Clinton executive order developed at all. After all, in the language of his executive order, President Clinton was merely formally recognizing that through a wide variety of statutes, regulations, and judicial decisions throughout this century, the United States has gradually been adopting of a new system of political governance and organization. That system is known more commonly as unitary or centralized government.

Therefore, it remains to be seen whether the debate sparked by President Clinton's executive order represents merely a rest stop on the road to unlimited national power or instead signifies a genuine concern, collectively held by many policymakers, organizations, and average citizens, that America's original system of governance–republican federalism–has been under attack throughout this century and that a return to constitutional first principles is needed.

Regardless of the answer to that question, this episode has sparked new interest—at least for the moment—in the constitutional foundations of the American Republic and the importance of federalism within that framework. And for the purposes of this book, it serves nicely to make the case that two very distinct visions of governance exist in America.

This book will examine these conflicting visions of federalism and extend its coverage and applicability to contentious jurisdictional disputes in several different fields. Specifically, this book is the product of several years of intellectual wrangling over the interplay of high-technology industries and the American federalist structure of government. Increasingly, each industrial or technological issue that has been debated in the public forum has raised heated federalism

Footnotes:
5. William J. Clinton, "Suspension of Executive Order 13083," White House, Office of the Press Secretary, August 5, 1998.

Preface and Acknowledgments

and jurisdictional issues which often have frustrated efforts to deregulate the high-tech sectors of America's free-market economy or to keep them free from regulation in the first place.

As a firm believer in state sovereignty and a vigorous interstate marketplace, I decided to look for answers to questions for which I had found few good answers: How, for example, can the sometimes competing values of state sovereignty and interstate commerce be balanced in a way that respects the ability of citizens to engage in creative self-governance at the state or local level but also preserves and enhances America's vibrant national marketplace?

The short answer: It's not easy.

In many ways, I regard the present undertaking as a work in progress, precisely because I could not find satisfactory solutions or answers to the many questions I have posed throughout the book. One lesson that I have learned from an extensive review of federalism literature, policymaking, and jurisprudence is that the world of federalism is painted not in black and white, but rather in shades of gray. Simply put, clear-cut solutions to jurisdictional disputes and federalism questions are not always evident or even possible. Although this is arguably the case in many fields of public policy and constitutional jurisprudence, I suspect it is even more true in the field of federalism policy making.

Nonetheless, it is also my contention throughout this book that the Constitution provides a set of enduring principles to guide this difficult process and that, to the extent that any firm answers are available, they flow directly from the words and spirit that are embodied in that amazing document. In the interest of contributing to the never-ending debate over constitutional interpretation, jurisdictional jurisprudence, and federalism in general, I offer this volume and ask the reader's forgiveness if I have left more questions unanswered than resolved.

I am grateful to the many fine scholars in the corporate community, academia, and other public policy research organizations who reviewed and critiqued early drafts of this book and provided substantive comments that helped shape its conclusions. Early critiques by Roger Pilon of the Cato Institute and Gerald O'Driscoll of Citicorp were particularly helpful in focusing my thoughts on issues or concepts I had not considered. The legal analysis provided by Leonard Leo of the Federalist Society and Michael Greve of the Center for Individual Rights was likewise crucial to the effort.

I am particularly indebted to The Heritage Foundation and its staff and leaders, who have encouraged my efforts in these fields and

The Delicate Balance

given me the time and support required to undertake and complete this project. Several Heritage colleagues deserve special recognition.

Heritage Senior Fellow in Legal Studies Todd Gaziano was of particular assistance in providing critical comments on my efforts from the first day of the project. Two distinguished alumni of the Reagan Administration who now work at Heritage were also very helpful. Becky Norton Dunlop, Vice President for External Relations, and Edwin Meese III, former Attorney General and current Ronald Reagan Fellow in Public Policy at Heritage, offered valuable insights from their years on the front lines of federalism battles. Former Heritage analyst John S. Barry and current Heritage researcher Alexander F. Annett must be singled out for their willingness to offer a sounding board for many of the ideas and concepts that did (and did not) make it into the book. Their patience is appreciated, and their critical feedback was extremely helpful. In addition, I must thank my direct superiors at Heritage: Stuart Butler, Vice President for Domestic Policy Studies, and Angela Antonelli, Director of the Thomas A. Roe Institute for Economic Policy Studies, provided me with the time and intellectual support necessary to work through a project of this magnitude. I am especially grateful also to the Alex C. Walker Educational and Charitable Foundation of Pittsburgh, Pennsylvania, long-time friends and generous supporters of The Heritage Foundation. I am privileged to be the Alex C. Walker Fellow in Economic Policy at Heritage.

In conclusion, many thanks to those who polished the volume and did such a fine job of bringing the final product together. Research Department Managing Editor Janice A. Smith, Design and Publishing Coordinator Michelle Smith, Publishing Services Director Ann Klucsarits, Copy Editors Margaret D. Bonilla and William T. Poole, Manager of Graphic Design Services Thomas J. Timmons, and Senior Editor Richard Odermatt all were integral to the successful completion of this book.

In the end, of course, any mistakes or omissions within the text should be attributed solely to the author.

Adam D. Thierer
January 1999

COMMERCIAL FEDERALISM AT THE DAWN OF THE 21ST CENTURY

In his widely cited textbook *Constitutional Law*, Gerald Gunther has noted that "The scope of the national legislature's authority to reach local affairs is a characteristic, never-ending problem of our federal system. It continues to breed conflicts and to generate searches for new accommodations...."[1] The dawn of the 21st century is uncovering new commercial sectors and fresh public policy issues that exacerbate these tensions and increase the need for new resolutions to these conflicts.

The past century has witnessed the birth or successful commercial development of remarkable new technologies and industries. Among them, to name only a few: wireline and wireless telephony, satellite telecommunications and television, the electrical power industry, rail and truck transportation and shipping, the financial services and securities industry, aerospace and commercial aviation, and, most recently, the computer and interactive services industry. But the very presence of these industries and technologies on America's national economic landscape poses troubling, ongoing questions with regard to the scope of the national legislature's authority and its reach into local affairs. These industries and technologies can be extremely parochial in nature while at the same time presenting national or even international implications in their overall scope and effect.

For example, there is perhaps nothing more local (or personal) than the act of picking up a telephone to call a friend. Yet with that same telephone line, one individual can reach out to millions of other individuals or organizations worldwide through millions of phone lines, cables, or satellite hookups. The rise of integrated, interactive

Footnotes:
1. Gerald Gunther, *Constitutional Law*, 12th Ed. (Westbury, N.Y.: Foundation Press, Inc., 1991), p. 77.

The Delicate Balance

computer networks and the Internet has brought the Information Age home as well. Now the wonders of the world are but a keystroke away from the computer in the average citizen's living room.

Likewise, virtually every American has access to a constant source of electrical power in the home. Yet that electricity is not an entirely local commodity, since it travels through a complex, interlocking grid of interconnected electricity lines, often crossing state lines in the process. Finally, rising numbers of Americans are taking advantage of at-home financial services which allow personalized money, stock, and asset management. Yet such funds and assets are likely to be dispersed across the globe and must be accessed through a tightly integrated financial services network using both the communications and electrical power technologies referred to above.

Thus, what may seem local in character is at the same time national, international, or even global in scope. Because these industries and technologies possess such seemingly contradictory characteristics, their regulation has forced difficult questions and dilemmas on policymakers. Lawmakers are challenged to search for ways to accommodate and encourage the flourishing commerce and economic liberty of the Technological Age while simultaneously preserving a proper sphere for state and local sovereignty and decision-making.

But although the technologies and industries may be new, these problems are as old as the nation itself. Indeed, the Constitution of the United States of America was put in place over two centuries ago primarily because the nation's Founding Fathers felt that America's first constitution—the Articles of Confederation—failed to create and protect national harmony, specifically *commercial* harmony and economic union among the states.

Hence, although most Americans do not realize or appreciate it today, in formulating and ratifying the Constitution, the Founding Fathers put in place an extraordinary solution to these problems that is still applicable to modern-day industries and technologies which they could not possibly have envisioned.

Their timeless solution, of course, is the system of governance known as federalism.

A CONFLICT OF FEDERALISM VISIONS

Although many definitions of federalism are available, perhaps the most concise and complete definition was provided by the Domestic Policy Council Working Group on Federalism. The Working Group, convened by President Ronald Reagan in the mid-1980s,

Commercial Federalism at the Dawn of the 21st Century

sought "to develop strategies for ensuring that federal law and regulations are rooted in basic constitutional federalism principles."[2] It defined "federalism" as follows: "Federalism is a constitutionally based, structural theory of government designed to ensure political freedom and responsive, democratic government in a large and diverse society."[3]

But why did the Founders feel the need to adopt a federalist system of governance for America, and, more profoundly, is their 200-year old political system really still applicable to the dynamic industries and technologies of the modern age? These are not easy questions, and how they are answered depends on the school of thinking to which policymakers or legal scholars subscribe. Throughout this volume, two distinct visions, or paradigms, will be referred to when discussing how policymakers, academics, legal scholars, and others think about federalism issues, jurisdictional disputes, and constitutional interpretation in general.

The first vision or paradigm is *broad constructionism*. Broad constructionists are so named because they believe generally that the Constitution, if it is to be consulted at all, should be interpreted broadly by policymakers and the courts in an effort to accommodate changing political preferences and socioeconomic conditions. That is, broad constructionists view the Constitution not as a constraint on national authority, but rather as an open-ended document from which the federal government can construe numerous powers to carry out a higher "common good."

Federalism is an amorphous concept to the broad constructionists. As defined above, the more traditional view of federalism focused on the proper balance of power between levels of government, constraints on national power, and a generous sphere of autonomy for states and localities. Most broad constructionists view this concept of federalism with suspicion, if not outright contempt. They see it as a radical, outdated notion of governance that is hopelessly at odds with modern political, social, and economic realities.

Consequently, the broad constructionists have sought to redefine federalism as a system of top-down, centralized, bureaucratic administration, within which state and local governments are viewed as administrative offices or districts of the federal government. Federal officials are seen as omniscient, benevolent guardians of the American Republic. They are called upon frequently to inter-

Footnotes:
2. *The Status of Federalism in America: A Report of the Working Group on Federalism of the Domestic Policy Council*, November 1986, p. 1.
3. Ibid., p. 2.

vene in even the most trivial and parochial of human affairs, either to supplement, replicate, or replace the responsibilities and activities of state and local governments or to prevent them from acting altogether. State and local flexibility is viewed as beneficial only insofar as it is used to legislate or regulate more stringently than federal standards allow.

The second constitutional vision or paradigm that will be discussed in the book will be referred to as *textualism* or *originalism*. The textualist school is more in line with the Founders' vision for America; proponents of this vision stress adherence to the letter and spirit of the Constitution as originally written. In emphasizing the importance of original intent when discussing constitutional interpretation, textualists argue that the Constitution's specific balance of powers must be sustained and that the national government should remain one of limited, enumerated powers.

Textualists define federalism exactly as did President Reagan's Working Group on Federalism in the above statement. Textualists place a high value on decentralized decision-making and argue that state and local sovereignty will breed a healthy degree of competition between different jurisdictions. Furthermore, textualists believe that the inherent tension between these competing levels of government will protect and enhance the liberty of individual Americans by providing reciprocal checks on abuse of power.

This book will adopt a textualist approach to federalism and provide a thorough critique of the broad constructionist philosophy that continues to dominate modern policy making and constitutional jurisprudence.

It is important to note that textualist thinking is not as homogeneous as suggested here, however. In fact, important disagreements have divided the textualists into two distinct camps. One theory, typically espoused by the more conservative wing of the textualist movement, stresses the benefits of state and local autonomy, devolution of power, and political decentralization as the primary objective of the Founders' constitutional vision of federalism. The other strand of textualism has a decidedly libertarian bent, regarding the protection of interstate commerce and individual liberties in general as the preeminent goal of the Founders' federalist system.

More important, this dispute has a direct bearing on the deregulation or protection of economic liberties within several industries that will be discussed throughout this book. Thus, this divide begs for a solution or compromise.

Commercial Federalism at the Dawn of the 21st Century

THE TEXTUALIST DIVIDE

To discover the nature and effect of this internal division within the textualist camp, it helps to step back and examine how federalism issues have unfolded and been discussed in the most recent, 105th Congress.

When Republicans took control of Congress after sweeping gains in the 1994 elections, "federalism" and "devolution" quickly became two of the most popular words in Washington's political lexicon. As part of their "Contract With America,"[4] many Republican candidates had taken strong stands during their campaigns against the over-centralization of power within the federal government in Washington and had called for a return to the federalist principles upon which the nation was founded. Specifically, to justify their intention to return programs and power to the states, many of these candidates employed the language of the Tenth Amendment of the Constitution. The Tenth Amendment declares that "The powers not delegated to the United States by the Constitution, nor prohibited by it to the States, are reserved to the States respectively, or to the people."

"States' rights" became the catch-phrase most commonly associated with the new devolution movement. Supporters of devolution argued that the most appropriate way to reform the modern Leviathan was to transfer control of many federal programs or policies back to state and local governments and begin once again to limit the scope of federal powers to constitutionally defined boundaries.[5] Clearly, the textualist vision dominated the day.

Yet, four years after this landmark election, it remains unclear just what, if any, difference this resurgent federalist impulse has made.

Devolutionists note that they can point to certain successes, including welfare reform, which relegated many programs back to the states; repeal of the national 55-mph speed limit; and passage of

Footnotes:
4. Representative Newt Gingrich, Representative Dick Armey, and the House Republicans, *Contract With America* (Washington, D.C.: Times Books, Random House, 1994).
5. For a general discussion, see Douglas Seay and Robert E. Moffit, "Transferring Functions to the States," in Stuart M. Butler and Kim R. Holmes, eds., *Mandate for Leadership IV: Turning Ideas Into Actions* (Washington, D.C.: The Heritage Foundation, 1997), pp. 87–127, and Peter H. Schuck, "Introduction: Some Reflections on the Federalism Debate," in *Yale Law & Public Policy Review / Yale Journal on Regulation*, Symposium Issue, "Constructing a New Federalism: Jurisdictional Competence and Competition," Vol. 14, No. 2 (March 1–2, 1996), pp. 1–22.

the Unfunded Mandates Act of 1995, which prohibits the imposition of expensive, unfunded federal mandates on state and local governments.

Yet this limited success left untouched many long-standing national programs and policies that remain firmly entrenched at the federal level. Overall, the size and scope of the federal government have not shrunk significantly in terms of spending or regulation. As a percentage of gross domestic product (GDP), government outlays have held fairly steady since the Republicans took office. Total government outlays (or spending) as a percentage of GDP, which stood at 21.4 percent in 1994, fell only slightly, to 20.1 percent in 1997, and it is estimated that this figure will stand at 20 percent at the end of 1998. Total government receipts (or taxes) as a percentage of GDP actually have grown slightly under Republican rule, rising from 18.4 percent in 1994 to 19.8 percent in 1997.

Moreover, federal regulatory activity continues to grow or at least remains constant. The total number of pages in the *Federal Register*, in which federal regulations are published, grew slightly from 68,108 in 1994 to 68,530 in 1997. And the total number of pages in the federal government's Code of Federal Regulations grew from 134,196 in 1994 to 138,186 in 1995, although it shrank slightly to 132,121 by the end of 1996.[6]

Some critics have claimed that this same devolutionist-minded Congress actually has reversed course and ushered in a new age of federal government expansion. This charge has left some legal scholars and political pundits asking whether the Republicans' Contract With America has resulted in a "devolution revolution" or, instead, just a "devolution dilution."[7] In fact, Joshua Wolf Shenk, a reporter for *U.S. News & World Report*, has argued that when Congress adjourned for recess in late 1997, "lawmakers were pushing a wide array of legislation that would *increase* Washington's control over state and local affairs, not reduce it."[8] To support this argu-

Footnotes:
6. For up-to-date information on the severity of the federal regulatory burden, see "The Regulation Home Page" Internet site: http://www.regulation.org/keyfacts.html#Numbers. See also Angela Antonelli, "Regulation: Demanding Accountability and Common Sense," in Stuart M. Butler and Kim R. Holmes, eds., *Issues '98: The Candidate's Briefing Book* (Washington, D.C.: The Heritage Foundation, 1998), pp. 65–97.
7. See Stanford F. Schram and Carol S. Weissert, "The State of American Federalism: 1996–1997," *Publius: The Journal of Federalism*, Vol. 27, No. 2 (Spring 1997), pp. 1–31.
8. Joshua Wolf Shenk, "Washington's Counter-Devolutionaries," *U.S. News & World Report*, November 24, 1997, p. 34.

ment, Shenk cited a number of recent congressional efforts that suggest a counter-devolutionary trend, including:

- The Citizen's Access to Justice Act. This act, passed by the House of Representatives in late 1997, would make it easier for citizens to pursue compensation claims against government bodies (including state and local) that take their property. Under the Citizen's Access to Justice Act, Americans would be able to take their grievances against governments directly to federal court to seek the compensation they are entitled to under the Fifth Amendment.

- The Internet Tax Freedom Act. The Internet Tax Freedom Act, which has gained bipartisan support in both the House and the Senate, would place a moratorium on the imposition of state and local taxes on the Internet. Many states and localities argue that they will need to be able to tax electronic transactions over the Internet in order to replace their shrinking tax bases.

- Federal electricity deregulation efforts. Throughout the 105th Congress, numerous bills were introduced in both the Senate and the House to deregulate America's $200 billion-per-year electricity industry. Although the bills varied considerably in terms of approach, at the heart of each bill was an effort to tear down interstate barriers to electricity competition in order to give all Americans the right to shop for cheaper electricity nationwide. Critics charge this is a state, not federal, responsibility.

On the surface, it might seem that Shenk is indeed correct in finding that these recent congressional actions take powers away from states and localities. Yet he fails to ask the more profound question that divides many textualists: *Should states and localities be able to exercise these powers in the first place?* If Congress is acting to prevent states or localities from exercising extraterritorial jurisdiction they do not possess, or to demand that the states tear down unjustifiable barriers to interstate commerce and trade, or to require the states to respect and honor the constitutional rights of all citizens, then is not such congressional action entirely consistent with constitutional first principles?

For example, shouldn't all governments, whether federal, state, or local, be required to compensate citizens if they confiscate their private property? And do the states, in any meaningful sense, have jurisdictional authority to tax or regulate the Internet, which is global in character? Finally, since electricity is increasingly an interstate commodity, bought and sold across state boundaries, doesn't Congress have the right to demand that interstate barriers to electricity competition be dismantled?

Textualists are somewhat divided on these questions because of the schism that exists between the two camps of constitutional scholars within the textualist school. This schism is most evident when textualists consider the proper scope of federal power with regard to the free flow of interstate commerce, and ultimately how best to honor and protect the economic rights of individuals within America's federalist system.

One strand of textualist thinking—to which a large number of conservative scholars and policymakers have always subscribed—can be referred to generically as *state sovereignty textualism*. State sovereignty textualists would argue that Congress and the courts should allow the states and localities extremely generous latitude in exercising authority over most economic issues and industries. State and local experimentation will likely produce the optimal result for consumers and producers. If citizens within a given jurisdiction do not like their current arrangement, they can simply pack their bags and move elsewhere.

Stephan Calabresi, associate professor at the Northwestern University School of Law, summarizes the benefits of this viewpoint: "Jurisdictional competition...is also beneficial because it leads to the protection of liberty. If I dislike the laws of my home state enough and feel tyrannized by them enough, I can always preserve my freedom by moving to a different state with less tyrannous laws."[9] Calabresi goes on to note that, in addition to the benefits of jurisdictional competition, the other arguments in favor of giving great deference to the states include their responsiveness to local tastes and conditions; the value of experimentation; the improved quality of political decision-making and administration; and the preservation of peace and harmony through the dispersion of political power.[10]

Another textualist camp—which is attracting an increasing number of adherents within Republican circles—advocates what can be

Footnotes:
9. Stephan G. Calabresi, "A Government of Limited and Enumerated Powers: In Defense of *United States v. Lopez*," 94 *Michigan Law Review*, p. 776. Another excellent summary of the benefits of a more decentralized system can found in Jacques Leboeuf, "The Economics of Federalism and the Proper Scope of the Federal Commerce Power," *San Diego Law Review*, Vol. 31 (Summer 1994), pp. 556–566.
10. Calabresi, "A Government of Limited and Enumerated Powers," pp. 774–779.

referred to generically as *libertarian textualism*. Libertarian-minded scholars and policymakers argue that, while great deference should be given to the states in tailoring rules and programs for many of the same reasons Calabresi lists, the overarching goal of lawmakers when considering jurisdictional disputes should be the maximization of individual liberty. Liberty is maximized through the protection of citizens' constitutional rights, including their economic freedoms.

Thus, libertarian textualists reject the notion that "states' rights" are ends in and of themselves. In fact, some of these thinkers reject the notion of states' rights altogether. As Clint Bolick, vice president of the Washington, D.C.-based Institute for Justice, argues, "[T]he very notion of states' rights is oxymoronic. States don't have rights. States have powers. People have rights. And the primary purpose of federalism is to protect those rights."[11] Therefore, Bolick argues, while the states should have a sphere of sovereignty and autonomy that is free from federal intervention, Congress and the courts should not shy away from taking constitutionally permissible actions to defend the rights of individual Americans when the states violate those rights.

Thus, although it is clear that constitutional textualists generally agree that America's state and federal governments have distinct and respective constitutional powers and spheres of responsibility, they differ among themselves regarding precisely where to draw the line.

In particular, as Chapter 4 will discuss in greater detail, the textualists are somewhat at odds regarding exactly what specific sections, clauses, or even words within the Constitution mean or signify. Among some of the issues that divide textualists:

- What constitutes "interstate" commerce and whether the courts should adjudicate interstate commerce disputes when Congress has not acted;

- The scope of protection provided by "the Contract Clause";

- The meaning and applicability of the Fourteenth Amendment's "Privileges and Immunities Clause," "Due Process Clause," and "Equal Protection Clause";

- The scope of legitimate state and local "police powers" when attempting to legislate on matters of health, safety, and public morals; and

Footnotes:
11. Clint Bolick, *Grassroots Tyranny: The Limits of Federalism* (Washington, D.C.: Cato Institute, 1993), p. 17.

The Delicate Balance

- The role of judicial review and the courts in general in protecting interstate commerce and economic liberty.

Although these philosophical disputes among the textualists over constitutional interpretation and federalism jurisprudence have raged in law journals and at academic conferences for decades, the rise of a Republican Congress and Republican-dominated governorships has brought this ivory-tower debate into the public policy arena in the 1990s. Consequently, the schism between conservative and libertarian legal scholars has become a prevalent feature within many policy debates, frequently pitting political allies against each other.

As a result, a number of attempts to deregulate certain industries or liberalize certain sectors of the economy have been frustrated or put on hold while philosophical differences are debated within conservative and libertarian circles. For example, recent efforts to deregulate electricity markets, the financial services industry, insurance markets, and the Internet have all been frustrated to some degree by the rift among constitutional textualists. Ironically, however, each group argues that its vision would better ensure that the economic liberties of the American people are honored and that its paradigm, if followed, is the one which will ensure that a vigorous national marketplace is both preserved and enhanced.

Thus, this esoteric and largely academic debate among textualists has spilled over into the policy arena, with the unintended consequence of shifting the focus away from what deregulation is supposed to be about: *getting government, in all its forms and at all levels, off the backs of companies and consumers.* Instead, free-market reformers remain locked in a frustrating internal debate about whose vision will do more to achieve this common goal. Perhaps more important, infighting among constitutional textualists has prevented them from repelling the advances made by broad constructionists. The broad constructionists, therefore, are free to continue their historically successful efforts to augment government power at the expense of the free market and of economic freedom in general.

To break this logjam and, it is hoped, resolve some of the differences that divide the textualists, this volume will pose—and seek to answer—two questions:

1. Which interpretation of federalism most accurately represents the Framers' constitutional vision of federalism?
2. From an economic point of view, which scheme of constitutional policy making and jurisprudence is most favorable to a

vibrant free-market economy and to the expansion of economic freedom in general?

Chapter 4 will clarify that, for a number of reasons, the modern, broad constructionist view of constitutional interpretation does not answer either of these two questions satisfactorily. In particular, proponents of the broad constructionist vision not only fail to abide by the letter or even the spirit of the Constitution, but freely diverge from it when doing so suits their shifting political desires. Adherents of this vision also place far too much faith in centralized planning, bureaucratic decision-making, and uniform solutions to policy dilemmas, all of which are incompatible with a vigorous free market and economic freedom generally.

The textualist school, on the other hand, is clearly more in line with the Founders' vision for America. Its proponents stress adhering to the letter and spirit of the Constitution, and in doing so promote a greater sphere of economic freedom.

But which strain of thought within the textualist school *better* satisfies these two objectives?

Should policymakers heed the logic of the proponents of greater state sovereignty by granting state and local governments the broadest possible discretion over economic issues? Or should Congress instead follow the advice of more libertarian-minded scholars whose jurisprudence would discourage most forms of meddling with the free-market economy, including actions taken at the state and local levels to advance parochial goals?

This philosophical divide within the textualist camp will be explored at much greater length, and a synthesis of the two visions will be proposed to solve this dilemma. Essentially, *The Delicate Balance: Federalism, Interstate Commerce, and Economic Freedom in the Technological Age* will argue that the truth lies somewhere between the two extremes of the textualist camp. Proper adherence to the Founding Fathers' original delicate balance between the protection of states' rights and an unfettered national marketplace will demand a series of balancing efforts and policy trade-offs to achieve the best economic outcomes. It is only by striking this balance that policymakers will enhance economic liberty and preserve the Founders' federalist framework well into the 21st century.

In certain cases, libertarian textualists will need to understand that unbridled individual economic liberty must take a back seat to state and local efforts to tailor policies to the wishes of their communities. Libertarians must be willing, therefore, to accept that states and localities will continue to exercise many legitimate "police power" functions that their citizens demand to protect public health and safety or moral standards.

On the other hand, state sovereignty textualists will need to understand that the states must give up some of their power to make such political determinations if, in exercising this power, they violate important constitutional rights held by all Americans or violate the free flow of interstate commerce. Conservative scholars and policymakers who support radical notions of states' rights absolutism must be willing to concede that the Constitution indeed contains broader protections for economic freedom and interstate commerce than they may care to admit.

In the end, any synthesis of these visions undoubtedly must involve a fair degree of pragmatism and a healthy respect for the difficult task at hand. When the Framers of the Constitution were designing the American Republic, many of them must have realized that the job would prove remarkably difficult and require much pragmatic compromise. Giving due weight to the need to preserve the sovereignty of the states while promoting the development of full nationhood and a vigorous national marketplace would require a careful balancing of powers that did not satisfy anyone completely. This is still the case today.

Again, to narrow the scope of this ambitious inquiry somewhat, the Framers' original constitutional balance of powers will be discussed primarily in the context of the economic regulation and deregulation of several important commercial sectors which currently present troubling jurisdictional headaches for policymakers. The hope is to provide policymakers with a useful framework within which difficult jurisdictional issues and federalism disputes can be addressed and resolved appropriately. These disputes could not have been envisioned by the Founders, dealing as they do with fields such as telecommunications, the Internet, and the electricity, transportation, and modern financial services industries.

As will be demonstrated, despite the Founders' inability to foresee the remarkable commercial innovations and developments within the American economy, their constitutional framework is still remarkably applicable to modern, high-tech markets and industries. Protecting the individual economic rights of American citizens and protecting the sovereignty and autonomy of the individual states are not mutually exclusive goals. In fact, they are two sides of the same coin, both of which are essential if the delicate balance of powers envisioned by the Framers is to be preserved.

Finally, since this book will focus primarily on jurisdictional disputes within various commercial sectors, many social policy issues that involve heated federalism disputes will not be discussed in detail, although the framework presented here will have some applicability to controversies in those fields. For example, the framework and recommendations found throughout this book could help resolve disputes over various social policy issues, including welfare, education, health care, or even crime control.

STEPS TOWARD A FEDERALISM REVIVAL

Finally, this book will move beyond the somewhat esoteric issues that need to be resolved within the textualist camp and call on policymakers to take steps immediately to begin restoring the proper balance of constitutional powers.

Chapter 5 will discuss emerging federalism issues and jurisdictional tensions brought on by the amazing technological developments of this century. Specifically, high-tech industries such as telecommunications, Internet/electronic commerce, electricity, aviation, transportation, and financial services will be discussed. These industries and technologies exhibit unique characteristics that often create tensions among policymakers who simultaneously claim jurisdictional authority within America's federal system.

> Protecting the individual economic rights of American citizens and protecting the sovereignty and autonomy of the individual states are not mutually exclusive goals. In fact, they are two sides of the same coin, both of which are essential if the delicate balance of powers envisioned by the Framers is to be preserved.

Chapter 5 will then develop a framework within which such controversies can be resolved in a manner that satisfies the previously stated objectives: honoring the Founders' constitutional vision of federalism while preserving and enhancing a vibrant free-market economy and economic freedom in general. A two-tiered test with multiple sub-tests and constitutional considerations will be proposed to achieve these objectives.

Essentially, the first tier of this test will demand strict scrutiny of the text of the Constitution to determine how best to resolve commercial disputes. This will demand that policymakers adhere to the literal textual requirements and overarching vision that the Founders established in the Constitution. It will also take into account subsequent statutory actions and regulatory arrangements, as well the body of jurisprudence that has developed since the founding.

The Delicate Balance

Although many laws, decisions, and regulatory arrangements must be reconsidered to restore the proper constitutional balance of powers, this first test will advise that great care be taken when reassessing these roles and responsibilities. In addition, it is important to recognize that, as a practical matter, a certain degree of deference should be given to past precedents and the traditional regulatory jurisdictional arrangements that have developed over time.

The second tier of the test will discuss interstate commerce considerations that must be addressed when considering how best to resolve commercial disputes. This will involve discussing the true nature of "interstate commerce," the purpose of the Commerce Clause, and how the increasingly complex technologies and industries of the modern age fit into the Founders' original framework.

Chapter 6 will examine how these and other, more comprehensive reforms can be adopted by policymakers to begin reinvigorating federalism immediately. The wisdom of a constitutional convention to restore the Founders' vision of federalism will be discussed, and a number of specific recommendations will be made that could be entertained either at such a convention or at any other type of federalism conference that might be held in the future.

Again, the primary focus of this study is the difficult jurisdictional questions and dilemmas involved in the regulation, or more appropriately *deregulation*, of commerce sectors and economic activity in the American Republic. This topic promises to be the subject of ongoing controversy and conflict between state and federal officials. The goal is to advance the deregulation of traditionally regulated industries or to expand the scope of economic freedom in general across many industry sectors as quickly as possible.

To be sure, much thought will need to be put into how to balance the often competing American values of state sovereignty and individual liberty. If this is done properly, through the application of the Founding Fathers' original constitutional balance of powers, American commerce and consumers will benefit into the 21st century. It is precisely this ambitious objective that will guide this inquiry.

2

THE FOUNDERS' VISION OF CONSTITUTIONAL FEDERALISM

Over two hundred years have passed since the Founders convened in Philadelphia to embark on the grand political experiment that would result in the adoption of the Constitution of the United States of America. The Constitution has proved a durable document and has served the nation well, but it is important to remember that this was not the Founders' first effort to establish a guiding document and form of political organization for the American polity. The Articles of Confederation governed the States of the Union for roughly ten years, from the period of the American Revolution until the period during which the Constitution was ratified in 1787–1788.[1] Understanding why the Founders abandoned the Articles of Confederation in favor of America's current Constitution is important to understanding why today—more than two centuries later—our constitutional framework remains the optimal form of political organization for the American Republic.

WHY THE FOUNDERS ABANDONED THE ARTICLES OF CONFEDERATION

In theory, the Articles of Confederation presented an appealing form of decentralized government capable of ensuring the states that no despotic national power similar to the one they had just defeated in the Revolution would be able to trample the rights of their inhabitants. Essentially, the Articles provided for loose federation among the independent, sovereign states. Under the Articles—which could be considered primarily a security pact among the states—the national Congress was given very limited powers to keep the peace among the states and deal with matters of war or piracy on the high seas.[2]

Footnotes:
1. The Articles of Confederation were adopted on November 15, 1777.

The Delicate Balance

Yet, as former Reagan Administration Attorney General Edwin Meese III noted in a 1985 speech, "There is no question that the Constitutional Convention grew out of widespread dissatisfaction with the Articles of Confederation."[3] There were many reasons for this discontent. In practice, the Articles were so extreme as to prohibit nearly all federal actions, including those that would benefit the country as a whole. These restrictions caused problems as the new nation struggled to raise enough money to ensure that adequate forces would exist to protect it. Coinage and currency problems which arose to prevent the development of an efficient monetary system accounted for a large share of the problem. Moreover, the federal government lacked the authority to enter into commercial treaties or agreements with other nations, and this hampered free and fair trade between foreign nations and the individual American states. Finally, the Articles contained no provisions for a federal judiciary or executive power to deal with such issues.

But perhaps the most problematic development of the Confederation period was the rise of state-by-state protectionism. Although the Founders had hoped America would develop into a peaceful, well-integrated nation, the Articles instead encouraged the rise of destructive forms of factionalism and protectionism that "prevented the emergence of full nationhood"[4] and discouraged the development of robust interstate commerce.

Unfortunately, under the Articles of Confederation, the states came to view themselves as miniature kingdoms that could regulate commerce at the expense of citizens in other states and regions of America. The federal government was essentially powerless to stop this protectionism, since the Articles of Confederation had not provided for a federal role in preventing these and other types of undesirable state actions. In fact, historian Clarence B. Carson has argued, "It is even doubtful that what existed under the Articles was a general government at all."[5] That is, there were no restrictions on state actions that imposed unjustifiable burdens on interstate com-

Footnotes:
2. For the complete text of the Articles of Confederation, see Appendix I.
3. Edwin Meese III, *Address Before the D.C. Chapter of the Federalist Society Lawyers Division*, November 15, 1985, reprinted in *Report to the Attorney General, Original Meaning Jurisprudence: A Sourcebook*, March 12, 1987.
4. Kermit L. Hall, William M. Wiecek, and Paul Finkelman, eds., *American Legal History: Cases and Materials* (New York: Oxford University Press, 1996), p. 80.
5. Clarence B. Carson, *A Basic History of the United States, Volume 2: The Beginning of the Republic 1775–1825* (Wadley, Ala.: American Textbook Committee, 1984; Sixth Printing, January 1991), p. 62.

merce; states were free to act with impunity, independent of the concerns and rights of citizens in other states.

Trade and commerce suffered as a result of this dysfunctional system of political organization. In fact, just a few years after America's war with Britain ended, the states were engaging in anti-competitive activities against each other which mimicked those that had driven the colonists to rebel against England.

> **Unfortunately, under the Articles of Confederation, the states came to view themselves as miniature kingdoms that could regulate commerce at the expense of citizens in other states and regions of America.**

In his 1935 *Constitutional History of the United States*, Andrew C. McLaughlin noted that, "[A]s the days went by disorganization rather than integration seemed to be gathering headway, until the more serious patriots and watchers of the night feared for the safety of their country. States with commodious harbors had an advantage over their neighbors and did not shrink from using it."[6] Moreover, notes legal scholar Richard A. Epstein of the University of Chicago Law School, "Many states had created extensive networks of public monopolies, franchises, and privileges, as well as wide arrays of local restrictions on trade and commerce."[7] Gerald Gunther concludes in his *Constitutional Law* textbook that "The poor condition of American commerce and the proliferating trade rivalries among the states were the immediate provocations for the calling of the Constitutional Convention."[8] And Bernard H. Siegan, distinguished professor of law at the University of San Diego, concurs, noting that "The tariffs and other economic barriers erected by the states against each other, are widely alluded to as a major source of discontent with the existing Confederation."[9]

Historian John Fiske summarized how these anti-competitive actions were carried out by the states in his 1888 book *The Critical Period in American History*:

Footnotes:
6. Andrew McLaughlin, *A Constitutional History of the United States*, reprinted in Leonard W. Levy, ed., *Essays on the Making of the Constitution* (New York: Oxford University Press, 1969, 1987), p. 56.
7. Richard A. Epstein, "Toward a Revitalization of the Contract Clause," *University of Chicago Law Review*, Vol. 51 (Summer 1984), p. 706.
8. Gerald Gunther, *Constitutional Law*, 12th Ed. (Westbury, N.Y.: Foundation Press, Inc., 1991), p. 93.
9. Bernard H. Siegan, "The Economic Constitution in Historic Perspective," in Richard B. McKenzie, ed., *Constitutional Economics: Containing the Economic Powers of Government* (Lexington, Mass.: Lexington Books, 1984), p. 40.

The Delicate Balance

> [T]he different states with their different tariff and tonnage acts, began to make commercial war upon one another. No sooner had...three New England states virtually closed their ports to British shipping than Connecticut threw hers wide open, an act which she followed by laying duties upon imports from Massachusetts. Pennsylvania discriminated against Delaware, and New Jersey, pillaged at once by both her greater neighbors, was compared to a cask tapped at both ends.[10]

Historians Frederic A. Ogg and P. Orman Ray aptly summarized the overall effects of the Confederation period in their 1932 textbook *Essentials of American Government*:

> The consequences were disastrous. No money for national use could be raised from tariff duties; no uniform commercial policy could be adopted; and the states laid duties, granted favors, and set up barriers as their individual interests dictated, sacrificing by their jealousies and bickerings splendid opportunities for advancing the new nation's trade, wealth, and prosperity. Enmeshed in a network of duties and tolls, trade languished; healthy commercial competition gave way to downright commercial warfare.[11]

Finally, in *The Federalist Papers*, James Madison and Alexander Hamilton clearly articulated the frustration of the Founders when crafting the new constitutional framework. As Hamilton noted in *Federalist* No. 22:

> The interfering and unneighborly regulations of some states, contrary to the true spirit of the Union, have, in different instances, given just cause of umbrage and complaint to others, and it is to be feared that examples of this nature, if not restrained by a national control, would be multiplied and extended till they become not less serious sources of animosity and discord than injurious impediments to the intercourse between the different parts of the Confederacy.[12]

Footnotes:
10. John Fiske, *The Critical Period of American History* (New York: Houghton Mifflin, 1888, 1916), p. 145.
11. Frederic A. Ogg and P. Orman Ray, *Essentials of American Government*, 6th Ed. (New York: Appleton–Century–Crofts, Inc., 1932, 1950), p. 10.
12. Alexander Hamilton, *Federalist* No. 22, in Clinton Rossiter, ed., *The Federalist Papers* (New York: NAL Penguin, 1961), pp. 144–145.

The Founders' Vision of Constitutional Federalism

Madison concurred in *Federalist* No. 42: "The defect of power in the existing Confederacy to regulate the commerce between its several members is in the number of those which have been clearly pointed out by experience."[13] More important, Madison went on to point out in *Federalist* No. 45 that "The regulation of commerce, it is true, is a new [national] power; but that seems to be an addition which few oppose and from which no apprehensions are entertained."[14]

In other words, the members of the state delegations who came together in Philadelphia in May of 1787 to draft the Constitution recognized that something would be gained by sacrificing a small degree of autonomy over interstate commercial activity. And since the federal government had no power under the Articles of Confederation to prohibit state-based protectionism, the Founders made it clear when drafting the new Constitution that a stronger federal role was needed to protect the economic liberties of all American citizens and encourage the expansion of industry through an integrated national economy. They were admitting, in other words, as constitutional historian Leonard W. Levy argues, that the lesson of the Confederation period was "that excessive localism was incompatible with nationhood."[15]

> **The Founders made it clear when drafting the new Constitution that a stronger federal role was needed to protect the economic liberties of all American citizens and encourage the expansion of industry through an integrated national economy.**

Consequently, the Founders included several provisions in the Constitution dealing with federal oversight of the states to end factionalism and protectionism among them. In addition, other affirmative powers were granted to the federal government to protect the economic liberties of the citizenry and to aid in the promotion of a more integrated national economy. These enumerated protections for commerce and enhancement of federal economic powers included:

> Article I, Section 8, Clause 3 (the Commerce Clause), which gave Congress the power "To regulate commerce with foreign nations, and among the several states, and with Indian tribes."

Footnotes:
13. James Madison, *Federalist* No. 42, in *ibid.*, p. 267.
14. James Madison, *Federalist* No. 45, in *ibid.*, p. 293.
15. Leonard W. Levy, "Introduction: The Making of the Constitution, 1776–1789," in Levy, ed., *Essays on the Making of the Constitution*, p. xix.

The Delicate Balance

Article I, Section 8, Clause 4 (the Bankruptcy Clause), which gave Congress the power "To establish...uniform Laws on the subject of Bankruptcies throughout the United States."

Article I, Section 8, Clause 5 (the Coinage Clause), which gave Congress the power "To coin Money, regulate the value thereof, and foreign Coin, and fix a Standard of Weights and Measures."[16]

Article I, Section 8, Clause 8 (patents and copyrights), which gave Congress the power "To promote the Progress of Science and useful Arts, by securing for limited Times to Authors and Inventors the exclusive Right to their respective Writings and Discoveries."

Article I, Section 9, Clauses 5 and 6 (non-discrimination in shipping and trading), which specify that "No tax or duty shall be laid on articles exported from any state. No preference shall be given by any regulation of commerce or revenue to the ports of one state over those of another: nor shall vessels bound to, or from, one state, be obliged to enter, clear, or pay duties in another."

Article I, Section 10, Clause 1 (prohibition of retroactive laws), which prohibits states from enacting legislation retroactively: "No State shall...pass any...ex post facto Law...."

Article I, Section 10, Clause 1 (the Contract Clause), which prohibits state interference with the right of voluntary contracts by specifying that "No State shall...pass any...Law impairing the Obligation of Contracts...."

Article I, Section 10, Clauses 2 and 3 (additional shipping and trading protections), which specify that "No state shall, without the consent of Congress, lay any imposts or duties on imports or exports...[or] lay any duty on tonnage."

Article IV, Section 2, Clause 1 (the Privileges and Immunities Clause), which specifies that "The citizens of each State are entitled to all the Privileges and Immunities of Citizens in the several States." This was intended to prevent states from discriminating against certain constitutional rights of out-of-state citizens.

Article VI, Clause 2 (the Supremacy Clause), which made it clear that when state laws came into conflict with each other or with

Footnotes:
16. Article I, Section 10 also prohibits the states from making "any Thing but gold and silver Coin a Tender in Payment of Debts."

The Founders' Vision of Constitutional Federalism

national laws, federal law was to prevail: "This Constitution...shall be the supreme law of the land."

Essentially, these functions were considered so crucial to the commercial development of the nation and to the preservation of national harmony that the Framers forbade the states and localities from legislating in these fields. The combined effect of these enumerated constitutional provisions was a clear declaration by the Founders that state-based protectionism would not be tolerated. The rights of individual consumers, where threatened by oppressive and unjustifiable state actions that adversely affected interstate commerce, would be prohibited by Congress and the courts.[17]

THE FRAMERS' CONSTITUTIONAL FRAMEWORK

It is important to note, however, that the Founders also went to great lengths to ensure that the power of the federal government would not become overly burdensome on the states and the people. Despising centralized power, the Founders made it abundantly clear that local control was almost always preferable to federal regulation.

To that end, the Founders listed only a handful of explicit, enumerated powers for the federal government and left the remaining rights and responsibilities largely to the states or, more important, directly to the citizens. As Madison argued in *Federalist* No. 39, "[Federal] jurisdiction extends to certain enumerated objects only, and leaves to the several States a residuary and inviolable sovereignty over all other objects."[18] And in *Federalist* No. 45, Madison noted even more succinctly that "The powers delegated by the proposed Constitution to the federal government are few and defined. Those which are to remain in the State governments are numerous and indefinite."[19]

Furthermore, the States were given a very direct role in constraining the powers of the federal government through their ability to appoint members of the Senate[20] as well as through their vital veto power over proposed amendments to the Constitution. Also, the written guarantee of the Tenth Amendment made it very clear that "The powers not delegated to the United States by the Constitution,

---

Footnotes:
17. For the complete text of the Constitution, see Appendix II.
18. James Madison, *Federalist* No. 39, in Rossiter, ed., *The Federalist Papers*, p. 245.
19. James Madison, *Federalist* No. 45, in *ibid.*, p. 292.
20. This was eliminated with passage of the Seventeenth Amendment in 1913.

nor prohibited by it to the States, are reserved to the States respectively, or to the people."

Finally, Article IV, Section 4—the Guarantee Clause—of the Constitution ("The United States shall guarantee to every State in the Union a Republican Form of Government...") was also intended to serve as an impediment to federal overreach. Although the Guarantee Clause has been read by some as merely a federal check on the power of states to abuse the rights of their citizens, the Clause also provides an equal check on federal efforts to undermine the republican nature of the states. As Deborah Jones Merritt, associate professor of law at the University of Illinois College of Law, has argued cogently, "[A] republican form of government is one in which the people make important decisions affecting their community. In order to accommodate that goal, the guarantee clause must grant the states a measure of autonomy in directing their government machinery."[21] After all, if the federal government does not allow the citizens of the individual states the flexibility to experiment freely with different political arrangements and policies, then it can hardly be claimed that it has guaranteed them a republican form of government.[22]

Again, however, it is important to remember that the Founders recognized that unconstrained state action and commercial regulation potentially could infringe the rights of individual Americans, which were preeminent. In fact, the Tenth Amendment ends with the phrase "... *or to the people*," and the Ninth Amendment notes that "The enumeration in the Constitution of certain rights shall not be construed to deny or disparage others retained *by the people*." Likewise, after noting in *Federalist* No. 39 that the states were to retain the great majority of public powers, Madison went on to reiterate the importance of an impartial federal authority vested in Congress to arbitrate disputes between the states to encourage national harmony:

> [I]n controversies relating to the boundary between two jurisdictions, the tribunal which is ultimately to decide is to be established under the general govern-

Footnotes:
21. Deborah Jones Merritt, "The Guarantee Clause and State Autonomy: Federalism for a Third Century," *Columbia Law Review*, Vol. 88 (January 1988), p. 44.
22. "At the same time, however, the guarantee clause does not give the states carte blanche to order their government systems. Other constitutional provisions impose a variety of restrictions on a state's freedom to structure its government process." Merritt, "The Guarantee Clause and State Autonomy," p. 44.

The Founders' Vision of Constitutional Federalism

ment.... The decision is to be impartially made, according to the rules of the Constitution.... Some such tribunal is clearly essential to prevent an appeal to the sword and a dissolution of the compact; and that it ought to be established under the general government rather than under the local governments, or to speak more properly, that it could be safely established under the first alone, is a position not likely to be combated.[23]

In other words, so that the rights of individuals would be protected from unjustifiable state actions that interfered with the free flow of interstate commerce and the voluntary interaction of producers and consumers across state boundaries, local control was to be tempered by a small degree of federal oversight. But these federal powers would be strictly limited.

> In essence, the Constitution established a delicate balance between federal and state responsibilities for the regulation of interstate commerce; neither extreme — absolute federal pre-emption or complete state control of national commercial activity — would be tolerated.

In essence, the Constitution established a delicate balance between federal and state responsibilities for the regulation of interstate commerce; neither extreme—absolute federal pre-emption or complete state control of national commercial activity—would be tolerated. America would be a nation that respected both federalism and capitalism to guarantee that the rights of the people would not be unjustly infringed. As Gunther has summarized, "Stronger [national] government was necessary, but government must not become too powerful: these were dominant concerns to the Framers, and the Constitution reflects their effort to accommodate these needs and risks."[24]

Thus, a system of "dual sovereignty" or "competitive federalism" was born that provided governmental authorities with plenary powers in their respective jurisdictional fields. In the very limited sphere of authority granted to the federal government through its enumerated powers under the Constitution, national power was to be exclusive. In the many other areas not delimited as being of national concern, the states were given plenary power to exercise jurisdictional authority. "The national government would clearly have as

Footnotes:
23. James Madison, *Federalist* No. 39, in Rossiter, ed., *The Federalist Papers*, pp. 245–246.
24. Gunther, *Constitutional Law*, p. 65.

The Delicate Balance

much power as its mandate required to break down local barriers to the exchange of persons or goods," notes Hadley Arkes, Professor of Jurisprudence and American Institutions at Amherst College. "But it was understood, beyond any need to state, that the Commerce Clause would not provide a virtual license for the displacing of local government in regulating all varieties of business, manufacturing, and exchange."[25]

The unique balance of powers established under this system of dual sovereignty or competitive federalism granted different sets of governmental entities powers that were intended to complement one another and preserve the natural rights of the citizenry. However, the interplay between these competing forces almost immediately would create constitutional questions about the limits of federal and state power relative to one another. The Supreme Court was left to face the difficult task of resolving many of these disputes and, in the process, developing a system of commercial jurisprudence for the young republic.

Footnotes:
25. Hadley Arkes, *The Return of George Sutherland: Restoring a Jurisprudence of Natural Rights* (Princeton, N.J.: Princeton University Press, 1994), p. 124.

3

THE JURISPRUDENCE OF AMERICAN COMMERCIAL FEDERALISM

THE 19TH CENTURY SUPREME COURT AND THE COMMERCE POWER

For many years after the ratification of the Constitution, the Founders' delicate balance was preserved and protected in numerous Supreme Court decisions through fairly sensible applications of the Commerce Clause and other constitutional clauses. Chief Justice John Marshall, who served from 1801–1835, authored a number of important decisions in the early 1800s which applied the Founders' intent to difficult commercial disputes that developed in the young nation. In such noted cases as *McCulloch v. Maryland* (1819),[1] *Gibbons v. Ogden* (1824),[2] *Brown v. Maryland* (1827),[3] *Willson v. Black Bird Creek Marsh Co.* (1829),[4] and *Weston v. Charleston* (1829),[5] Marshall worked to preserve this balance by striking down state actions that unduly affected interstate commerce.[6]

In *Gibbons v. Ogden*, the first and most important case dealing directly with the question of the reach of the Commerce Clause, Chief Justice Marshall authored a unanimous decision striking down a New York law which had granted a monopoly to the use of the Hudson River by a steamboat operator. Marshall and the Court held in favor of Thomas Gibbons, who was represented by noted statesman Daniel Webster. The Court agreed with Webster's reasoning during argumentation that, where state laws came into conflict with each other or

Footnotes:
1. 4 Wheat. 17 U.S. 316 (1819).
2. 9 Wheat. 22 U.S. 1 (1824).
3. 12 Wheat. 25 U.S. 419 (1827).
4. 2 Pet. 27 U.S. 245 (1829).
5. 2 Pet. 27 U.S. 449 (1829).
6. For a comprehensive listing of the many Supreme Court cases that involve commercial federalism, see Appendix III.

The Delicate Balance

with national laws, federal action was required to settle the matter. Importantly, Marshall further noted that in order for the Commerce Clause to have its intended effect—the prohibition of state-based protectionism and discrimination—the term "commerce" would have to be defined to include more than just simple goods transported across state boundaries. It would have to include other activities and entities, such as steamboats and the passengers they transported. These are sometimes referred to as the "instrumentalities of commerce."

Although Marshall's opinion in *Gibbons v. Ogden* remains somewhat controversial in its application of the Founders' balance,[7] legal and economic experts agree that its significance in encouraging the development of a vibrant American commercial sector cannot be overestimated or over-appreciated. As legal scholars Ezra Parmalee Prentice and John G. Egan noted in their seminal 1898 study *The Commerce Clause of the Federal Constitution*:

> In reading that momentous decision, apprehending, as we do now, the interests which were at stake...one cannot help pausing to wonder what might have been the result had that decision been in any way different from what it was. Had the utterance of the court upon the powers of the States been more ambiguous; had the expression upon the relation of the States to the Federal government been avoided, and the element of nationality involved been less explicitly disclosed and asserted; had it been allowed to cripple the commercial power of the nation in any way—where would the influence of that decision have led us now?[8]

While the general thrust of most Marshall-era decisions mimicked *Gibbons v. Ogden*, some on the Court feared that pro-nationalist forces might be moving too far.[9] Balance was restored under the guidance of Chief Justice Roger Brooke Taney, who served from

Footnotes:
7. For a critique of Marshall's reasoning in the case, see Raoul Berger, "The Commerce Clause," in *Federalism: The Founders' Design* (Norman, Okla.: University of Oklahoma Press, 1987), pp. 120–157.
8. Ezra Parmalee Prentice and John G. Egan, *The Commerce Clause of the Federal Constitution* (Chicago, Ill.: Callaghan and Company, 1898), p. 16.
9. "The Marshall Court applied the national powers enumerated in Article I very broadly but was not insensitive to the need to recognize breathing room for state and local regulation, especially when it did not have spill-over effects on other citizens." William N. Eskridge, Jr., and John Ferejohn, "The Elastic Commerce Clause: A Political Theory of American Federalism," *Vanderbilt Law Review*, Vol. 47 (1994), p. 1371.

The Jurisprudence of American Commercial Federalism

1835–1864. Under Taney, a number of important decisions were handed down that further attempted to clarify how the Founders' balance was to apply as national commercial markets grew larger and the overall number of states in the Union multiplied. The key Taney-era cases were *New York v. Miln* (1837),[10] *Bank of Augusta v. Earle* (1839),[11] *Swift v. Tyson* (1842),[12] the *License Cases* (1847),[13] the *Passenger Cases* (1849),[14] *Genesee Chief v. Fitzhugh* (1852),[15] and *Cooley v. Board of Wardens of the Port of Philadelphia* (1851).[16]

Cooley v. Board of Wardens of the Port of Philadelphia was probably the most important Commerce Clause–related decision of the Taney era. In *Cooley*, the Court upheld a Pennsylvania law that regulated vessels entering or exiting the port of Philadelphia, on the grounds that the matter was local in nature. The Pennsylvania statute required that any ship entering the port of Philadelphia must employ a local pilot to guide it through the port, or else pay a fine or fee to the government to help fund a retirement system for Pennsylvania ship pilots or widows and dependents of deceased pilots.

The Court argued that while such a law could stand, other laws and issues that were clearly national in scope would demand federal attention. This approach has come to be known as the "*Cooley* Doctrine of selective exclusiveness." That is, in select commercial areas where national uniformity may be needed, Congress has exclusive jurisdiction to legislate if it desires to do so. However, when the commercial activity is local in character or Congress has not acted, the states are free to legislate. Prentice and Egan summarize the *Cooley* Doctrine of selective exclusiveness as follows:

> In matters admitting uniform regulation throughout the country and affecting all the States, the inaction of Congress is to be taken as a declaration of its will that commerce shall be "free and unrestricted" so far only as concerns any general regulation by the States.... On the other hand, in matters of local nature, such as are auxiliary to commerce rather than part of it, the inaction of Congress is to be taken as an indication that for

Footnotes:
10. 11 Pet. 36 U.S. 102 (1837).
11. 38 U.S. 519 (1839).
12. 16 Pet. 41 U.S. 1 (1842).
13. *Thurlow v. Massachusetts*, *Fletcher v. Rhode Island*, and *Peirce v. New Hampshire*, 5 How. 46 U.S. 504 (1847).
14. *Smith v. Turner* and *Norris v. Boston*, 7 How. 48 U.S. 283 (1849).
15. 12 How. 53 U.S. 443 (1852).
16. 12 How. 53 U.S. 299 (1852).

The Delicate Balance

the time being, and until it sees fit to act, they may be regulated by State authority.[17]

Hence, in the *Cooley* case, the Court viewed the issue at hand (pilotage regulation) as a purely local matter that did not require national attention. The distinction between those issues that demanded "national uniformity" and those that where "purely local," however, remained unclear.

While the Taney Court did lean toward state sovereignty over commercial affairs before allowing or encouraging federal action, the Court's decisions during this period continued to balance the two in the interest of promoting the commercial development of the nation. University of Missouri–St. Louis Professor of History and Education Walter Ehrlich notes that:

> Contrary to popular misconception, then, Taney did not reverse the Marshall trend and institute radical agrarian egalitarianism and state sovereignty. On the contrary, he preserved and redefined the main lines of Marshall's constitutional law, opened economic opportunities for many Americans, and retained a strong national power redefined to accommodate a judicious dual sovereignty.[18]

In this sense, the Founders' delicate balance between unfettered, nationally enforced capitalism and outright state-based control was preserved through the evolution of American common law court cases.

RECONSTRUCTION, THE FOURTEENTH AMENDMENT, AND SUBSTANTIVE DUE PROCESS

Although the federal government did create a handful of new powers for itself in the post-Civil War Reconstruction period, the Founders' original balance of power was preserved, for the most part, by Congress and the courts. But the adoption of the Fourteenth Amendment to the Constitution in 1868 marked a watershed moment in the history of commercial federalism in America.

The Fourteenth Amendment required that the protections of individual liberty found within the Constitution and the Bill of Rights

Footnotes:
17. Prentice and Egan, *The Commerce Clause of the Federal Constitution*, pp. 27–28.
18. Walter Ehrlich, "Roger Brooke Taney," in Kermit L. Hall, ed., *The Oxford Companion to the Supreme Court of the United States* (New York: Oxford University Press, 1992), p. 859.

subsequently would cover the states. In other words, the states generally would be required to honor the specific protections of the Constitution in the same way the federal government did, including protections for economic ownership and liberty.

Section 1 of the amendment provides that "No State shall make or enforce any law which shall abridge the privileges and immunities of citizens of the United States; nor shall any State deprive any person of life, liberty, or property, without due process of law; nor deny to any person within its jurisdiction the equal protection of the laws." As Bernard Siegan noted in 1987:

> The importance of [this provision of the Fourteenth Amendment] derives from the fact that there are few other provisions in the Constitution that protect citizens or other persons against violation of their rights by the states.... The provision under discussion was designed to accord maximum protections for liberty at the state level. Each of its three clauses—privileges and immunities, due process, and equal protection—was directed toward this end, and collectively they constitute a formidable barrier against state excesses and oppression.[19]

Thus, Congress pushed through the Fourteenth Amendment during the Reconstruction period not only to remedy the injustices of slavery, but also to provide important safeguards against future violations of individual rights by state and local governments.

Yet, from the start, it was unclear just how this new balance of powers would be struck. Constitutional historian William E. Nelson, in his book *The Fourteenth Amendment: From Political Principle to Judicial Doctrine*, argues cogently that the drafters of the amendment were not clear in their intention. Was their primary goal simply to guarantee equal rights and equal treatment of individuals within the states? Or was the Fourteenth Amendment intended, in a more radical sense, to guarantee that the fundamental, absolute natural rights of all citizens would be protected by the federal government in all cases? As Nelson summarizes:

> What the proponents [of the Fourteenth Amendment] did not do effectively was to explain how federal enforcement of principles designed to affect nearly

Footnotes:
19. Bernard H. Siegan, "Economic Liberties and the Constitution: Protection at the State Level," in James A. Dorn and Henry G. Manne, eds., *Economic Liberties and the Constitution* (Fairfax, Va.: George Mason University Press, 1987), p. 138.

every aspect of human endeavor could be limited so as not to undermine the plenary lawmaking power of the states. The most cogent explanation was that the Fourteenth Amendment would not, in and of itself, create rights, but would leave that task to state law; the amendment's sole restriction on state legislative freedom would lie in its requirement that the states confer equal rights on all.

But not all of the amendment's proponents accepted this view. Consistently with the antislavery heritage, some Republicans claimed that the amendment did more than protect rights equally; it protected absolutely certain fundamental rights such as those specified in the Bill of Rights and those given by common law to enter contracts and own property.[20]

Nelson notes that this immediately created headaches for the courts, since "The Fourteenth Amendment thus had at least two possible meanings as it emerged from the congressional and state ratification debates. It could be read as guaranteeing either equal rights or absolute rights.... As a result, the amendment first came into the courts with more than one possible meaning."[21]

Nonetheless, during the Reconstruction period, and up until the time of the New Deal, the Supreme Court attempted to apply a higher standard of constitutional review in cases involving interstate commerce, property rights, and economic liberty in general—what is often referred to as "substantive due process" analysis. Yet, despite the expanded protections many thought would be afforded by the Fourteenth Amendment, the actual results during this period were quite varied.

For example, in the *Slaughter-House Cases* (1873) and *Munn v. Illinois* (1887), the Court handed down decisions that granted state and local officials greater regulatory leeway, primarily on "police power" grounds (i.e., the authority of the states to pass legislation regulating health, safety, and public morality). In *Slaughter-House*,[22] the Court held that a Louisiana law granting a monopoly to a private slaughterhouse company in the New Orleans area did not violate

Footnotes:
20. William E. Nelson, *The Fourteenth Amendment: From Political Principle to Judicial Doctrine* (Cambridge, Mass.: Harvard University Press, 1988), p. 150.
21. *Ibid.*, p. 151.
22. 83 U.S. (16 Wall.) 36 (1873).

other butchers' Fourteenth Amendment economic rights to engage freely in business in the New Orleans area.

This case greatly limited the scope of the Fourteenth Amendment's protections, such as the Privileges and Immunities Clause, and set back the cause of substantive due process as a guarantee of economic freedom in general. In his noted dissent in *Slaughter-House*, Justice Stephan J. Field lamented that the Court had not taken steps to preserve "the right of free labor, one of the most sacred and imprescriptible rights of man...."[23] Field's classic statement of substantive due process jurisprudence concluded:

> This equality of right, with exemption from all disparaging and partial enactments, in the lawful pursuits of life, throughout the whole country, is the distinguishing privilege of citizens of the United States. To them, everywhere, all pursuits, all professions, all avocations are open without other restrictions than such as are imposed equally upon all others of the same age, sex, and condition. The State may prescribe such regulations for every pursuit and calling of life as will promote the public health, secure the good order and advance the general prosperity of society, but when once prescribed, the pursuit or calling must be free to be followed by every citizen who is within the conditions designated, and will conform to the regulations. This is the fundamental idea upon which our institutions rest, and unless adhered to in the legislation of the country our government will be a republic only in name.[24]

Essentially, Field and his fellow dissenters in *Slaughter-House* and other cases[25] argued that a "reasonableness standard" must be adhered to when interpreting the limits of state and local police powers. That is, when a state or locality was regulating business or commerce equally and fairly to further the public good "legitimately" or "reasonably," it would not violate a citizen's or a corporation's "right to free labor," as Field referred to the economic freedoms guaranteed under the Fourteenth Amendment.

Footnotes:
23. Justice Stephan J. Field (dissenting opinion), *In re Slaughter-House Cases*, 83 U.S. (16 Wall.) 36, 110 (1873).
24. Justice Stephan J. Field (dissenting opinion), *In re Slaughter-House Cases*, 83 U.S. (16 Wall.) 36, 110–111 (1873).
25. See, for example, *Mugler v. Kansas*, 123 U.S. 623 (1887).

The Delicate Balance

Again, the ambiguity of the Fourteenth Amendment was problematic in this regard. The drafters failed to spell out the "legitimate" scope of "reasonable" state and local police powers when they were debating the amendment in the late 1860s. As Nelson notes, "The fact is that no one in 1866 was engaged in precise doctrinal analysis of what the concept of reasonableness might mean."[26] This meant that the courts were given the sometimes hopeless task of trying to strike this balance on their own.

The Court would face this dilemma again in *Munn v. Illinois*.[27] In *Munn*, private grain elevator owners asked the Court to strike down, on Fourteenth Amendment substantive due process grounds, an Illinois statute regulating the maximum price that grain elevator operators could charge customers for storing their grain. Instead of upholding the right of the grain elevators to contract freely with customers and arrange prices voluntarily, the Court ruled that the business of grain elevator storage was "affected with the public interest" since, in the words of Chief Justice Morrison Waite, "Property [becomes] clothed with the public interest when used in a manner to make it of public consequence, and affect the community at large."

Not only did the *Munn* decision cast further doubt on what constitutional protections were extended to industry and commerce under the Constitution and the Fourteenth Amendment, but it also raised a more profound question regarding regulation of industry in general. That issue has been summarized aptly by Ernest Gellhorn and Richard J. Pierce, Jr., authors of *Regulated Industries in a Nutshell*:

> More difficult to explain, indeed left unanswered by the Court's over-long opinion, is its unsupported conclusion that grain elevators were like common carriers affected with a public interest and thus properly subject to government regulation. What was it that distinguished them from other businesses such as tailors and shoemakers (who, it was conceded were not common carriers subject to maximum price regulation)?[28]

In other words, if it could be claimed that a grain elevator was "clothed with the public interest" and therefore subject to common carrier regulation of rates, prices, service quality, and the like, then

Footnotes:
26. Nelson, *The Fourteenth Amendment*, p. 122.
27. 94 U.S. 113 (1887).
28. Ernest Gellhorn and Richard J. Pierce, Jr., *Regulated Industries in a Nutshell* (St. Paul, Minn.: West Publishing Co., 1987), p. 73.

why shouldn't any other business that offers its goods or services to the public also be regulated accordingly?

In summary, although it can be claimed legitimately that, through *Slaughter-House* and *Munn*, the Supreme Court was attempting to strike the Framers' balance between an uninhibited marketplace and the right of state and local governments to exercise their police powers over industry and commerce, there can be no doubt that these two cases had particularly devastating consequences for economic commerce and freedom in future American industries. The *Slaughter-House* decision's acceptance of the political establishment and legitimization of local franchise monopolies, coupled with *Munn's* creation of the "public interest doctrine," set the stage for the rise of the 20th century glut of regulatory agencies and state-created monopolies which have denied consumers choice in service ever since.

Furthermore, by undermining the substantive due process protections required by a strict application of the Fourteenth Amendment, the Court opened the door to a flood of regulation at all levels of government. These rules inevitably interfered with the right of individuals to pursue their economic affairs free of the stifling hand of government intervention. In many ways, this century's avalanche of licensing requirements, occupational restrictions, zoning laws, business controls, and various forms of industry regulation can be traced directly to the decisions handed down by the Court in *Slaughter-House* and *Munn v. Illinois*.

At the same time, however, a handful of other cases decided in this era cut in the opposite direction, favoring freedom of contract and unbridled commercial activity over state and local regulatory intervention. Notably, in *Allgeyer v. Louisiana* (1897),[29] *Lochner v. New York* (1905),[30] *Adkins v. Children's Hospital* (1923),[31] and *New State Ice Co. v. Liebmann* (1932),[32] the Court rigorously developed the doctrine of economic due process "under which," according to Gellhorn and Pierce, "it reviewed the constitutionality of state and federal legislation against charges that it arbitrarily and unnecessarily interfered with the liberty of contract between an employer and his employees or otherwise served no legitimate state end."[33]

Footnotes:
29. 165 U.S. 578 (1897).
30. 198 U.S. 45 (1905).
31. 261 U.S. 525 (1923).
32. 285 U.S. 262 (1932).
33. Gellhorn and Pierce, *Regulated Industries in a Nutshell*, p. 78.

The *Lochner* decision, which remains controversial to this day, struck down a New York law that restricted working hours in bakeries. Although *Lochner* represented the height of the ascendancy of economic due process jurisprudence on the Supreme Court, many other decisions during the same period employed a reasonableness test that balanced competing interests and weighed in favor of state and local rule. For example, in 1908, just three years after the *Lochner* decision, the Court ruled in *Muller v. Oregon*[34] that an Oregon statute limiting the number of hours that women were allowed to work in factories and laundries was a legitimate exercise of the state's police powers.

Therefore, it is clear that the purpose and scope of the Fourteenth Amendment's substantive due process protections for economic freedom and commercial activity were much debated in the late 1800s and early 1900s. As Chapter 4 will discuss in greater detail, modern conservative and libertarian legal scholars, policymakers, and judges continue to disagree over the question of just how much freedom from state and local regulatory action is guaranteed under the Constitution generally and the Fourteenth Amendment in particular.[35] Just as the *Slaughter-House* and *Lochner* cases divided the Court a century ago, these controversial decisions continue to divide conservative and libertarian theorists over the proper scope and extent of judicial intervention to protect economic liberties.

For purposes of this historical discussion, however, it is enough to note that the impact of substantive due process jurisprudence was short-lived and that, as Gellhorn and Pierce have noted, "the Supreme Court has not invalidated any economic regulation on substantive due process grounds since 1936."[36]

THE CORRUPTING INFLUENCE OF THE NEW DEAL

Clearly, over the course of the nation's first 150 years, there were numerous legislative and judicial disagreements regarding the proper scope of the economic protections found within the Constitution, as well as the degree to which federal officials could intervene to prevent certain state policies from interfering with commerce. These disagreements were only heightened by the pas-

Footnotes:
34. 208 U.S. 412 (1908).
35. See, in general, "Are There Unenumerated Constitutional Rights?" The Seventh Annual National Federalist Society Symposium on Law and Public Policy—1988, *Harvard Journal of Law and Public Policy*, Vol. 12, No. 1 (Winter 1989), pp. 1–192.
36. Gellhorn and Pierce, *Regulated Industries in a Nutshell*, p. 83.

The Jurisprudence of American Commercial Federalism

sage of the Fourteenth Amendment, with its new restrictions on state or local efforts to interfere with economic activity.

Despite these disagreements, it is equally clear that, from 1789 until the dawn of the New Deal, most scholars and policymakers agreed generally that the Constitution did not grant the federal government sweeping powers to use such clauses and subsequent amendments as a positive tool of social, political, and economic experimentation.

The New Deal radically changed this understanding by ushering in an era of progressive-minded government activism. The period spawned a new form of constitutional jurisprudence. Adopting an attitude that had not existed previously, lawmakers and the courts came to interpret the Fourteenth Amendment, the Commerce Clause, and other vague clauses within the Constitution as tools for the transfer of power from the states and the people to the federal government.

"The result," argues legal scholar David Bernstein in a 1992 study for the Cato Institute, "was a revolution in the American constitutional system, which was transformed from a system in which strict limits were placed on the powers of the national government to one in which the national government's powers were almost limitless, particularly in the commercial sphere."[37] David Forte, professor of law at Cleveland State University, concurs, noting that "Subsequent to 1938, any real judicial concern for maintaining the federal system quickly evaporated. Through a virtually unlimited definition of the Commerce Power, and especially through an unrestrained use of the Spending Power, Congress was able to supplant the states as the primary policy making force in the country."[38]

As Supreme Court Justice Clarence Thomas noted in a recent decision regarding the post–New Deal contortion of Commerce Clause jurisprudence, "[F]rom the time of the ratification of the Constitution to the mid-1930s, it was widely understood that the Constitution granted Congress only limited powers, notwithstanding the Commerce Clause.... To be sure, congressional power pursuant to the Commerce Clause was alternatively described less narrowly during this 150-year period."[39] Once the New Deal juris-

Footnotes:
37. David Bernstein, "Equal Protection for Economic Liberty: Is the Court Ready," Cato Institute *Policy Analysis*, October 5, 1992, p. 5.
38. David F. Forte, "Conservatism and the Rehnquist Court," Heritage Foundation *Lecture* No. 438, June 12, 1992, p. 4.
39. Justice Clarence Thomas (concurring opinion), *United States v. Lopez*, 115 S.Ct. 1624, 1649 (1995).

The Delicate Balance

prudence became commonly accepted, however, this narrow definition of federal authority that Justice Thomas describes lost favor among intellectuals and policymakers.

The result was a series of Supreme Court cases that upset the Founders' delicate balance and served as a catalyst for the augmentation of federal powers at the expense of the states and individual citizens. The Court accomplished this by reading too much into legal phrases and terms of art, such as "interstate commerce," "commerce among the several states," and actions that "affected other states."

Most notably, the Court came to equate "commerce" with manufacturing and production, which clearly are not the same types of activities as commerce and trade. Manufacturing and production give birth to commerce and trade—one necessarily must precede the other. As legal historian and federalism expert Raoul Berger has argued, "the Founders conceived of 'commerce' as 'trade,' the interchange of goods by one State with another."[40] And as Chief Justice Melville Weston Fuller correctly argued in the 1895 case of *United States v. E. C. Knight Co.*, "Commerce succeeds to manufacture, and is not a part of it."[41]

Despite Chief Justice Fuller's admonition, the courts and Congress abandoned the constraints imposed on the federal government by the Constitution and instead decided to apply their own personal judgments to matters of commercial regulation by broadly interpreting the meaning of "interstate commerce" and the purpose of the Commerce Clause. In fact, in 1905, just a decade after the *E. C. Knight* decision, the Court began to abandon this commerce-manufacturing distinction in *Swift & Co. v. United States*.[42] Although the Court tried to revive this distinction in the 1918 case of *Hammer v. Dagenhart*,[43] subsequent cases gradually abandoned attempts to separate the two. A noble effort to halt this constitutional transformation was made during the New Deal period by the so-called Four Horsemen—Justices George Sutherland, Pierce Butler, Willis Van Devanter, and James McReynolds—who fought to uphold the Constitution's original design of checks and balances and limited, enumerated federal powers. But this effort proved futile because the nine activist judges appointed during Franklin Delano Roosevelt's

Footnotes:
40. Raoul Berger, "Judicial Manipulation of the Commerce Clause," *Texas Law Review*, Vol. 74, Issue 4 (March 1996), p. 703.
41. Chief Justice Melville Weston Fuller, *United States v. E. C. Knight Co.*, 156 U.S. 1, 12 (1895).
42. 196 U.S. 375 (1905).
43. 247 U.S. 251 (1918).

The Jurisprudence of American Commercial Federalism

long tenure as President during the New Deal were committed to creating a bold new world of jurisprudence that would overthrow the old constitutional order.

And they did. By wandering far off the course charted by the Framers, the Court produced the twisted legal reasoning found in such New Deal-era cases as *N.L.R.B. v. Jones & Laughlin Steel Co.* (1937),[44] *U.S. v. Darby* (1941),[45] *Wickard v. Filburn* (1942),[46] and other subsequent decisions.[47] In these cases, the New Deal justices seemed comfortable contorting the confines of the Commerce Clause into an affirmative grant of seemingly unlimited federal power. This was strikingly at odds not only with the Founders' original balance of constitutional powers, but also with the vast majority of Supreme Court opinions for the preceding 150 years of American history, as Justice Thomas has argued. As Raoul Berger summarizes, "The Court's repeatedly shifting construction of the Commerce Clause indicates that it does not speak with the voice of the Constitution, but rather reflects a given majority's personal predilections."[48] From the time of the New Deal onward, these personal judicial predilections almost always were tilted toward the expansion of federal power and responsibility at the expense of individual liberty, economic freedom, and the autonomy of the states and localities.

> **As Raoul Berger summarizes, "The Court's repeatedly shifting construction of the Commerce Clause indicates that it does not speak with the voice of the Constitution, but rather reflects a given majority's personal predilections."**

In *Wickard*, for example, the Court construed the Commerce Clause to find that the federal government's regulatory reach under the Second Agricultural Adjustment Act of 1938 extended all the way down to the wheat that a farmer grew on his property for personal consumption. In other words, the New Deal Court reasoned tortuously, even though a farmer was growing an agricultural product purely for personal use and in no way intended to enter the

Footnotes:
44. 301 U.S. 1 (1937).
45. 312 U.S. 100 (1941).
46. 317 U.S. 111 (1942).
47. For a thorough discussion and critique of this modern, expansionary-minded Commerce Clause jurisprudence, see Richard A. Epstein, "The Proper Scope of the Commerce Power," *Virginia Law Review*, Vol. 73, No. 8 (November 1987), pp. 1387–1455.
48. Berger, "Judicial Manipulation of the Commerce Clause," p. 717.

stream of interstate or even intrastate commerce, the Commerce Clause could be interpreted to cover such activity. The Court's argument: The wheat conceivably might have at least some incidental impact or indirect effect upon interstate commerce.

Professor of History John W. Johnson of the University of Northern Iowa argues that *Wickard* was "the decision which best indicated how completely the Court had come in acquiescing to the nationalist economic philosophy of President Franklin Roosevelt and the Democratic majorities in both houses of Congress...."[49] More important, as Justice Thomas has pointed out, *Wickard* and its related body of New Deal Supreme Court case law signified an end to roughly 150 years of fairly constrained Commerce Clause jurisprudence. "The New Deal cases systematically removed each of the previous limitations on the scope of the commerce clause," notes legal scholar Richard A. Epstein of the University of Chicago Law School.[50] The creation of an extremely vague "indirect effects" test as the new standard of Commerce Clause review meant, in effect, that any conceivable form of economic activity, *no matter how local in character*, could be construed as having at least some sort of marginal or incidental impact on interstate commerce. Therefore, the vast majority of such activities were brought under federal control. Moreover, Congress and the courts came to view the Commerce Clause as a tool that allowed them to *prescribe* specific programs and policy actions, in contrast to the Founders' original understanding that the Commerce Clause should be used primarily to *proscribe* state or local policies that discriminated unjustly against interstate commerce.

Wickard v. Filburn and other New Deal Commerce Clause cases dealt an almost fatal blow to the American system of dual sovereignty. Thenceforth, a new hierarchy existed within the American Republic that placed the powers of the federal government on a higher plane relative to the states and localities. But the worst was yet to come. The knockout blow to federalism came roughly four decades later, in 1985, when the Supreme Court handed down its decision in *Garcia v. San Antonio Metro. Transit Authority*.[51]

In *Garcia*, the Court foolishly reversed its sensible 1976 ruling in *National League of Cities v. Usery*,[52] which had held that Congress could not extend wage and hour regulation to cover state or local

Footnotes:
49. John W. Johnson, "Wickard v. Filburn," in Hall, ed., *The Oxford Companion to the Supreme Court of the United States*, p. 930.
50. Epstein, "The Proper Scope of the Commerce Power," p. 1443.
51. 469 U.S. 528 (1985).
52. 426 U.S. 833 (1976).

employees. While the *National League of Cities* decision held out a brief glimmer of hope that the Court would continue to enforce at least some minimal protections against federal overreach, *Garcia* abandoned all such judicial safeguards, including the rather ambiguous "indirect effects" tests used throughout the New Deal period.

Under the new *Garcia* test written by Justice Harry Blackmun, the Court argued basically that the best protection against potential federal overreach was the federal electoral process which, at least in theory, allows the states equal representation in Congress. The Court concluded that "State sovereign interests...are more properly protected by procedural safeguards inherent in the structure of the federal system than by judicially created limitations on federal power."[53] With *Garcia*, the Court essentially abandoned any notion that it should play a legitimate refereeing role in the protection of federalism and left all decisions regarding the proper scope of the Commerce Clause to Congress.[54]

The problem is that allowing Congress to be the sole judge in every federalism dispute is about as fair as allowing the members of a football team to provide their own coaches as referees in every game they play. As Justice Lewis F. Powell explained in his dissent in *Garcia*, "More troubling than the logical infirmities in the Court's reasoning is the result of its holding, i.e., that federal political officials, invoking the Commerce Clause, are the sole judges of the limits of their own power. This result is inconsistent with the fundamental principles of our constitutional system."[55] As Deborah Jones Merritt argues, "Nothing in the structure of federal poli-

Footnotes:
53. Justice Harry Blackmun, *Garcia v. San Antonio Metro. Transit Authority*, 469 U.S. 528, 552 (1985).
54. In taking this view, the Court essentially was adopting the opinions of a handful a modern legal scholars who had argued incorrectly, in the words of Herbert Wechsler, that "[T]he national political process in the United States—and especially the role of the states in the composition and selection of the federal government—is intrinsically well adapted to retarding or restraining new intrusions by the center on the domain of the states." See Herbert Wechsler, "The Political Safeguards of Federalism: The Role of the States in the Composition and Selection of the National Government," *Columbia Law Review*, Vol. 54, No. 4 (April 1954), p. 558. This assessment is even more wrong-headed in light of the fact that in 1913, 40 years before Wechsler authored this famous article claiming that the states could safeguard their authority through the national electoral process, the enactment of the Seventeenth Amendment to the Constitution had stripped the state legislatures of their former constitutional power to appoint Senators to Congress. Thus, the states had lost their most important check on the growth of national power.

tics...guarantees that these representatives will promote the institutional interests of state and local governments."[56] Finally, writing about *Garcia* in 1986, Lawrence A. Hunter and Ronald J. Oakerson of the United States Advisory Commission on Intergovernmental Relations observed that "Because Congress has the advantage of national supremacy (within the scope of the enumerated powers), the states can never be fully equal to the federal government."[57]

> With *Garcia*, the Court essentially abandoned any notion that it should play a legitimate refereeing role in the protection of federalism and left all decisions regarding the proper scope of the Commerce Clause to Congress.

In effect, *Garcia* marked the culmination of corrupt New Deal–era, pro-federal jurisprudence. The Court had abdicated its constitutional responsibility to protect the rights of the states by giving Congress free reign to exercise virtually unlimited authority over "interstate commerce" through the Commerce Clause. The Court, in *Garcia*, subjected Americans to the very sort of federal tyranny the Framers had tried so hard to prevent; regaining the delicate balance, if it occurs, will be a long and arduous process.

THE BEGINNINGS OF A FEDERALISM BACKLASH

Surprisingly, however, a small but much-needed backlash against this tortured constitutional jurisprudence has begun, both in the courts and in Congress, in recent years.

The Reagan Administration initiated this movement in the early 1980s by introducing its New Federalism initiative.[58] In his first inaugural address in 1981, President Ronald Reagan announced, "It is my intention to curb the size and influence of the federal establishment and to demand recognition of the distinctions between the powers granted to the federal government, [and] those reserved to

Footnotes:
55. Justice Lewis F. Powell (dissenting opinion), *Garcia v. San Antonio Metro. Transit Authority*, 469 U.S. 528, 567 (1985).
56. Deborah Jones Merritt, "The Guarantee Clause and State Autonomy: Federalism for a Third Century," *Columbia Law Review*, Vol. 88 (January 1988), p. 16.
57. Lawrence A. Hunter and Ronald J. Oakerson, "An Intellectual Crisis in American Federalism: The Meaning of *Garcia*," reprinted in *Federalism and The Constitution: A Symposium on Garcia* (Washington, D.C.: Advisory Commission on Intergovernmental Relations, July 1987), p. 5.
58. See C. Boyden Gray, "Regulation and Federalism," *Yale Journal of Regulation*, Vol. 1, No. 1 (1983), pp. 94–96.

The Jurisprudence of American Commercial Federalism

the states...."[59] As part of its New Federalism initiative, the Administration proposed bold reductions in federal spending and domestic grants as well as the elimination of many regulations, restrictions, and mandates on the states.[60] *The Status of Federalism in America*, a report released in November 1986, was drafted by the Administration's Working Group on Federalism to summarize these goals and initiatives.[61]

Yet, in spite of an ambitious start and a handful of limited victories (mostly in the form of the block grants to the states), President Reagan's calls for federalism reforms fell on deaf ears in Congress and slowly lost momentum. Substantively, therefore, very little occurred to restore the proper balance of powers between the states and the federal government during the 1980s, despite President Reagan's efforts at reform.

Significantly, however, the most enduring portion of President Reagan's New Federalism effort was the issuance of Executive Order 12612[62] in October 1987. E.O. 12612 directed Cabinet agencies and executive branch offices to "restore the division of governmental responsibilities between the national government and the States that was intended by the Framers of the Constitution and to ensure that the principles of federalism established by the Framers guide the Executive departments and agencies in the formulation and implementation of policies...."

As part of the strict guidelines outlined in Section 3 of Executive Order 12612,[63] executive branch agencies were ordered to follow specific Federalism Policymaking Criteria "when formulating and implementing policies that have federalism implications:"

Footnotes:
59. Ronald Reagan, *First Inaugural Address*, Washington, D.C., January 20, 1981.
60. See Richard L. Cole and Delbert A. Taebel, "The New Federalism: Promises, Programs, and Performance," *Publius: The Journal of Federalism*, Vol. 16, No. 1 (Winter 1986), pp. 3–10.
61. *The Status of Federalism in America: A Report of the Working Group on Federalism of the Domestic Policy Council*, November 1986.
62. President Ronald Reagan, Executive Order No. 12612, "Federalism," October 26, 1987, in *Federal Register*, Vol. 52, No. 210 (October 30, 1987), pp. 41685–41688.
63. See James Miller III, Director, Office of Management and Budget, "Implementation of Executive Order No. 12612, Federalism," Memorandum for the Heads of Executive Departments and Agencies, December 16, 1987, and President George Bush, "Federalism Executive Order," Memorandum to the Heads of Executive Departments and Agencies, February 16, 1990.

(a) There should be strict adherence to constitutional principles. Executive departments and agencies should closely examine the constitutional and statutory authority supporting any Federal action that would limit the policymaking discretion of the States, and should carefully assess the necessity for such action. To the extent practicable, the States should be consulted before any such action is implemented....

(b) Federal action limiting the policymaking discretion of the States should be taken only where constitutional authority for the action is clear and certain and the national activity is necessitated by the presence of a problem of national scope....

(c) [T]he national government should grant the States the maximum administrative discretion possible. Intrusive, Federal oversight of State administration is neither necessary nor desirable.

(d) When undertaking to formulate and implement policies that have federalism implications, Executive departments and agencies shall:

(1) Encourage States to develop their own policies to achieve program objectives and to work with appropriate officials in other States.

(2) Refrain, to the maximum extent possible, from establishing uniform, national standards for programs and, when possible, defer to the States to establish standards.

(3) When national standards are required, consult with appropriate officials and organizations representing the States in developing those standards.

Although widely ignored by most regulatory agencies, President Reagan's Executive Order 12612 was an important acknowledgment of the federal government's overwhelming power. For the first time in many decades, federal officials formally recognized the problems associated with national overreach while simultaneously reaffirming the potential benefits of returning to the Framers' original model of federalism. On a more practical level, E.O. 12612 provided a road map showing how to return to the Founders' model by encouraging federal officials to work more closely or in direct consultation with the states to devolve certain powers or better craft federal policies that continued to be deemed essential national functions.[64]

Footnotes:
64. For the complete text of Executive Order 12612, see Appendix IV.

Twelve years later, however, in a stunning about-face on executive branch federalism policy, President Clinton revoked President Reagan's executive order and replaced it with his own set of Federalism Policymaking Guidelines. As mentioned in the Preface to this volume, on May 14, 1998, President Clinton signed Executive Order 13083, revoking President Reagan's E.O. 12612 and putting into place a radically different federalism vision.

It should be noted, however, that although President Clinton's new Executive Order 13083 called for revocation of the Reagan executive order, the Clinton order also borrowed much of the good language from the earlier document with respect to what constitutes "Fundamental Federalism Principles." In fact, Section 2 of the Clinton order sounds strikingly similar to the Reagan executive order:

> [T]he Constitution is premised upon a system of checks and balances.... The sovereign powers not granted to the Federal Government are reserved to the people or the States.... Federalism reflects the principle that dividing power between the Federal Government and the States serves to protect individual liberty. Preserving State authority provides an essential balance to the power of the Federal Government.... The people of the States are at liberty, subject only to the limitations of the Constitution itself or in Federal law, to define the moral, political, and legal character of their lives.... Effective public policy is often achieved when there is competition among the several States.... Policies of the Federal Government should recognize the responsibility of—and should encourage opportunities for—States, local governments, private associations, neighborhoods, families, and individuals to achieve personal, social, environmental, and economic objectives through cooperative effort.[65]

Unfortunately, however, the language of Section 2 of E.O. 13083 proved to be nothing more than lip service to those who believe in the Framers' original federalist model. Indeed, under the "Federalism Policymaking Criteria" laid out in Section 3 of the Clinton order, guidelines are established that the Clinton Administration believes justify federal regulatory intervention in the affairs of state

Footnotes:
65. President William J. Clinton, Executive Order No. 13083, "Federalism," May 14, 1998, in *Federal Register*, Vol. 63, No. 96 (May 19, 1998), pp. 27651–27655.

and local governments. Among the more ambiguous and open-ended criteria supposedly justifying federal action are the following:

- "When decentralization increases the costs of government thus imposing additional burdens on the taxpayer."
- "When States would be reluctant to impose necessary regulations because of fears that regulated business activity will relocate to other states."
- "When placing regulatory authority at the State or local level would undermine regulatory goals because high costs or demands for specialized expertise will effectively place the regulatory matter beyond the resources of State authorities."
- "When the matter relates to Federally owned or managed property or natural resources, trust obligations, or international obligations."

These criteria for federal action represent a significant distortion of the Founders' original federalist framework. Nowhere in the Constitution is there any mention of such justifications for federal regulatory activity. Nor can these new criteria be justified on the grounds that such rules and regulations might be needed to protect "interstate commerce." President Clinton's executive order on federalism consequently represented a major step backward in the ongoing effort to restore the Founders' vision of limited government, because it provided far too much leeway for federal regulatory intervention.[66]

Luckily, as already stated, political pressure from Members of Congress, state and local officials, and other interested parties grew so intense that by the summer of 1998, President Clinton was forced to "suspend" E.O. 13083.[67] The efforts of Representative David McIntosh (R–IN)[68] and Senator Fred Thompson (R–TN)[69]

Footnotes:
66. See Adam D. Thierer, "President Clinton's Sellout of Federalism," Heritage Foundation *Executive Memorandum* No. 536, June 25, 1998, and Adam D. Thierer, "Federal Power Forward Creep," *The Washington Times*, July 28, 1998, p. A16.
67. President William J. Clinton, "Suspension of Executive Order No. 13083," The White House, Office of the Press Secretary, August 5, 1998.
68. The House Government Reform and Oversight Committee's Subcommittee on National Economic Growth, Natural Resources, and Regulatory Affairs, chaired by Representative McIntosh, held a widely attended hearing on July 28, 1998. The hearing brought together representatives from the major state and local organizations who uniformly criticized President Clinton's proposed federalism policies as embodied in E.O. 13083. See Internet site: *http://www.house.gov/reform/neg/hearings/index.htm*.

The Jurisprudence of American Commercial Federalism

were crucial in drawing attention to the President's actions and unifying congressional opposition to the Clinton order.

The suspension of the Clinton order leaves the Reagan E.O. 12612 in effect. However, the White House stressed in press statements that it would seek to engage in future consultation or negotiations with state and local groups to discuss whether a new federalism executive order is needed.

On the legislative front, recent years have witnessed renewed congressional interest in finding new ways to grant states flexibility or relief from the growing burdens of federal mandates. Besides the previously mentioned increase in block grants to accomplish policy goals, the newly elected Republican Congress passed the Unfunded Mandates Reform Act of 1995 to check the costs imposed on state or local governments by Congress and federal agencies. The Act also requires closer review of federal rules that might have an impact on other levels of government.

In addition, several Members of Congress have suggested that a much more ambitious structural reorganization of government needs to be undertaken. To that end, in May of 1995, Representative J. D. Hayworth (R–AZ) announced the formation of the Constitutional Caucus. In a "Dear Colleague" letter, Representative Hayworth noted that "During this century the federal government has assumed a vast and unprecedented set of powers. The mass accumulation of power at the federal level is antithetical to both the letter and spirit of the Constitution." The mission of the Constitutional Caucus, therefore, would be to "explore ways to return power to the states and the people and restore limited, constitutional government."[70]

Even more significantly, on the judicial front, a clear shift in the Supreme Court's thinking on federalism issues appears to have taken place in just the past few years. In such cases as *Gregory* v. *Ashcroft* (1991),[71] *New York* v. *United States* (1992),[72] *U.S.* v. *Lopez* (1995),[73] *Printz* v. *United States* (1997),[74] and *City of Boerne* v. *Flores*

Footnotes:

69. Senator Thompson introduced and successfully secured passage of a sense of the Senate resolution calling on President Clinton to withdraw E.O. 13083. See Senator Fred Thompson, "The Thompson Federalism Amendment," *Congressional Record*, Vol. 144, No. 99 (July 22, 1998), p. S8747. The Thompson resolution on federalism was adopted as an amendment to the Commerce–State–Justice Appropriations bill on July 22, 1998. The bill was passed unanimously the following day.
70. Representative J. D. Hayworth, "Dear Colleague," May 2, 1995.
71. 501 U.S. 452 (1991).
72. 505 U.S. 144 (1992).

The Delicate Balance

(1997),[75] the Court handed down decisions that attempted to breathe new life into the more traditional understanding of federalism.

In *Gregory v. Ashcroft*, for example, Justice Sandra Day O'Connor wrote for the Court that "[E]very schoolchild learns [that] our Constitution establishes a system of dual sovereignty between the States and the Federal Government. This Court also has recognized this fundamental principle."[76] In *New York v. United States*, Justice O'Connor again wisely remarked that "States are not mere political subdivisions of the United States. State governments are neither regional offices nor administrative agencies of the Federal Government."[77] And in the *Lopez* and *Printz* decisions, the Court struck down federal gun laws that Congress had attempted to enforce by using a spurious Commerce Clause defense.

Despite this renewed interest in constitutional federalism, however, there is much that remains to be done if the disturbing imbalance of powers created during this century is to be corrected. Chapter 6 will outline several measures that could be discussed or implemented to help restore the Framers' proper balance.

As the turn of the century approaches and the United States anticipates the celebration of its 225th birthday in 2001, it seems clear that the foundations of American federalism have been shaken severely. But is the underlying structure of the American federal republic fractured beyond repair? Hardly. The framework for a vibrant federal republic still exists. What is needed is the political will to repair and strengthen the Founders' original framework to ensure that the proper balance of constitutional powers is restored.

Footnotes:
73. U.S. 93–1260 (1995).
74. U.S. 95–1478 (1997).
75. U.S. 95–2074 (1997).
76. Justice Sandra Day O'Connor, *Gregory v. Ashcroft*, 501 U.S. 452, 457 (1991).
77. Justice Sandra Day O'Connor, *New York v. United States*, 505 U.S. 144, 188 (1992).

4

COMPETING THEORIES OF FEDERALISM

The preceding historical analysis of the development of commercial federalism in the United States discussed why the Founders felt so deep a need to establish and maintain a delicate balance in the federalist structure of the young nation's government. It also outlined how the courts and Congress have interpreted and implemented this balance in the years following the framing of the Constitution.

What remains to be explained is how competing philosophical visions of the meaning of federalism have been formed by legal scholars, economists, and policymakers over the course of America's history. To simplify the discussion, these competing visions will be refined into two schools of thought:

- The broad constructionist vision, based on an expansive reading and understanding of the text and spirit of the Constitution, views federalism as a somewhat outmoded system of governance. Broad constructionists call for a national government with substantial, sometimes unlimited powers to address socioeconomic ills and argue that state and local flexibility is appropriate when used to raise the bar above federal standards.

- The textualist vision, based on strict adherence to the text and spirit of the Constitution, views federalism as the protector of liberty and a check on the growth of governmental power. Textualists believe in a national government of limited, enumerated powers that provides ample room for political experimentation at the state or local level.

The strengths and weaknesses of each vision or interpretation of the Constitution and America's federalist framework will be discussed in turn. After the broad constructionist vision is discussed, the textualist vision will be broken down into two further schools of thought and critiqued accordingly. As mentioned in the introduction, two questions will be posed to guide this inquiry. Specifically:

1. *Which interpretation of federalism most accurately represents the Framers' constitutional vision of federalism?*

2. *From an economic point of view, which scheme of constitutional policy making and jurisprudence is most favorable to a vibrant free-market economy and to the expansion of economic freedom in general?*

THE BROAD CONSTRUCTIONIST VISION

Overview of Broad Constructionist Federalism. This first vision of federalism is the modern view that has dominated the thinking of Congress and the courts roughly since the time of the New Deal. Broad constructionists are so labeled because they believe in the malleability of words, phrases, and concepts in the Constitution. The term "living Constitution" or "evolving Constitution" is frequently invoked by advocates of broad constructionism to signify their desire to allow policymakers, and judges in particular, to read new ideas or powers into the text of the Constitution.

Broad constructionists generally argue that, as traditionally defined, federalism is a relic of America's political past. A literal reading of the Constitution is impractical if not impossible, they contend, and changing conditions in any event demand shifting constitutional priorities. Therefore, prudence dictates that national programs and solutions ought not to be rejected automatically, simply because they do not fit the Founders' original federalist framework. Expansive national bureaucracies, all-encompassing uniform standards and regulations, and a host of federal spending initiatives and programs are accepted and even encouraged.

Thus, under the logic of broad constructionism, Congress and the courts are encouraged to prescribe national remedies for any perceived socioeconomic ills that may arise. To the extent that federalism is accepted at all, it is a top-down process in which states and localities are viewed as implementational vehicles for federal policies and programs. Once centralized, one-size-fits-all national solutions are determined, and federal laws and regulations are promulgated, the states and localities are to carry out or comply with these rules or programs. Although some flexibility may be granted to a state with respect to how it carries out this task, this flexibility as a rule is limited to allowing the state to pass statutes that would strengthen or expand the coverage of the federal statute.

This theory has important ramifications for interstate commerce and economic freedom since, according to the logic of the broad constructionist school, experimentation among states and localities is acceptable when such experimentation is intended to raise the regulatory bar above nationally imposed standards. Consequently, the broad constructionists' idea of flexibility is the issuance of state and local waivers or exemptions from federal rules or requirements. "Voting with one's feet," whether by a consumer or by a business, is discouraged if not simply prohibited.

Critique of Broad Constructionist Federalism. This concept of federalism cannot be regarded as historically appropriate, since it is devoid of any serious grounding in the Constitution. In fact, the top-down federalism espoused by the broad constructionists really is not federalism at all—it is unilateral or unitary government. It basically allows federal legislators and judges to craft laws and regulations based on their own tastes and preferences, without reference to the Constitution, and then simply pass along a series of edicts to the states regarding how these constitutionally ungrounded policies should be implemented.

On a more practical note, top-down federalism does not work well because a single, national solution to most political problems rarely exists. Such one-size-fits-all centralized planning stifles the innovative decision-making and parochial experimentation that often are needed to devise workable solutions to political problems.

To be fair, a handful of situations do exist that demand national attention and for which this top-down model therefore may be appropriate. For example, even the Framers recognized that uniform naturalization procedures, currency standards, bankruptcy laws, and standards for copyright and patent protection were desirable goals, and they listed these among the federal government's few enumerated powers. Such rules fostered the development of a more efficient commercial union among the states.

Modern politicians and jurists, however, have blown this efficiency defense for national regulation out of all proportion to reality, arguing incorrectly that the vast majority of commercial situations demand national attention to achieve optimal outcomes. Such thinking was fundamental to the corrupt constitutional jurisprudence of *N.L.R.B. v. Jones & Laughlin*, *U.S. v. Darby*, *Wickard v. Filburn*, and *Garcia v. San Antonio*, and the corresponding New Deal era of a federal government without restraints was born.[1]

Luckily, as noted in Chapter 3, some recent Supreme Court decisions have begun to reverse this trend. In several cases this decade, the Court has decimated the logic of this warped modern jurispru-

The Delicate Balance

dence by proving that it is completely at odds with the Framers' true federalist framework. In 1992, for example, Justice Sandra Day O'Connor noted sagaciously in *New York v. United States* that:

> The Federal Government undertakes activities today that would have been unimaginable to the Framers in two senses; first, because the Framers would not have conceived that any government would conduct such activities; and second, because the Framers would not have believed that the Federal Government, rather than the States, would assume such responsibilities.[2]

> **One-size-fits-all centralized planning stifles the innovative decision-making and parochial experimentation that often are needed to devise workable solutions to political problems.**

Finally, it should be clear from the previous chapter's discussion why the Founders gave the national government pre-emptive authority under the Commerce Clause: They desired to end economic protectionism between the states and ensure that a free capitalist marketplace could develop nationwide. In an 1829 correspondence with J. C. Cabell, James Madison made the purpose of the Commerce Clause absolutely clear: "[It] grew out of the abuses of the power by the importing States in taxing the non-importing, and was intended as a negative and preventative provision against injustice among the States themselves, rather than as a power to be used for positive purposes of the General Government...."[3]

Likewise, Cato Institute constitutional law scholar Roger Pilon argues that the purpose of the Commerce Clause was "not so much to convey a power 'to regulate'—in the affirmative sense in which we use that term today—as a power 'to make regular' the commerce that might take place among the states."[4] As former Judge Robert Bork has written, "[E]veryone agrees that the historic, central func-

Footnotes:
1. For an excellent overview of the growth of government from the New Deal period onward, see Robert Higgs, *Crisis and Leviathan: Critical Episodes in the Growth of American Government* (San Francisco: Pacific Research Institute for Public Policy, 1989).
2. Justice Sandra Day O'Connor, *New York v. United States*, 505 U.S. 144, 157 (1992).
3. Letter from James Madison to J. C. Cabell, February 12, 1829, quoted in Raoul Berger, "Judicial Manipulation of the Commerce Clause," *Texas Law Review*, Vol. 74, Issue 4 (March 1996), p. 705.

tion of the commerce clause was to empower Congress to eliminate state-created obstacles to interstate trade."[5] In other words, the Founders' concern was primarily *economic*, or more specifically, to guarantee economic union and commercial harmony among the states by *proscribing* the discriminatory treatment of interstate commerce by the states. Nowhere in the Framers' writings is there any reference to the use of the commerce power for any broader purpose.

To summarize, the Commerce Clause was intended—as its title obviously implies—to protect the free flow of *commerce* among the states; it most assuredly was not intended to be a *prescriptive* tool that social engineers could use to re-craft the states in the image of the national government's preference. Thus, the modern reach of the Commerce Clause under the top-down, federalist approach of the broad constructionists has come to encompass almost every conceivable form of human activity. This sweeping power is without doubt a gross distortion of the Framers' original intent, and deserves no further consideration other than to say that it must be rescinded and the Framers' original concept restored.

THE TEXTUALIST VISION

The textualist, or originalist, vision represents a better interpretation of the Framers' original model of constitutional federalism. Textualists regard broad constructionism as a betrayal of the federalist framework because it places little value on adhering to the letter and spirit of the Constitution as originally written. In particular, textualists are gravely concerned that the integrity of the Constitution is seriously compromised when broad constructionist philosophy is embraced by policymakers. The Constitution becomes infinitely malleable and subject to continuous revision, especially by the Courts, under broad contructionist theory.

Textualists fear that such thinking subordinates the rule of law to the rule of men. In other words, textualists believe that just because the times change does not mean that the context of the Constitution should change as well. Legal standards should remain fixed and comprehensible. Any attempts to change America's constitutional

Footnotes:
4. Roger Pilon, "Freedom, Responsibility, and the Constitution: On Recovering Our Founding Principles," in David Boaz and Edward H. Crane, eds., *Market Liberalism: A Paradigm for the 21st Century* (Washington, D.C.: Cato Institute, 1993), p. 42.
5. Robert H. Bork, "Federalism and Federal Regulation: The Case of Product Labeling," Washington Legal Foundation, *Critical Legal Issues*, Working Paper Series No. 46, July 1991, p. 10.

structure of government should be accompanied by adherence to strict procedures and should never be undertaken lightly.

In emphasizing the importance of original intent when discussing constitutional interpretation, textualists argue that the Constitution's specific balance of powers must be adhered to and that the national government should remain one of limited, enumerated powers as established in the document. The expansion of federal powers and programs should be constrained, and unconstitutional advances that have been made by the federal government at the expense of the states should be reversed.

Federalism to the textualists is the federalism created by the Founders: limited, enumerated powers for the national government; checks and balances within the respective branches and levels of government; and a generous sphere for autonomous state, local, and especially individual action.

Textualists place a high value on decentralized decision-making and argue that state and local sovereignty will breed a healthy degree of competition between different jurisdictions. They further believe that the inherent tension between these competing levels of government will protect and enhance the liberty of individual Americans by providing reciprocal checks on the abuse of power.

In an important essay examining "Common-Law Courts in a Civil Law System," Supreme Court Justice Antonin Scalia provides a vigorous defense of textualism, even while conceding that the textualist or originalist school is not perfectly unified on all issues:

> [O]riginalists [do not] always agree upon their answer. There is plenty of room for disagreement as to what original meaning was, and even more as to how that original meaning applies to the situation before the court. But the originalist at least knows what he is looking for: the original meaning of the text. Often—indeed, dare I say usually—that is easy to discern and simple to apply. Sometimes (though not very often), there will be disagreement regarding the original meaning; and sometimes there will be disagreement as to how that original meaning applies to new and unforeseen phenomena....
>
> But the difficulties and uncertainties of determining original meaning and applying it to modern circumstances are negligible compared with the difficulties and uncertainties of the philosophy that says that the Constitution *changes*; that the very act that it once pro-

hibited it now permits, and that it once permitted now forbids; and that the key to that change is unknown and unknowable. The originalist, if he does not have all the answers, has many of them.[6]

Thus, textualism or originalism is a superior vision of constitutional interpretation, since it attempts to adhere to the Founders' constitutional vision for America and their federalist system of governance. However, as Justice Scalia points out, textualist thinking is not perfectly homogeneous. In fact, important disagreements have divided the textualist camp into two distinct factions.

One theory, typically espoused by the more conservative wing of the textualist movement, stresses the benefits of state and local autonomy, devolution of power, and political decentralization as the primary objectives of the Founders' constitutional vision of federalism. The other brand of textualism exhibits a decidedly libertarian bent, regarding the protection of interstate commerce and individual liberties (including economic liberties) as the Founder's preeminent goal.

Needless to say, this dispute can have, and has had, a direct bearing on the regulation or deregulation of many important nationwide industries and the protection of economic liberties in general. As mentioned in Chapter 1, these internal disputes often have divided the textualists and resulted in textualist scholars and policymakers spending time feuding among themselves instead of fighting the unconstitutional advances made by the broad constructionists. As a consequence, efforts to deregulate these sectors and grant consumers the economic freedom to which they should be entitled have been frustrated. This schism begs for a solution, or at least a compromise.

Thus, the issue becomes (to restate the two questions posed above, but in a more focused manner) which of these two views of constitutional textualism better corresponds with the Framers' original constitutional federalist framework, and which better guarantees the expansion of economic freedom and vigorous interstate commerce?

Each of these textualist theories will be discussed and critiqued in turn to answer these questions.

Footnotes:
6. Antonin Scalia, *A Matter of Interpretation: Federal Courts and the Law* (Princeton, N.J.: Princeton University Press, 1997), pp. 45–46.

STATE SOVEREIGNTY TEXTUALISM

Overview of State Sovereignty Textualism. Adherents of the state sovereignty theory of constitutional textualism would argue their vision is more in line with the Founders' original intent because the Framers placed a high value, perhaps even the highest value of all, on the autonomy of the individual states of the Union. The founding of the United States of America began with the states collectively seeking to enter into a cooperative union to ensure their mutual protection from foreign invaders as well as to ensure peace and tranquillity among the several states.[7] Thus, since all national authority originally sprang entirely from the states, America must return to a system in which states' rights are once again the guiding star of federalism jurisprudence and, for that matter, all political decision-making.

"Further, in a pluralistic society, reasonable people should be left room to differ on...value judgments," argues Earl M. Maltz, professor of law at Rutgers University. "Recognition of the importance of federalism allows states to adapt their policies to fundamentally different value systems to an extent unattainable in a world governed by uniform national rules."[8]

Concerning the more practical question of how to preserve commercial harmony throughout the Union, the traditional defense of state sovereignty textualism or states' rights federalism is an enduring one. States' rights federalism presents the most efficient way to govern a society and an economy because it allocates government responsibility and power according to which level of government is best suited to a particular task. The level of government best suited to the task of governing is typically that which is closest to the issue, industry, or individuals in question. Therefore, while a handful of political concerns will demand national governance, the vast majority of life's political issues and troubles are best addressed by state and local officials, who have the ability to experiment with different systems and solutions. When citizens are dissatisfied with the outcome, they can pack their bags and move elsewhere, or elect new public officials to govern them.[9]

Footnotes:
7. See Raoul Berger, "The Commerce Clause," in *Federalism: The Founders' Design* (Norman, Okla.: University of Oklahoma Press, 1987).
8. Earl M. Maltz, "Individual Rights and State Autonomy," *Harvard Journal of Law and Public Policy*, Vol. 12, No. 1 (Winter 1989), p. 184.
9. For an excellent summary and discussion of the benefits of a more decentralized political system, see Michael W. McConnell, "Federalism: Evaluating the Founders' Design," *University of Chicago Law Review*, Vol. 54 (1987), pp. 1484–1512.

Competing Theories of Federalism

Critique of State Sovereignty Textualism. While a federalist system of governance possesses these advantages, such a simplistic justification for the American system of constitutional federalism falls short of providing a complete explanation of the Founders' true framework. As analysts Douglas Seay and Wesley Smith argued in a 1996 Heritage Foundation study:

> [A]ll these arguments in favor of federalism are subsidiary to its central purpose: *limiting the power of governments at all levels*. The national and state governments were intended to constrain one another, not to work hand-in-glove or parcel out functions to that level of government which will perform them best. Thus the new government was given the power to prevent the states from abusing their authority through such actions as erecting trade barriers against one another, and national legislation was given preeminence over state and local law in those limited areas reserved to the national government. In turn, the states were expected to constrain Washington, as they were regarded as the only effective means of doing so.[10]

Legal scholar Stephan Calabresi has argued similarly that "It is...no accident that Americans have thought from the time of the founding onward that liberty would be preserved by having two levels of government that serve as checks on one another."[11] As the Supreme Court summed up in *Gregory v. Ashcroft*:

> Perhaps the principal benefit of the federalist system is a check on abuses of government power.... Just as the separation and independence of the coordinate Branches of the Federal Government serve to prevent the accumulation of excessive power in any one Branch, a healthy balance of power between the States and the Federal Government will reduce the risk of tyranny and abuse from either front.[12]

Finally, even within its highly disappointing decision in *Garcia v. San Antonio Metro. Transit Authority*, the Court correctly pointed out

Footnotes:
10. Douglas Seay and Wesley Smith, "Federalism," in Stuart M. Butler and Kim R. Holmes, eds., *Issues '96: The Candidate's Briefing Book* (Washington, D.C.: The Heritage Foundation, 1996), p. 413; emphasis added.
11. Stephan G. Calabresi, "A Government of Limited and Enumerated Powers: In Defense of *United States v. Lopez*," *Michigan Law Review*, Vol. 94 (1995), p. 785.
12. Justice Sandra Day O'Connor, *Gregory v. Ashcroft*, 501 U.S. 452 (1991).

that "[T]he constitutionally mandated balance of power between the States and the Federal Government, [was] designed to protect our fundamental liberties."[13] Hence, the Founders had a higher purpose in mind than simply parceling out government functions to the most efficient level when they adopted a federalist system for America over two hundred years ago. As will be summarized below, the libertarian federalists argue that this higher purpose is the preservation and maximization of individual liberty.

Although most adherents of the state sovereignty view of textualism would concede these points, proponents of this vision still fall prey to the temptation to repeat the mantra of "states' rights" or "devolution" as a seemingly universal cure for all political problems or jurisdictional disputes. This is not always the case. But even when states' rights or devolution do represent the proper policy response for textualists to offer (as, more often than not, they do), these remedies should be invoked in the name of expanding individual liberty and economic freedom. They should not serve simply as a knee-jerk response that might sound more politically appealing to the electorate.

An equally important critique of the state sovereignty model is that, if taken to the extreme as it was during the Articles of Confederation period, an absolutist vision of states' rights federalism would threaten the competitive commercial vitality of the national economy through balkanization, factionalism, and protectionism. America grew rich over the past two centuries precisely because its internal markets were open to trade. For the most part, states have not been permitted to establish barriers to commercial trade and interaction. Single market standards have evolved freely, and consumers have been free to contract voluntarily with producers from a variety of geographic venues.

In this sense, the American federalist system is best understood as one of the world's first, and certainly one of its most successful, multilateral free trade systems. Multilateral free trade systems, such as the General Agreement on Tariffs and Trade (GATT) and the North American Free Trade Agreement (NAFTA), are created by autonomous governments to expand trade between members. Governments agree to remove barriers to trade and accord equal treatment to the goods and services imported from other states, regions, or nations. This unique American contribution to future political and economic trading systems should not be underestimated and must

Footnotes:
13. Justice Harry Blackmun, *Garcia v. San Antonio Metro. Transit Authority*, 469 U.S. 528 (1985).

Competing Theories of Federalism

rank among the primary achievements of the Founders' constitutional framework.[14] Such a system would not have been possible under the Articles of Confederation, and state sovereignty textualists need to understand and appreciate this fact.

This American common market system has been protected by the Supreme Court even when Congress has chosen not to take affirmative steps to prohibit discriminatory or protectionist state policies; specifically, the Court has intervened to enforce Commerce Clause protections even though Congress was silent on the matter at hand. This area of jurisprudence has come to be known as the Negative Commerce Clause or Dormant Commerce Clause theory.

> **The American federalist system is best understood as one of the world's first, and certainly one of its most successful, multilateral free trade systems.**

The Negative or Dormant Commerce Clause, summarizes Roger Pilon, "restricts states from intruding on federal authority over interstate commerce even when there has been no federal legislation in a given area...."[15] In the words of Jacques Leboeuf of the Oakland, California-based law firm of Crosby, Heafey, Roach & May, "State regulations affecting interstate commerce, whose purpose or effect is to gain for those within the state an advantage at the expense of those without, or to burden those out of state without any corresponding advantage to those within, have been thought to impinge upon the constitutional prohibition *even though Congress has not acted.*"[16]

Many legal scholars and judges who lean toward the state sovereignty theory of textualism argue that the Dormant or Negative Commerce Clause is a fictional creation of the courts and therefore has no legitimate place in federalism jurisprudence.[17] For example, in *Bendix Autolite Corp. v. Midwesco*, Justice Antonin Scalia has noted that he would "abandon the 'balancing' approach to...negative Commerce Clause cases...and leave essentially legislative judgments

Footnotes:
14. See also Daniel A. Farber and Robert E. Hudec, "Free Trade and the Regulatory State: A GATT's Eye View of the Dormant Commerce Clause," *Vanderbilt Law Review*, Vol. 47 (1994), pp. 1401–1440. Farber and Hudec conclude that, "Despite the great conceptual difficulties posed by regulatory trade barriers, both U.S. and international tribunals seem largely to have struggled their way to defensible results." *Ibid.*, p. 1440.
15. Pilon, "Freedom, Responsibility, and the Constitution," p. 42.
16. Jacques Leboeuf, "The Economics of Federalism and the Proper Scope of the Federal Commerce Power," *San Diego Law Review*, Vol. 31 (Summer 1994), p. 611; emphasis added.

The Delicate Balance

to Congress."[18] And in his polemical concurring opinion in *Lopez*, Justice Clarence Thomas has cast similar doubts on the usefulness and legitimacy of balancing tests and the notion of the Dormant Commerce Clause.[19]

Negative or Dormant Commerce Clause jurisprudence is well-established, however, and cannot be claimed to be entirely a creation of the modern Court. In fact, Chief Justice John Marshall is widely credited with being the first person to elucidate a general theory of the Dormant Commerce Clause as early as 1824 in the famous case of *Gibbons v. Ogden*.[20] Other cases handed down throughout the 1800s also employed the logic of Dormant Commerce Clause jurisprudence, including *Willson v. Black Bird Creek Marsh Co.* (1829),[21] *Cooley v. Board of Wardens* (1851),[22] and *Welton v. Missouri* (1875).[23]

Regarding so-called balancing tests, which will be discussed in more detail in the next chapter, they too have been employed in many cases throughout U.S. history. In one sense, every jurisdictional dispute or federalism case has involved *some* degree of "balancing." Regrettably, trade-offs necessarily will be made in many Commerce Clause cases regarding the regulation of interstate commerce, since not every case lends itself well to a black-and-white resolution of the dispute at hand. Instead, the world of federalism jurisprudence is painted in shades of legal gray.

As the next chapter will make clear, however, at the heart of every such balancing effort should be an effort to uncover potentially protectionist, discriminatory, or extraterritorial actions by states or localities, as well as violations of sacred, constitutionally protected liberties. If violations of these core constitutional imperatives are not

Footnotes:
17. See, notably, Lino A. Graglia, "The Supreme Court and the American Common Market," in A. Dan Tarlock, ed., *Regulation, Federalism, and Interstate Commerce* (Cambridge, Mass.: Oelgeschlager, Gunn & Hain, Publishers, Inc., 1981), pp. 67–75, and Martin H. Redish and Shane V. Nugent, "The Dormant Commerce Clause and the Constitutional Balance of Federalism," *Duke Law Journal*, No. 4 (1987), pp. 569–617.
18. Justice Antonin Scalia (concurring opinion), *Bendix Autolite Corp. v. Midwesco Enterprises*, 486 U.S. 888, 897 (1988).
19. Strong academic support for this belief can be found in Redish and Nugent, "The Dormant Commerce Clause and the Constitutional Balance of Federalism," pp. 569–617.
20. 22 U.S. (9 Wheat.) 1 (1824).
21. 27 U.S. 252 (1829).
22. 53 U.S. (12 How.) 299 (1851).
23. 91 U.S. 275 (1875).

evident, then the balance should tilt clearly in favor of the states and localities, as supporters of states' rights would rightly demand.

With regard to the claim made by many state sovereignty textualists that all Commerce Clause or economic liberty disputes should be handled within the legislative arena instead of by the Court, such a luxury is not always possible. Inevitably, the Court will be forced to deal with many jurisdictional disputes or questions of economic freedom about which Congress has not been able to reach agreement, or which Congress simply has not had the time or interest to cover. Many of these cases will involve conflicting state laws, and settlement will require Supreme Court adjudication. Article III, Section 2 of the Constitution specifies clearly that "The judicial Power shall extend…to Controversies between two or more States," meaning the Court has the power to deal with such commercial disputes. Furthermore, Article IV, Section 2 requires that "The citizens of each State shall be entitled to all Privileges and Immunities of Citizens in the several States."

If the protections afforded by the Privileges and Immunities Clause of Article IV and the Fourteenth Amendment are read in conjunction with the intentions of the Commerce Clause, then it seems that Dormant Commerce Clause jurisprudence rests on sound constitutional foundations. Consequently, when disputes over interstate commerce arise between the states, the Court may be forced to render a verdict. In doing so, it should not shy away from its constitutional duty to uphold the spirit of the Constitution; the Court should act as an institutional defender of the Framers' federalist system and of economic liberty in general.

Some conservative textualists may claim that protectionist or discriminatory state laws ought to stand until such time as Congress sees fit to take steps to prevent such political mischief. But this view ignores the role the Court traditionally has played in protecting free trade among the states. When congressional guidance is available, the Court obviously must defer to legislative judgments on the matter at hand. But when Congress has failed to act and states are behaving in a facially discriminatory manner against the interests of other states, the Court, for both principled and practical reasons, has provided a check against state actions that upset the Founders' constitutional balance of powers.

On grounds of principle, it is worth reiterating that in abandoning the Articles of Confederation and adopting the modern Constitution, the Framers made it abundantly clear that state interference with the free flow of interstate commerce would not be tolerated. Therefore, under the logic of both the Commerce Clause and the

Privileges and Immunities Clause, the Supreme Court has a right to strike down protectionist, discriminatory, or extraterritorial state laws that come before the Court when these laws would create economic discord among the states and injure the cause of interstate commerce.

On a more practical note, it seems far-fetched to believe that Congress can legislate on every potential violation of interstate commerce that arises from the existence of discriminatory state laws. As the brief survey of Supreme Court cases in Appendix III makes evident, interstate commerce disputes between the states involve everything from broad macroeconomic issues, such as monetary policy and trade on the open seas, to trivial microeconomic issues involving the type of mud flaps on trucks and the packaging and transportation of cantaloupes. Congress should not have to establish new national policies for each of these issues or industries every time a state law discriminates against interstate commerce in a new field. As Justice Stephan Field aptly concluded as long ago as 1875 in *Welton v. Missouri*, "The fact that Congress has not seen fit to prescribe any specific rules to govern inter-State commerce does not affect the question. Its inaction on this subject...is equivalent to a declaration that inter-State commerce shall be free and untrammeled."[24]

Therefore, the Courts can provide a legitimate check on discriminatory and protectionist actions by the states that interfere with the interstate market for trade in goods and services. The Founders made it clear in formulating the Constitution that such behavior was incompatible with national harmony and the common market structure of the American Republic. Furthermore, the lack of congressional action to protect interstate commerce should not be read as an affirmative grant to the states to legislate over interstate affairs. Rather, the courts should assume that the nation's lanes of interstate trade and commerce should be kept free of restraints unless Congress authorizes state interference within a given field.

The benefits of an open internal marketplace are substantial, and the judicial doctrine of the Dormant Commerce Clause is well-entrenched in constitutional jurisprudence and therefore has *stare decisis* importance, or precedential value. Even Justice Scalia, the current Court's most vociferous critic of balancing and Dormant Commerce Clause jurisprudence, has noted that for *stare decisis* or precedential reasons alone, the anti-discrimination policies already penned in previous Dormant Commerce Clause cases should be

Footnotes:
24. 1 U.S. 275 (1875).

respected and preserved. Thus, Scalia has cast a skeptical eye toward the Dormant Commerce Clause and balancing jurisprudence in cases such as *New Energy Co. of Indiana v. Limbach* (1988),[25] *Bendix Autolite Corp. v. Midwesco Enterprises, Inc.* (1988),[26] and *West Lynn Creamery, Inc. v. Healy* (1994)[27] while also acknowledging the beneficial nature of commercial law in the field.

Conservative textualists like Scalia argue that the Dormant Commerce Clause lacks firm constitutional footing because the power to regulate interstate commerce is found only within Article I of the Constitution, meaning it should be reserved exclusively to Congress and not the Courts. In other words, even while admitting the practical benefits of the Court's Dormant Commerce Clause jurisprudence, the conservatives argue that these substantial benefits do not necessarily justify a loose reading of the Constitution.

Michael DeBow, professor of law at Samford University's Cumberland School of Law, has proposed a very practical yet principled solution to this problem in a recent law review article. DeBow proposes that Congress codify the Dormant Commerce Clause in statutory form to preserve its anti-discrimination policy as the law of the land and give it the legitimacy of the legislative branch.[28] Congress should immediately undertake efforts to implement such a proposal to ensure that the nation's common market system is preserved and enhanced; moreover, until such time as Congress sees fit to do so, the Court should continue to respect the commerce-enhancing nature and precedential value of previous Dormant Commerce Clause cases.

On a similar note, and likewise problematic for some conservatives, will be judicial efforts to address broader disputes over economic liberty that involve state and local efforts to infringe upon constitutionally protected economic rights. Some textualists, such as Hadley Arkes, have argued that "Conservative jurists will need to become far more active in flexing the discipline of the courts against the meretricious use of the powers of licensing and zoning, and the restriction, in countless ways, of the right to earn a living in a lawful business."[29] Conservative textualists will contend that this power should be tailored very narrowly to protect legitimate and verifiable

Footnotes:
25. 486 U.S. 269 (1988).
26. 486 U.S. 888 (1998).
27. 512 U.S. 186 (1994).
28. Michael DeBow, "Codifying the Dormant Commerce Clause," *Public Interest Law Review*, Vol. 69 (1995), pp. 69–86.
29. Hadley Arkes, *The Return of George Sutherland: Restoring a Jurisprudence of Natural Rights* (Princeton, N.J.: Princeton University Press, 1994), p. 31.

individual rights so that a generous sphere for state and local experimentation can continue to exist. This is obviously a somewhat controversial topic among textualists and will be discussed at greater length below and in the next chapter.

Counterpoint and Summary of State Sovereignty Textualism. Regardless of these criticisms, the state sovereignty textualists make an important point about the foundation of American federalism: There is no chicken-and-egg dispute when it comes to which came first, state governments or the federal government. The states were first, and ceded the national government limited powers to handle disputes beyond the scope of their individual authority. The Framers were deeply concerned about the power of the national government and sought to do everything possible to restrain its power and future growth so as to preserve the rights of the states.

> There is no chicken-and-egg dispute when it comes to which came first, state governments or the federal government. The states were first, and ceded the national government limited powers to handle disputes beyond the scope of their individual authority.

The question is, was this the highest or most important goal or value associated with America's founding? The challenge for modern conservative jurists and scholars is to articulate a clear jurisprudence that more coherently supports such a contention and simultaneously supports a vigorous market for interstate commerce and greater individual and corporate economic freedom. Libertarian scholars believe they have a more consistent and principled jurisprudence to answer this challenge, as will be discussed below.

The state sovereignty camp also should be credited with casting much doubt on modern federalism jurisprudence and the entire top-down school of broad constructionism that has developed during this century. Conservative scholars, judges, and policymakers have worked arduously to de-legitimize much of the corrupt, New Deal-era jurisprudence and its corresponding national programs. Good questions have been raised, however, regarding whether the state sovereignty textualists might be going too far and essentially advocating throwing out the baby with the bathwater by calling for such a radical devolution of power to the states and localities. Other critics feel that conservative jurists and scholars provide too much discretion to the majoritarian impulses of the electorate, which often ignores the protections afforded by the Constitution. Many of these criticisms are made by advocates of liberty-maximizing or libertarian textualism, to which we now turn.

LIBERTARIAN TEXTUALISM

Overview of Libertarian Textualism. Those adhering to the liberty-maximizing or libertarian conception of textualism—or originalism—would argue that their model is in line with the Founders' original intent because the Framers placed perhaps their highest value on the protection and maximization of individual liberty. As *U.S. News & World Report* reporter Joshua Wolf Shenk has noted, ever-larger numbers of Republican legislators in Congress are coming to believe "that devolution's ultimate goal is not to transfer federal power to state governments but to strip power from government entirely."[30] These legislators believe that the rights of individual citizens were of utmost importance to the Founders and the vision they established in the Declaration of Independence and the Constitution, and it is to this vision that the nation must return.

It takes little more than a cursory reading of American history to understand the importance of liberty to the Founders. Whether it is the text of their writings on the Revolution, the Declaration of Independence, the Constitution, *The Federalist Papers*, or the many other letters and documents authored by America's Founders, individual liberty is clearly paramount. America came into being precisely because colonial patriots claimed, and successfully convinced the other people of their time, that their liberty was threatened by Britain and that a revolution was necessary to preserve and protect their natural rights from a tyrannical government.

It is against this backdrop that libertarian federalists argue their case. When a government body infringes on the rights of the people, *regardless of what level of government is in question*, the federal government should have the ability (often through express judicial activism) to take action to reverse the policy in question.

To support this belief, libertarians place heavy emphasis on constitutionally enumerated powers such as the Contracts Clause, Article IV's Privileges and Immunities Clause, the Fifth Amendment's Takings Clause, and the Ninth Amendment, which specifies that "The enumeration in the Constitution of certain rights shall not be construed to deny or disparage others retained by the people." Combined with the Fourteenth Amendment's Privileges and Immunities Clause, Due Process Clause, and Equal Protection Clause,

Footnotes:
30. Joshua Wolf Shenk, "Washington's Counter-Devolutionaries," *U.S. News & World Report*, November 24, 1997, p. 34.

these provisions of the Constitution constitute the core of libertarian jurisprudence with regard to the protection of commerce activity and economic liberty in general.

Ironically, some libertarians also cast a skeptical eye at arguments that any sort of "balancing" between federal and state powers is necessary, since the language of the Constitution and the Fourteenth Amendment clearly forbids many of the legislative actions governments undertake. Hence, they argue, no balancing is necessary.

For example, during the Reconstruction period, a number of judges who sat on the Supreme Court embraced a more laissez-faire approach to jurisprudence. These jurists argued that the substantive due process protections of economic liberty and commerce found in the Constitution rendered many state and local laws and regulations unconstitutional. Most notable in this regard are the comments of Justice Stephan J. Field in his famous polemical dissent in the *Slaughter-House Cases*. Field criticized the logic of the Court and made a passionate plea for the protection of economic liberty through the substantive due process protections of the Fourteenth Amendment:

> The first clause of the fourteenth amendment changes this whole subject, and removes it from the region of discussion and doubt. It recognizes in express terms, if it does not create, citizens of the United States, and it makes their citizenship dependent upon the place of their birth, or the fact of their adoption, and not upon the constitution or laws of any State or the condition of their ancestry. A citizen of a State is now only a citizen of the United States residing in that State. The fundamental rights, privileges, and immunities which belong to him as a free man and a free citizen, now belong to him as a citizen of the United States, and are not dependent upon his citizenship of any State. The exercise of these rights and privileges, and the degree of enjoyment received from such exercise, are always more or less affected by the condition and the local institutions of the State, or city, or town where he resides. They are thus affected in a State by the wisdom of its laws, the ability of its officers, the efficiency of its magistrates, the education and morals of its people, and by many other considerations. This is a result which follows from the constitution of society, and can never be avoided, but in no other way can they be affected by the action of the State, or by the residence

of the citizen therein. They do not derive their existence from its legislation, and cannot be destroyed by its power.[31]

Justice Joseph P. Bradley agreed with Field, noting in his own *Slaughter-House* dissent that "[T]he right of any citizen to follow whatever lawful employment he chooses to adopt (submitting himself to all lawful regulations) is one of his most valuable rights, and one which the legislature of a State cannot invade, whether restrained by its own constitution or not."[32] As Justice George Sutherland, who fought the onset of the New Deal from the bench, argued in *New State Ice Co. v. Liebmann* (1932):

> The principle is imbedded in our constitutional system that there are certain essentials of liberty with which the state is not entitled to dispense in the interest of experiments.... [A] regulation which has the effect of denying or unreasonably curtailing the common right to engage in a lawful private business...cannot be upheld consistent with the Fourteenth Amendment.[33]

Modern-day libertarians agree with this reasoning, believing that a broader reading of the Contract Clause, the constitutional prohibition of *ex post facto* laws, and the substantive due process protections found in the Fourteenth Amendment renders many federalism/interstate commerce disputes moot. The libertarians hold that no jurisdictional authority has the right to "legislate away" constitutionally protected liberties.

With respect to the scope of the Contract Clause, for example, Richard Epstein notes that "[P]roperly construed, the clause extends substantial protection to economic liberties against legislative, and perhaps judicial, interference.... [T]he internal logic of the clause, like the theory of governance that inspired it, points to a sharp restriction of the power of individual states to regulate economic affairs."[34] And Bernard Siegan argues that had certain constitutional clauses such as the Contract Clause and the prohibition against the passage of *ex post facto* laws not been undermined by various court

Footnotes:
31. Justice Stephan J. Field (dissenting opinion), *In re Slaughter-House Cases*, 83 U.S. (16 Wall.) 36, 96–97 (1872).
32. Justice Joseph P. Bradley (dissenting opinion), *In re Slaughter-House Cases*, 83 U.S. (16 Wall.) 36, 114–115 (1872).
33. Justice George Sutherland, *New State Ice Co. v. Liebmann*, 285 U.S. 262, 278–279 (1932).
34. Richard A. Epstein, "Toward a Revitalization of the Contract Clause," *University of Chicago Law Review*, Vol. 51 (Summer 1984), p. 705.

cases, "they would have curbed the power of the state and local legislatures to restrict existing prerogatives of ownership. In short, they would be barriers to the imposition of zoning and historical landmarks, rent and condominium conversion controls, among other property restraints."[35]

Stephan Macedo, author of *The New Right vs. the Constitution*, unabashedly defends national intervention to protect individual rights and simultaneously argues against the tendency by many modern conservatives to associate themselves too closely with a more radical, absolutist states' rights point of view. Explains Macedo:

> It is one thing to argue that the federal government has assumed powers reserved to the states, making a mockery of both federalism and a government of enumerated powers. It is quite another thing, however, and far more difficult, to maintain that the federal government has overstepped its bounds in defending constitutional rights against the states.[36]

A more recent and quite articulate elucidation of libertarian textualism or liberty-maximizing federalism can be found in Clint Bolick's 1993 book, *Grassroots Tyranny: The Limits of Federalism*. In an important polemical challenge to other competing theories of federalism, the vice president and chief of litigation for the Washington, D.C.-based Institute for Justice argues that the hierarchy of constitutional values can be summarized as follows: Individual liberty trumps the power of state governments, and the authority of state governments trumps the authority of the national government. More precisely:

1. Conflicts between individual liberty and the power of the national government should be resolved in favor of individual liberty, unless the conflict involves an expressly delegated power, which should be exercised in a manner that infringes upon individual rights as little as possible.

2. Conflicts between individual liberty and the power of the state governments should be resolved in favor of individual liberty, unless the conflict involves an exercise of legitimate state police

Footnotes:
35. Bernard H. Siegan, "The Economic Constitution in Historic Perspective," in Richard B. McKenzie, ed., *Constitutional Economics: Containing the Economic Powers of Government* (Lexington, Mass.: Lexington Books, 1984), p. 42.
36. Stephan Macedo, *The New Right vs. The Constitution* (Washington, D.C.: Cato Institute, 1987), p. 21.

powers exercised in a way that infringes upon individual rights as little as possible.

3. Conflicts between state governments and the national government should be resolved in favor of the states, unless the national government is acting pursuant to an expressly delegated power, including the power to protect individual liberty.[37]

"This is federalism, as the Framers of the Constitution and the Framers of the Fourteenth Amendment created and understood it," argues Bolick.

Critique of Libertarian Textualism. But is this really federalism as the Framers of the Constitution and the Fourteenth Amendment understood it? This is an important question, but the libertarian concept of textualism poses an even more obvious problem: Taken to the extreme, the libertarian federalist model would strip state and local governments of almost all policy-making power. In one sense, this may well sound appealing, but it also poses two significant problems:

1. It opens the door to overreach by national legislators and judges, and
2. It assumes that people do not want state or local governments to have the power to form distinct political systems and unique communities that reflect the preferences of their citizens.

The first critique of libertarian federalism is fairly straightforward: Any government that has enough power to protect all the rights of the people also has enough power to take away those same rights. Therefore, why not entrust the protection of individual rights (including economic liberty) to the lowest levels of government possible so that a national leviathan cannot spring up, as it has this century, to usurp not only the authority of the states, but also the rights of the people? After all, critics of libertarian textualism would argue, the government that is closest to the people is also the government that is most accountable to the people. "The smaller size of the state government jurisdictions," as Calabresi summarizes, "thus makes it far easier for citizens to exercise a greater and more effective degree of control over their government officials."[38]

Libertarian federalists would respond that the nature of government has changed profoundly over the past century not only at the federal level, but also at the state and local levels. The problem with

Footnotes:
37. Clint Bolick, *Grassroots Tyranny: The Limits of Federalism* (Washington, D.C.: Cato Institute, 1993), p. 65.
38. Calabresi, "A Government of Limited and Enumerated Powers," p. 778.

The Delicate Balance

federalism today, libertarians would retort, is not just that the federal government has grown too large, but that *all* governments—federal, state, and local—have grown too large and fail to respect the rights of the people. As journalist Richard Miniter documented in a recent issue of *The American Enterprise*:

> [W]hile it is tempting to think of state and local governments as nimble Davids to the federal Goliath, if you look closer you will see that there are really two Goliaths. Below the federal level the U.S. now has more than 82,000 individual units of government. State and local governments have more than 500,000 elected officials and more than 13 million employees—compared to fewer than 600 elected officials at the federal level and slightly more than 2 million non-military federal employees. In other words, local government is more than six times as populous as the national government.[39]

Libertarians also cite the rise of multitudes of unelected, unaccountable taxing boards, regulatory authorities, and other bureaucratic entities at the state and local levels. Do these government bodies fit into the Framers' original model of federalism? Did the Framers expect their federalist structure to support or withstand the pressure of this much government activity? And if federal legislators and judges are capable of abusing the rights of the people, is it not also equally conceivable that this rapidly increasing army of state and local officials is just as likely to trample the rights of Americans?

Indeed, libertarians have a good point in arguing that all levels of government have grown too powerful in recent decades and that this power somehow needs to be checked. And there certainly will be times when the federal government will have the right to act within its constitutionally defined sphere of authority to check the abuses of the states and localities. Yet these situations in all probability will be unique, or at least more limited than some libertarian federalists might suggest.

Encouraging federal legislators and judges to come up with a quick fix for every problem posed by abusive state or local government activity could, by itself, open the door to abusive federal activity. Unless a clear and unambiguous constitutional imperative is at stake—for example, the protection of interstate commerce, the civil rights of individual citizens, the protection of private property

Footnotes:
39. Richard Miniter, "Small Towns, Big Government," *The American Enterprise*, November/December 1997, pp. 32–33.

rights, or the protection of other rights explicitly enumerated in the Constitution—it seems obvious that federal officials have very little standing over commercial matters. However, when such standing exists, the federal government may act in the manner libertarian textualists desire to defend those constitutionally protected liberties that have been deemed beyond the reach of state or local interference.

The question then becomes: What constitutes a "constitutional imperative," or national goal or value, that is so overriding that it warrants federal action to prevent or repeal offensive state or local legislative or regulatory action?

While it is clear that civil rights violations by the states represent such a case, libertarians argue that the Fourteenth Amendment ensured that individual rights would be construed broadly to include not only social and political rights, but also economic liberties. Moreover, they argue, if the Contract Clause, Takings Clause, Commerce Clause, Privileges and Immunities Clause, and other constitutional clauses are to serve as shields against excessive state and local "grassroots tyranny," then the courts will need to pay greater attention to their protections. Therefore, these constitutional rights will have to be read more broadly if the economic rights of the people are to be upheld and economic development of the nation is to continue unhampered by excessive state and local regulation.

But, again, while most libertarian scholars agree that these clauses should provide plenary protection against state and local infringements of economic liberty, it is unclear just how far some libertarians are willing to extend these restrictions on local self-government. Significantly, most libertarians do allow for some exceptions to such a stringent Contract Clause prohibition, or from other substantive due process restrictions on state or local government action.

Specifically, many libertarian-leaning textualists allow for a "police power" limitation so that states or localities can pass laws to prevent crimes, fraudulent activity, property violations, or other torts, and regulate to protect public health and safety. As Judge Stephan Field noted in *Barbier v. Connolly* (1885):

> [N]either the [Fourteenth] amendment—broad and comprehensive as it is—nor any other amendment, was designed to interfere with the power of the state, sometimes termed its police power, to prescribe regulations to promote the health, peace, morals, education, and good order of the people, and to legislate so as to increase the industries of the state, develop its resources, and add to its wealth and prosperity. From

> the very necessities of society, legislation of a special character, having these objects in view, must often be had in certain districts, such as for draining marshes and irrigating arid plains. Special burdens are often necessary for general benefits—for supplying water, preventing fires, lighting districts, cleaning streets, opening parks, and many other objects. Regulations for these purposes may press with more or less weight upon one than upon another, but they are designed, not to impose unequal or unnecessary restrictions upon any one, but to promote, with as little individual inconvenience as possible, the general good.[40]

Even Justice George Sutherland, one of the much-vilified "Four Horsemen" who resisted the onslaught of the New Deal's corrupt jurisprudence, realized that unrestrained economic liberty must sometimes give way to the police functions of the state. As he noted in *Adkins v. Children's Hospital* (1923):

> The liberty of the individual to do as he pleases, even in innocent matters, is not absolute. It must frequently yield to the common good, and the line beyond which the power of interference may not be pressed is neither definite nor unalterable, but may be made to move, within limits not well defined, with changing needs and circumstances. Any attempt to fix a rigid boundary would be unwise as well as futile.[41]

Furthermore, some modern libertarian scholars are willing to admit that, despite their distaste for modern local zoning ordinances and other types of local economic regulation, some of this regulatory authority will necessarily escape the coverage of the Contract Clause and other constitutional restrictions. As Epstein notes:

> [O]n balance it seems that while the contract clause prevents one major type of legislative abuse, it does not reach all such abuses.... The contract clause, properly interpreted, protects rights of disposition over things, whether exercised before or after the challenged legislation is passed. Zoning restrictions on land use, of course, may well impose heavy "burdens" on the right of sale, but it is doubtful that such restrictions are reached by the contract clause, which simply does not

Footnotes:
40. Justice Stephan Field, *Barbier v. Connolly*, 113 U.S. 32, 33 (1885).
41. Justice George Sutherland, *Adkins v. Children's Hospital*, 261 U.S. 525, 561 (1923).

Competing Theories of Federalism

govern all aspects of social life in which factions can operate. It is enough, however, that the contract clause imposes a powerful constraint on government actions within its limited domain: the right to dispose of property on terms thought fit to its owners.[42]

This is an important concession, but it begs additional questions regarding the many other variations of state and local grassroots tyranny that occur with regularity, including locally imposed health and safety standards, labor protections, or the myriad of occupational licensing restrictions.

This leads to a second and far more profound critique of libertarian or individual rights-based federalism: An extreme application of libertarian philosophy assumes that people do not want state or local governments to have the power to form distinct political systems and unique communities that reflect the preferences of their citizens. Critics of libertarian textualism would argue that if Americans are truly free, they should have the right to surrender certain liberties and enter into community arrangements that might place a higher value on unique rules and lifestyle restrictions. The Amish, for example, are free to live in sheltered, antiquated communities where they choose voluntarily to deny themselves modern amenities. More important for purposes of this discussion, they enforce a strict code of living that severely restricts both the social and economic liberties of the individuals within their communities.

Under a strict application of libertarian federalism, it could be argued that the Amish way of life should be prohibited, or at least opened to outside economic and social influences. If the community is establishing rules that might violate the rights of individual members of the community to speak or act as they wish, such restrictive codes of living would have to be prohibited because the rights of these individuals trump the rights of the local government.

Libertarians answer this second critique by noting that there is an important difference between "a local government" and "a community." Local governments, they argue, have coercive taxing and regulatory powers over citizens; communities, on the other hand, are purely voluntary associations that do not exercise such coercive powers. Furthermore, members of a private community are free to leave whenever they do not feel comfortable with its rules, but a local government might have the authority to restrict this freedom by holding individual citizens accountable under tax laws or regulatory edicts even after they have left its jurisdiction. Therefore, the

Footnotes:
42. Epstein, "Toward a Revitalization of the Contract Clause," p. 747.

The Delicate Balance

case of the Amish is not relevant because theirs is a private community with private rules.

The problem with this argument lies in the rhetorical or definitional dilemma of where the line between "community" and "local government" is to be drawn. There are roughly 82,000 different units of government in modern America. Many of the smallest probably started as "communities" with private rules and, over time, evolved into full-fledged governments. Yet many other communities remain that enforce strict codes of living on their citizens. Where does one draw the line between the two?

More important for purposes of this discussion, should communities, or even very small units of local or municipal government, be allowed in any way to restrict the flow of interstate commerce? While state sovereignty textualists would be much more willing to grant local communities or local governments the flexibility to restrict the flow of commerce, some libertarian federalists might insist that goods and services should be allowed to flow freely across state, local, and community boundaries.

The Supreme Court has tried to deal with this issue by arguing, in such cases as *Pike v. Bruce Church, Inc.* (1970),[43] that balancing tests must be employed that weigh legitimate local interests alongside the rights of citizens and businesses to engage in interstate commerce. Some of these tests will be discussed in the next chapter. As noted above, Justices Scalia and Thomas, along with other scholars of the state sovereignty school of textualism, have argued that such balancing tests are inappropriate because they are not strictly authorized by the Constitution or may unfairly favor the interests of the national government over the states. And many libertarian scholars argue that balancing represents an affront to the Constitution and to the rights and liberties of the citizens protected therein. Yet scholars and judges from each camp admit that some degree of pragmatic balancing must take place if the often competing values of economic liberty and local self-governance are to coexist peacefully.

Counterpoint and Summary of Libertarian Textualism. Despite the criticisms outlined above, libertarian scholars make many important, valid, and undeniable points regarding federalism, interstate commerce, and economic liberty in general.

There *are* certain enumerated rights under the Constitution that apply to every citizen of the United States regardless of the state, local, county, municipal, or other government under which he or

Footnotes:
43. 397 U.S. 137 (1970).

Competing Theories of Federalism

she lives. Furthermore, for better or for worse, the Fourteenth Amendment extends most of the rights found throughout the Constitution and the Bill of Rights to all citizens. For example, no state or local government has the right to enslave a citizen or deny any citizen due process under the law. And although some conservatives may disagree,[44] the historical record makes it clear that the Framers of both the Constitution and the Fourteenth Amendment intended certain economic liberties to be protected by the national government, as the libertarians claim.

What remains difficult is knowing where to draw the line between constitutionally protected economic rights and the right of citizens at the state and local levels to engage in creative self-governance that may involve the sacrifice of certain liberties. Part of the answer appears to involve a better elucidation of what represents a "legitimate" exercise of state and local police powers.

> **What remains difficult is knowing where to draw the line between constitutionally protected economic rights and the right of citizens at the state and local levels to engage in creative self-governance that may involve the sacrifice of certain liberties.**

As noted above, libertarian judges like Stephan Field and George Sutherland, among others, undertook to make such a distinction in the late 1800s and early 1900s. In *Mugler v. Kansas* (1887), for example, the Court attempted to establish a "reasonableness standard" that fairly weighed the interests of state and local prerogatives alongside the interest in preserving economic liberty and commercial activity in general:

> It does not at all follow that every statute enacted ostensibly for the promotion of [public morals, public health, or public safety] is to be accepted as a legitimate exertion of the police powers of the state. There are, of necessity, limits beyond which legislation cannot rightfully go. While every possible presumption is

Footnotes:
44. Notably, Judge Robert Bork, in his book *The Tempting of America*, argues that the libertarian belief that economic rights are protected by the Constitution or the Fourteenth Amendment is wholly fallacious. Bork condemns libertarian judicial activism and the application of substantive due process in several cases and argues for an extremely constrained interpretation of the constitutionally protected economic liberties. See Robert H. Bork, "Judicial Activism in the Service of Property and Free Enterprise," in *The Tempting of America: The Political Seduction of the Law* (New York: Simon & Schuster Inc., 1990), pp. 36–49.

> to be indulged in favor of the validity of a statute, the courts must obey the Constitution rather than the lawmaking department of government, and must, upon their own responsibility, determine whether, in any particular case, these limits have been passed.... The courts are not bound by mere forms, nor are they to be misled by mere pretenses. They are at liberty, indeed, are under a solemn duty, to look at the substance of things, whenever they enter upon the inquiry whether the legislature has transcended the limits of its authority. If, therefore, a statute purporting to have been enacted to protect the public health, the public morals, or the public safety, has no real or substantial relation to those objects, or is a palpable invasion of rights secured by the fundamental law, it is the duty of the courts to so adjudge, and thereby give effect to the constitution.[45]

In the words of Justice Rufus Peckham, writing for the majority in the famous liberty of contract case of *Lochner v. New York*:

> It is a question of which of two powers or rights shall prevail, the power of the state to legislate or the right of the individual to liberty of person and freedom of contract. The mere assertion that the subject relates, though but in a remote degree, to the public health, does not necessarily render the enactment valid. The act must have a more direct relation, as a means to an end, and the end itself must be appropriate and legitimate, before an act can be held to be valid which interferes with the general right of an individual to be free in his person and in his power to contract in relation to his own labor.[46]

Despite these efforts, however, a more precise definition of what represents an "appropriate and legitimate" exercise of the police power remains elusive. "For two centuries," notes Harry N. Scheiber, Associate Dean and Professor of Law and History at the University of California–Berkeley, "judges and scholars alike have repeatedly affirmed that the concept of the 'police power' resists a clear definition. Indeed, it seems that the leading characteristic of the police power is that its definition changes with shifting social

Footnotes:
45. *Mugler v. Kansas*, 123 U.S. 623, 661 (1887).
46. *Lochner v. New York*, 198 U.S. 45, 58 (1905).

economic realities and with changing political conceptions of the legitimate reach of governmental authority."[47]

But if one assumes the development by legislators and legal theorists of a more rigorous yet balanced police power test which fairly balances these competing values and interests, the libertarian paradigm becomes all the more attractive and amenable to economic activity. Although some libertarian legal scholars appear unwilling to accept any "balancing" efforts when competing interests or rights are at stake, they should not be so resistant, since many decisions made during the height of the substantive due process era involved just such pragmatic decision-making. The argument that the Contract Clause, the Privileges and Immunities Clause, the Due Process Clause, and other constitutional protections must be applied strictly, without concession or compromise, in every case ignores the obvious fact that doing so would leave very little room for government action at *any* level.

> If legislators and legal theorists could develop a more rigorous yet balanced police power test which fairly balanced competing values and interests, the libertarian paradigm becomes all the more attractive and amenable to economic activity.

Indeed, if modern libertarians maintain that balancing tests are always inappropriate and that these clauses of the Constitution are absolute in their coverage, they would seem to be saying, in effect, that there are *no* appropriate state police powers. This did not appear to be the position of such libertarian judges as Justices Field, Peckham, and Sutherland. They were willing to make reasonable accommodations for legitimate state and local police powers, even when certain economic liberties had to give way. To reiterate, then, the challenge for modern libertarian scholars is to define more precisely the situations and circumstances under which state and local officials may intervene in the economic affairs of individuals by exercising legitimate police powers in support of goals and values shared by the broader community.

Footnotes:
47. Harry N. Scheiber, "Police Power," in Kermit L. Hall, ed., *The Oxford Companion to the Supreme Court of the United States* (New York: Oxford University Press, 1992), p. 639.

SYNTHESIZING THE TEXTUALIST SCHOOLS OF THOUGHT

It would be easy to conclude from the preceding discussion that the Framers' original model of federalism is unclear or unknowable. Both state sovereignty textualists and libertarian textualists appear to make important and entirely valid statements about this country's founding and the nature of American federalism. And therein lies the secret to unlocking the truth, both about the Founders' intent and about the true nature of our system: *The truth lies somewhere between these two extremes.*

State sovereignty and individual rights work hand in hand; in many ways, they are two sides of the same coin. The Framers of the Constitution created a system of dual sovereignty or competitive federalism precisely to defend these values. As Heritage Foundation analysts Douglas Seay and Wesley Smith noted in 1996, "Federalism is not based on the assumption that one level of government is necessarily better than another; instead, it holds that limited, constitutional government is the goal and that the different levels are needed to restrain one another."[48] The reason these different levels of government were established to restrain one another was to protect the liberties of the individual citizens of the United States. "By dispersing centers of government power," says Judge Bork, federalism "protects against the dangers associated with concentrating power in the hands of a few."[49]

In other words, the preservation of state autonomy and the defense of individual liberty are not mutually exclusive goals; they are values that can, and often do, come into conflict in terms of priority of importance. The delicate balancing act between these goals, therefore, requires that some trade-offs be made; the Court frequently will be forced to make such judgments when Congress has failed to act to protect economic liberties or has acted in a way that infringes on the sovereignty of the states.

In certain cases, libertarians will need to understand that unbridled individual economic liberty must take a back seat to state and local efforts to tailor government policies to the desires of the community. In other words, they must be willing to accept that states and localities will continue to exercise many legitimate police power functions demanded by their citizens. These police powers might include emergency health and safety precautions; immunization or quarantine procedures during certain epidemics; fire hazard precau-

Footnotes:
48. Seay and Smith, "Federalism," p. 436.
49. Bork, "Federalism and Federal Regulation," p. 8.

tions and regulations; police and law enforcement efforts; many public works and construction matters; zoning procedures, historical landmark protections, and land use policy in general; and dam or waterway safety, water quality in general, and other parochial environmental, sanitation, and pollution concerns. Libertarians will need to accept a role for state and local governments in these and other similar matters.

On the other hand, the states will have to give up some of their power to make such determinations if, in exercising this power, they are violating either important constitutional rights held by all Americans or the free flow of interstate commerce. Many conservative scholars and policymakers who support radical notions of states' rights absolutism must be willing to concede that the Constitution contains broader protections for economic freedom and interstate commerce than they previously believed. These freedoms or liberties should include stronger protections for the liberty of contract, the freedom to engage in a line of work or create a commercial enterprise without overwhelming or unnecessary legislative or regulatory encumbrance, freedom from retroactive state and local legislative actions, and protection from unwarranted attempts by states and localities to take private property without just cause or compensation. Conservatives should support stricter constitutional scrutiny of these matters and accept a certain degree of national legislative or judicial oversight to safeguard these important economic liberties.

In the end, any synthesis of these visions undoubtedly will involve a fair degree of pragmatism and respect for the complex task at hand. Indeed, when the Framers of the Constitution were designing the American Republic, many of them must have realized that such an enormous undertaking would prove remarkably difficult and require much pragmatic compromise. Preserving the sovereignty of the states while promoting the development of full nationhood and a vigorous national marketplace would require a careful balancing of powers that would not satisfy anyone completely. As Christopher Wolfe, associate professor of political science at Marquette University, noted in a 1987 study:

> No one at the Constitutional Convention of 1787 "proposed" the principle of federalism. The federalism that emerged in the Constitution was the result of laborious, often acrid, debate and eventual, reluctant compromise. This does not mean, however, that there is no intelligible "principle" that informs this part of the Constitution's design.[50]

The Delicate Balance

Thus, although it would be far more convenient if every jurisdictional dispute could be resolved in black-and-white terms by reference to concrete principles or codes of commercial conduct, such a clear-cut resolution is not always possible in the American common law system. As Wolfe notes, such agreement was not even possible when the Founders were devising America's federalist system in the late 1700s.

> **Although it would be far more convenient if every jurisdictional dispute could be resolved in black-and-white terms by reference to concrete principles or codes of commercial conduct, such a clear-cut resolution is not always possible in the American common law system.**

Yet, while federalism cases typically involve a careful weighing and balancing of the sometimes competing values of state sovereignty, vigorous interstate commerce, and individual rights, as Wolfe notes, this does not mean that the process operates without a guiding set of principles. The Founders cherished the same values espoused by modern-day conservative and libertarian textualists and sought to protect and promote them by preserving certain spheres of action for different levels of government. At the same time, they also understood the need to devise checks on the power of government at all levels to protect the rights of individual citizens.

While honoring this delicate balance between federalism, interstate commerce, and economic liberty has never been easy, it can and should remain a goal of America's lawmakers. As University of Minnesota law professors Daniel A. Farber and Robert E. Hudec have aptly noted, "[T]here are no clear-cut solutions, and…the best that can be done is a rough-and-ready compromise of the competing goals of free trade and local regulatory autonomy."[51]

The question then becomes: *How do policymakers know when and how to make these pragmatic compromises and practical trade-offs*, especially in the ambiguous field of interstate commerce, the primary focus of this book? As Chief Justice William Rehnquist noted in *United States v. Lopez*, an important federalism decision handed down in 1995, "These are not precise formulations, and in the nature of things they cannot be."[52]

Footnotes:
50. Christopher Wolfe, "The Contemporary Supreme Court and Federalism: Symposium Discussion," in *Federalism and the Constitution: A Symposium on Garcia* (Washington, D.C.: Advisory Commission on Intergovernmental Relations, July 1987), p. 56.
51. Farber and Hudec, "Free Trade and the Regulatory State," p. 1418.
52. William Rehnquist, *United States v. Lopez*, 115 S.Ct. 1624, 1634 (1995).

Competing Theories of Federalism

Thus, finding more precise formulations will be the task undertaken in the next chapter.

5

NEW FEDERALISM TENSIONS AND A FRAMEWORK FOR THE FUTURE

At the time of the American founding, commerce (or, more specifically, interstate commerce) was a far more rudimentary concept than we understand it to be today. The most prevalent form of interstate commerce was waterborne commerce; thus, early court cases and legislative action dealt primarily with trade on navigable waters or with port and harbor regulation issues. Disputes also arose over agricultural trade, bridge and highway policy, taxation of goods in transit, and routine border controversies.

In general, disputes over interstate commerce were drawn rather narrowly, so very few were controversial or complex enough to be considered by the Supreme Court. In fact, according to Ezra Parmalee Prentice and John G. Egan, authors of the 1898 study *The Commerce Clause of the Federal Constitution*, "Before the year 1840, the construction of [the Commerce Clause] had been involved in but five cases submitted to the Supreme Court of the United States."[1]

Today, by way of comparison, a roughly equal number of cases invoking the Commerce Clause may be presented to the Supreme Court for consideration during any given year. Although the Court does not rule on every case presented to it that invokes the Commerce Clause, there is no doubt that such cases are more frequent. The Supreme Court now rules on the legal reach and applicability of commerce power far more often than it did either during the period of America's founding or in subsequent decades.

Footnotes:
1. Ezra Parmalee Prentice and John G. Egan, *The Commerce Clause of the Federal Constitution* (Chicago, Ill.: Callaghan and Company, 1898), p. 15. This book contains an excellent overview of early American commercial law.

The Delicate Balance

More important, today's disputes over interstate commerce, commercial law, and economic liberty are far more complex and contentious than the Commerce Clause cases of the Founders' age. The reasons for this, and for the rise in the overall number of such cases, include:

- The continuous expansion of America's internal marketplace for goods and services;
- The ever-expanding consumer sector, with its remarkably widespread and sophisticated customer demands;
- The expansion, subdivision, and diversification of American industries and the enormous growth of business start-ups or incorporation in general;
- Diminished barriers to international trade resulting in the rise of integrated global markets;
- The ever-changing nature of technology, industrial processes, and chains of distribution;
- The increase in the overall number of government entities at all levels of power dealing with commercial matters; and
- The continued use of the Commerce Clause by federal officials to justify a multitude of national programs and activities.

As a result of these trends, today's federal, state, and local legislators and judges must deal with a huge volume of commercial disputes. Consider how some of these complicated—and sometimes esoteric—commercial activities have created new federalism questions and significant jurisdictional headaches for modern policymakers:

- In the telecommunications sector, analog wavelengths and digital bits of information can pass instantaneously through wireline networks or wirelessly through antennas, cellular dishes, and satellites in space. Yet, despite the interstate or even global nature of much communications and computing activity, the companies that provide these services must utilize a great deal of fixed infrastructure—such as computers, wires, transmitters, and switching stations—that resides within multiple government jurisdictions.
- Electrical power companies produce and then distribute electrons nationwide through a complex, interconnected electrical grid. However, these power providers have immobile production factories and equipment located in different states and

New Federalism Tensions and a Framework for the Future

localities that have very different energy-related environmental standards and requirements.

- In the financial services field, everything from stocks, bonds, futures, and mutual funds to life, fire, and auto insurance policies is marketed to consumers across America by a multitude of companies. Yet state laws vary regarding the provision of insurance policies and traditionally have strictly curtailed the sale of bundled financial services, especially from out-of-state companies.
- Many environmental problems are simultaneously interstate and intrastate in nature. Often, overlapping sets of federal, regional, state, county, and municipal regulators can claim jurisdiction over a perceived environmental problem involving air, water, land, or natural resources.
- Product liability laws can differ widely from state to state. Thus, because companies conduct business in many states at once and consequently face multiple and sometimes contradictory tort systems, they face a potentially broader risk of liability.
- In recent years, growing numbers of states and municipalities have attempted to express their dissatisfaction with oppressive foreign governments or dictatorial regimes by imposing unilateral trade sanctions, despite the fact that such powers traditionally have been exercised exclusively by the federal government.
- Interstate mail-order businesses continue to skyrocket in popularity. With the rise of this vast national market, individual states are increasingly concerned that their tax revenues are being compromised, and that their health and safety standards or quality regulations are being evaded.

Which level of government can claim jurisdictional authority in these respective examples? How should the balance of powers be struck if the jurisdictional authority is not clear for these industries? How should these sophisticated industries and technologies be regulated or, more appropriately, *deregulated*? More important for purposes of this discussion, is it still appropriate to apply the Founders' original vision of federalism to modern, high-tech industries the Founders never could have foreseen? And is this vision still appropriate in light of this century's corrupted jurisprudence, which has shifted too much power to the federal level?

Questions such as these will be discussed throughout this chapter. A framework will be suggested to assist policymakers in the laborious and often thankless task of bringing such conflicts and controversies to a satisfactory resolution. Although this reconciliation will not be simple or without controversy, it must be accomplished if the Founders' original vision of constitutional federalism is to be upheld in the technological age. As Justice Scalia has noted, "The originalist must often seek to apply that earlier age's understanding of various freedoms to new laws, and to new phenomena, that did not exist at the time [of the founding]."[2]

A FRAMEWORK FOR DEALING WITH FEDERALISM DISPUTES INVOLVING INTERSTATE COMMERCE AND ECONOMIC LIBERTY

The following framework will apply a set of tests for policymakers to consider when attempting to resolve difficult disputes regarding interstate commerce or economic liberty. Specifically, in line with the focus of this book, these tests will focus primarily on commercial issues within high-tech fields.

Before proceeding, however, a word of caution is appropriate. "No matter how a legal test is articulated," as Professors Daniel Farber and Robert Hudec have noted, "it cannot satisfactorily resolve the tensions between local autonomy and free trade in all conceivable cases. In the end, the law must have a certain irreducible messiness in dealing with such fundamental tensions."[3] With this admonition in mind, these tests and considerations can be outlined as follows:

Tier 1 Test: Strict Textual Analysis

1. Literal Textual Requirements and Prohibitions Flowing from the Constitution.
2. "National Needs" and Constitutionally Protected Economic Rights.
3. Historical Regulatory Forum Considerations.
4. *Stare Decisis* Considerations.

Tier 2 Test: Practical Interpretory Considerations
Regarding Interstate Commerce

1. The Purpose of the Commerce Clause.
2. A More Rigorous "Interstate Commerce" Test.
3. Substantial Interstate Spillover/Negative Externalities Considerations.

Footnotes:
2. Antonin Scalia, *A Matter of Interpretation: Federal Courts and the Law* (Princeton, N.J.: Princeton University Press, 1997), p. 140.
3. Daniel A. Farber and Robert E. Hudec, "Free Trade and the Regulatory State: A GATT's Eye View of the Dormant Commerce Clause," *Vanderbilt Law Review*, Vol. 47 (1994), p. 1438.

New Federalism Tensions and a Framework for the Future

4. Technological Complexity and Network Externality Considerations.

Each part of this two-tier test and its corresponding considerations will discussed in turn.

TIER 1 TEST: STRICT TEXTUAL ANALYSIS

This first test is rather straightforward: Do the Constitution or other legal statutes and judicial precedents explicitly prohibit or encourage federal or state action in the given field? In other words, how do the Constitution and the body of law that evolved from it speak to the issue at hand? If the Constitution speaks directly to an economic or commercial matter, then no further analysis is necessary.

Literal Textual Requirements and Prohibitions Flowing from the Constitution. It should be abundantly clear from preceding discussions that Congress has the right to act only when explicitly mandated by the Constitution. However, where enumerated national powers are found in the Constitution, they are plenary in nature. That is, Congress, through the Supremacy Clause, is granted the absolute right to carry out its constitutionally defined tasks when the language of the Constitution specifies that such action is warranted. This test or consideration can be referred to as Textual Literalism.

The Constitution, for example, leaves all issues of national security, defense, and trade policy to the federal government. Yet, in recent years, this allocation of power has not stopped a growing number of states and municipalities from acting unilaterally to express their dissatisfaction with oppressive foreign governments or dictatorial regimes. These local governments have imposed unilateral trade sanctions despite the fact that throughout the nation's history, such powers have been exercised exclusively by the federal authorities.

David Schmahmann and James Finch, authors of a recent *Vanderbilt Journal of Transnational Law* article on state and local efforts to enact unilateral trade sanctions against companies doing business within Burma, correctly argue that such policies are tantamount to an unconstitutional foray by local authorities into the field of foreign policy making—a field within which, traditionally, federal officials have exercised plenary jurisdiction.[4] Only Congress is granted the power to regulate trade with foreign nations via the Commerce Clause, and Congress and the executive branch have exclusive rights to enact foreign policies through a wide variety of specifically enumerated powers within Articles I and II of the Constitution and Article VI's Supremacy Clause.

Furthermore, although state and local efforts to express opposition to a foreign regime may sound harmless and perhaps even commendable, in reality such unilateral trade actions run the risk of directly contradicting foreign policy positions established by Congress or the executive branch. If allowed to proliferate, multiple and contradictory foreign policies within the United States could damage America's position in the global theater.

Therefore, either states and localities should end all efforts to enact their own foreign policies or the federal government should act to ensure that they do so. Court challenges by private interests against these state and local enactments may also give the courts the chance to strike down such policies before other federal officials act. Whenever possible, the courts should not hesitate to strike down these unconstitutional laws immediately.

There are other domestic economic issues or commercial policies that are literally demanded or prohibited by the text of the Constitution. Chapter 2 listed some of the federal government's enumerated powers over commerce, including the power to establish uniform bankruptcy, patent, and copyright laws; the power to coin money and regulate its value; and the power to prohibit states from imposing duties on shipped cargo. These textual requirements or prohibitions are fairly unambiguous and noncontroversial.

Yet, although the text of the Constitution provides literal justification for the establishment of uniform commercial laws in these fields, as well as unambiguous justification for striking down state or local efforts to interfere with national security or international trade policy, other domestic trade and economic policy issues are somewhat more difficult to handle. In particular, while such a Textual Literalism Test clearly establishes Congress's right to regulate interstate commerce, it does not provide further guidance with regard to what really constitutes interstate commerce and what the scope of the Commerce Clause should be in modern America. These difficult questions will require far greater analysis by policymakers, especially in light of the amazing developments in America's commercial marketplace. Therefore, the Tier 2 Test described below is

Footnotes:
4. David Schmahmann and James Finch, "The Unconstitutionality of State and Local Enactments in the United States Restricting Ties with Burma (Myanmar)," *Vanderbilt Journal of Transnational Law*, Vol. 30, No. 2 (March 1997), pp. 175–207.

intended to deal exclusively with interstate commerce and Commerce Clause considerations.

Equally problematic, however, will be questions regarding what types of "national needs" or constitutional rights demand national attention or justify federal pre-emption of the states and localities under the text of the Constitution.

"National Needs" and Constitutionally Protected Economic Rights. A somewhat more ambiguous but still useful test for determining when congressional intervention in commercial matters might be justified is the National Need Test. Essentially, this test asks whether there is a clear and overriding national need for congressional action in a given field or matter. Many notable conservatives have employed such language when attempting to identify those rare cases in which federal intervention may be necessary or permissible.

As Robert Bork has argued, "[T]he constitutional concept of federalism, as the name indicates, does not prohibit all federal intervention. Although Congress and the executive should not intervene in wholly local matters, as they frequently have, the principles of federalism at times require them to take affirmative steps to deal with *truly national problems*."[5] Similarly, President Reagan's Executive Order 12612 on federalism wisely specified that "Federal action limiting the policymaking discretion of the States should be taken only where constitutional authority for the action is clear and certain and the national activity is necessitated by the presence of *a problem of national scope*."[6]

More succinct is the argument made by Wendell L. Willkie II and Alden F. Abbott, former General Counsel and Counselor to the General Counsel of the Department of Commerce, respectively, in a 1992 study: "The federal government should only regulate when there is a *demonstrated national need*, such as when a state law imposes substantial economic burdens on out-of-state consumers and producers greater than any benefits that may be bestowed on in-state citizens.... [T]he principle must only be applied where state action results in a major negative effect on commerce."[7]

As noted in Chapter 3, in the early Commerce Clause case of *Cooley v. Board of Wardens of the Port of Philadelphia*,[8] the Court

Footnotes:
5. Robert H. Bork, "Federalism and Federal Regulation: The Case of Product Labeling," Washington Legal Foundation, *Critical Legal Issues*, Working Paper Series No. 46, July 1991, pp. 4–5; emphasis added.
6. President Ronald Reagan, Executive Order No. 12612, October 26, 1987; emphasis added.

crafted a crude National Need Test that has come to be known as the "*Cooley* Doctrine of selective exclusiveness." Under the *Cooley* standard, Congress has exclusive jurisdiction to legislate over commercial matters that demand national uniformity; where commercial activity is local in character or Congress has not acted, the states are free to legislate.

But just what constitutes a national need? This is certainly more subjective and difficult to define than what constitutes interstate commerce. Variants of such an open-ended National Need Test have been used from time to time by Congress and the Court to justify national intervention in many fields not explicitly justified by the text of the Constitution.

Nevertheless, Judge Bork and President Reagan, as well as Willkie and Abbott, had good reasons to argue that such a principle is worth supporting. Some textual justification for such a National Need Test can be drawn from the Supremacy Clause, which the Framers included to make it clear that when state laws came into conflict with each other or with national laws, federal law was to prevail. "This Constitution," wrote the Founders unambiguously in Article VI, "shall be the supreme law of the land."

As discussed above, the strict enumeration of certain commercial or economic requirements or prohibitions in the Constitution makes it clear that the Founders thought there was a clear national need for federal oversight of national security and trade issues, patent and trademark protection, the maintenance of a sound monetary system, the formation of uniform bankruptcy laws, the prohibition of *ex post facto* laws, and the protection of contracts.

Yet, precisely because the Framers enumerated so few federal powers, it is equally evident that America's truly national needs were, and remain, extremely limited both in number and in scope. In fact, these originally enumerated powers probably remain the only national needs over which Congress should exercise *complete* control. Unless a commercial issue can satisfy the requirements set out in the other tests discussed in this chapter, it is doubtful that there is a genuine national need for *any* federal intervention.

More specifically, some textualists—especially those of a more libertarian bent—contend that a national need can exist where there

Footnotes:
7. Wendell L. Willkie II and Alden F. Abbott, "Who Should Regulate Business? Assessing the Federal–State Balance of Power," Washington Legal Foundation, *Critical Legal Issues*, Working Paper Series No. 48, August 1992, pp. vi–vii; emphasis added.
8. 12 How. 53 U.S. 299 (1852).

New Federalism Tensions and a Framework for the Future

are cherished, constitutionally protected rights to which all citizens are entitled regardless of jurisdictional residence. Notably, the civil rights of individual Americans are protected through various statutes, clauses in the Constitution, and the Fourteenth Amendment in particular. The rights of free speech and uninhibited travel throughout the United States have found similar protection by Congress and the courts. Regarding economic liberties, the Fourteenth Amendment's Due Process, Equal Protection, and Privileges and Immunities Clauses extended the coverage of certain constitutional protections to citizens throughout the country.

For example, it is clear from the plain language of the Fifth Amendment that the Framers placed a very high value on the protection of personal property rights, since the amendment demands that private property "not be taken for public use without just compensation." The Fourteenth Amendment reiterated and extended this protection to make it clear that state and local governments would not escape its coverage. This means that, as a society and as a nation, Americans have decided that the protection of private property represents a paramount civil right to which all citizens are entitled. Therefore, no government—federal, state, county, or local—can take an individual's private property for public use with compensating that individual for the fair value of his or her property: A "national need" exists to protect this important constitutional right.[9]

This issue has created a heated jurisdictional squabble between state and federal lawmakers. Congress has considered a bill, the Citizen's Access to Justice Act, which would make it easier for citizens to pursue compensation claims against government entities (state and local as well as federal) that take their property. Under the Citizen's Access to Justice Act, citizens would be able to take grievances directly to federal court against governments that take their property, and the injured party or parties could seek the compensation to which they are entitled under the Fifth Amendment.[10]

This effort by Congress represents a wise use of both the National Need and Constitutional Rights Tests. Admittedly, certain regulatory activities at the state and local levels might be curtailed if such a proposal were to become law, but when sacred and explicitly defined constitutional rights are at stake, such as the protection of

Footnotes:
9. The Rehnquist Court has been moving in this direction in a handful of recent cases which struck down state and local land zoning ordinances, largely on Fifth Amendment takings grounds. See *Nollan v. California Coastal Commission*, 483 U.S. 825 (1987); *First English Evangelical Lutheran Church of Glendale v. County of Los Angeles*, 482 U.S. 304 (1987); and *Lucas v. South Carolina Coastal Council*, 505 U.S. 1003 (1992).

an individual's right to be compensated for the confiscation of his private property, federal intervention is justified to protect the people from unjust government action.

Other constitutionally protected economic rights, such as the right to contract freely and the prohibition of *ex post facto* laws, also can be given greater protection by Congress and the courts under the National Need Test or Constitutional Rights Test. As discussed above, however, these rights must be balanced against the exercise of legitimate state and local police powers that do not constitute egregious violations of individual economic liberties or burdens on interstate commerce. Clearly, this balancing act demands much continued discussion and debate among jurists, legal scholars, and policymakers at all levels of government.

Historical Regulatory Forum Considerations. Further complicating Tier 1 analysis will be the question of how much weight should be given to precedential considerations when debating disputes over commercial law and jurisdictional authority. A Historical Regulatory Forum Test can be developed to take such matters into account.

Congress and the courts have acted well beyond their constitutionally defined sphere of power throughout the past century. For example, numerous federal laws have been passed, and programs implemented, that have unconstitutionally expanded the scope of national power by proactively using the Commerce Clause to prescribe how states, localities, and individuals should act. Simultaneously, the courts have refused to defend the rights of states, localities, and individuals from federal encroachment or, worse yet, have placed their stamp of approval on these congressional efforts or else have invented case law that expands the scope of the Commerce Power.

In most cases, if the federal government creates a mess, it will have to clean up that mess. For example, despite its lack of constitutional authority, Congress has created a number of large federal power programs, such as the Tennessee Valley Authority (TVA). It

Footnotes:
10. For more information, see Alex F. Annett, "How Congress Can Enhance Property Owners' Access to Justice," Heritage Foundation *Executive Memorandum* No. 492, September 12, 1997; Alex F. Annett, "Justice Delayed Is Justice Denied: How Congress Can Increase Property Owners' Access to Justice," Heritage Foundation *F.Y.I.* No. 158, October 31, 1997; and Alex F. Annett, "How Congress Can End the 'Regulatory Limbo' Blocking Property Owners' Access to Justice," Heritage Foundation *F.Y.I.* No. 154, October 1, 1997.

also has established authoritarian regulatory agencies, including the Federal Communications Commission (FCC) and the Environmental Protection Agency (EPA), and laws that regulate a multitude of human social and economic activities that were supposed to be well beyond the reach of the federal government. In addition, a huge body of administrative regulatory law and judicial case law has grown out of this congressional overreach. Most of the problems associated with America's health care system, for instance, can be traced to the bewildering array of federal regulatory requirements and federal tax policies that have created perverse market incentives and driven up the cost of health care.[11] Consequently, state and local efforts to address health care problems are likely to be ineffective or counterproductive in the absence of federal reform efforts.[12]

The Historical Regulatory Forum Test must take such issues into consideration. Congress will have to deal with privatization of the TVA, for example, and rein in over-zealous regulatory agencies like the FCC and the EPA, as well as the many other programs and agencies created throughout this century. Finally, some state policies may have been developed in response to federal efforts to push national issues back to the state or local level, often to stunt the growth of a maturing industry. Congress or the Supreme Court may have to deal with these potentially unconstitutional laws that have been passed at their behest.

In general, however, this Historical Regulatory Forum Test would provide greater justification for calls to devolve most programs and political decision-making to lower levels of government. The very enumeration of a small number of limited powers within the Constitution clearly suggests that the Framers intended most activities to be handled outside the national forum. And for the great majority of industries and economic issues, the states and localities traditionally have taken the lead in devising their own independent regulatory schemes and programs, with the federal government then following suit by initiating its own regulatory programs and agencies.

Over time, federal and state agencies have developed various methodologies to settle questions of jurisdictional responsibility; however, these guidelines often were crude, rudimentary, and illogical. For example, jurisdiction within the electricity sector is divided

Footnotes:
11. See, generally, Carrie J. Gavora, "Back to the Drawing Board: Why Tax Reform Is the Key to Health Care Reform," Heritage Foundation *Backgrounder* No.1189, June 9, 1998.
12. See Melinda L. Schriver and Grace-Marie Arnett, "Uninsured Rates Rise Dramatically in States with Strictest Health Insurance Regulations," Heritage Foundation *Backgrounder* No. 1211, August 14, 1998.

The Delicate Balance

essentially between retail and wholesale transactions. Retail transactions in the electricity marketplace involve the sale of power directly to consumers from utility companies; wholesale transactions involve the sale of electricity from one utility to another. Traditionally, retail transactions have been regulated by the states and wholesale transactions have been regulated by federal authorities.

Unfortunately, although this ad hoc approach has worked in a monopolistic setting for the past century, it is increasingly ill-suited to the modern electricity market, which could soon witness countless retail, utility-to-consumer transactions taking place across state boundaries on a daily basis. Therefore, traditional regulatory questions regarding jurisdiction may need to be re-assessed in light of such developments. At a minimum, the states may have to accept certain federal laws aimed at deregulating the national electricity marketplace on a fairly harmonious timetable.

Furthermore, for many of the same reasons discussed above, a literal reading of this test does not necessarily provide a definitive answer to the question of whether Congress now has the right to take action under the Commerce Clause to remove discriminatory or protectionist barriers to interstate commerce.

For example, the states for many decades have been the dominant forces in electricity and telecommunications regulation. As part of their regulatory programs, they devised exclusive franchise service territories within which only certain telecom and electricity monopolies were allowed to offer service. It was evident from the start that these franchise service territories were intentional restraints on competitive entry and the free flow of commerce. When such anti-competitive or protectionist laws have been placed on the books by the states, either because the federal government encouraged them to do so or because federal authorities simply overlooked such regulation despite its unconstitutional nature, Congress has the right to reassess such policy with a view to determining whether it violates the Commerce Clause. Similarly, under the Bank Holding Company Act and other New Deal-era banking laws, the federal government "restricted the ability of corporations to escape state charter restrictions on interstate operations."[13] This has prohibited consumers from freely entering into agreements with financial service companies outside their home states.

Footnotes:
13. Edmund W. Kitch, "Regulation and the American Common Market," in A. Dan Tarlock, ed., *Regulation, Federalism, and Interstate Commerce* (Cambridge, Mass.: Oelgeschlager, Gunn & Hain, Publishers, Inc., 1981), p. 43.

New Federalism Tensions and a Framework for the Future

Congress should have prohibited such anti-competitive arrangements long ago, since they infringe directly on the rights of out-of-state telecom and electricity providers to offer services to customers. Instead, because Congress tacitly approved these monopolistic franchise territories, today—many decades after they were initiated—telecom and electricity monopolies remain within these industries. Likewise, Congress's refusal until recently to deal with state-based restraints on interstate trade in financial services has greatly limited innovation and competition in the field. Where such state-created anti-competitive restraints on the free flow of interstate commerce remain, Congress can act to remove them.

These cases will be quite limited, however. More often than not, traditional regulatory forums should and will remain fixed for most industries or issues. For example, it is preposterous to assume that legislators need to rethink the logic of uniform federal systems for patents and copyrights, or national oversight of bankruptcy laws. These systems of commercial regulation have worked well and have improved market efficiency. They do not need to be changed.

At the same time, however, it is equally apparent that the states remain the optimal forum to resolve matters dealing with the enormous range of activities that remain purely *intra*state in focus. For example, state and local governments for decades have dealt with environmental policy matters, including land use policy; air, water, and land pollution regulation; local sanitation regulations and systems; and a host of similar concerns. Such matters should remain locally administered.

Another recent example of a jurisdictional squabble that could be resolved easily under the Historical Regulatory Forum Test is the current debate in Congress over an "auto choice" proposal aimed at reducing automobile insurance premiums for drivers. The Auto Choice Reform Act introduced by House Majority Leader Dick Armey (R–TX) and Senator Mitch McConnell (R–KY) would give all American automobile drivers the option of remaining part of a traditional tort-based system of automobile accident compensation. Alternatively, consumers could opt out of the tort system and enter a no-fault system. Simply put, the bill aims to convert the American auto insurance system from a third-party (tort-based) compensatory system to a first-party (no-fault) compensatory system.[14]

Footnotes:
14. For an excellent overview of the auto choice proposal and the current system of auto insurance compensation, see Robert R. Detlefsen, "Escaping the Tort-Based Auto Accident Compensation System: The Federal Auto Choice Reform Act of 1997," Citizens for a Sound Economy *Issue Analysis* No. 72, June 1, 1998.

The Delicate Balance

This auto choice proposal has garnered widespread bipartisan support, fueled primarily by a growing body of academic literature establishing that substantial economic benefits will flow to auto insurance customers if it is adopted. The proposal would help reduce the costs associated with America's inefficient tort system by speeding up the accident compensation process, eliminating excessive lawyer fees, minimizing or eliminating non-economic "pain and suffering" claims, and decreasing the overall incidence of auto insurance fraud.[15]

The fact that a proposal like the auto choice bill might have beneficial economic effects nationwide, however, is not necessarily enough to justify the implementation of such a scheme at the federal level. Clearly, it would not be the proverbial end of the world if this federal initiative was passed, since it would grant citizens greater economic freedom of choice and decrease the power of state insurance regulators in the process. Yet, because there is nothing inherently "interstate" about automobile insurance and because insurance has been regulated for so long at the state level, there seems little reason to federalize the system now, especially when state experimentation in this field has occurred already and works fairly well. Many states have no-fault insurance compensation systems. Others maintain a more traditional, tort-based system of compensation. If automobile drivers want to move toward the system proposed in the federal Auto Choice Reform Act, they can push their state legislators to implement state versions of the federal choice proposal.

Although the current auto choice proposal contains an opt-out feature for states wishing to forgo the new system, the very fact that this is viewed as necessary begs obvious questions regarding the need for, and wisdom of, any federal effort in the first place. Auto choice supporters argue that the inclusion of an opt-out provision for the states serves to protect the states from federal pre-emption and therefore should minimize federalism concerns. They also argue

Footnotes:
15. See, generally, Dan Miller, *Auto Choice: Relief for Businesses & Consumers*, Joint Economic Committee, U.S. Congress, July 1998; Dan Miller, *Auto Choice: Impact on the Cities and the Poor*, Joint Economic Committee, U.S. Congress, March 1998; Stephan Carroll, Allan Abrahamse, and Mary Vaiana, *The Costs of Excess Medical Claims for Automobile Personal Injuries* (Santa Monica, Cal.: Rand Institute, 1995); Jeffrey O'Connell, Stephen Carroll, Michael Horowitz, Allan Abrahamse, and Daniel Kaiser, "The Costs of Consumer Choice for Auto Insurance in States Without No-Fault Insurance," *Maryland Law Review*, Vol. 54, No. 2 (1995), pp. 281–351; and Jeffrey O'Connell, Stephen Carroll, Michael Horowitz, and Allan Abrahamse, "Consumer Choice in the Auto Insurance Market," *Maryland Law Review*, Vol. 52, No. 4 (1993), pp. 1016–1062.

that such a mechanism serves as an excellent precedent for future federal legislative or regulatory efforts, since the states could cite the auto choice opt-out provision in the event of jurisdictional conflict to minimize or nullify the effects of federal pre-emption.

Yet, despite the benefits that probably would be associated with passage of a federal auto choice proposal, the Historical Regulatory Forum Test would discourage the federalization of automobile insurance compensation policy, both because the system has always been state-based and because continued experimentation with differing compensatory mechanisms remains possible. Moreover, such a federal effort is difficult to justify. This is likewise true under the Tier 2 Test, examined below, since the auto insurance business remains almost entirely *intra*state in nature, and there exist no substantial interstate spillover effects associated with state-based systems of insurance regulation. There are no complex network externalities with which federal policymakers need to be concerned, such as those that exist with telecommunications or electricity networks.

To conclude, the Historical Regulatory Forum Test demands that great deference be given to the jurisdictional body that traditionally has overseen a particular industry or issue. Yet it does not say that historical regulatory responsibilities should never be re-assessed. In particular, the test should not be seen as a bar to reversing many of this century's statutes, regulations, and legal cases that have shifted too much power to the federal forum. On the other hand, it also should not be seen as an impediment to national efforts, either by Congress or by the courts, to prohibit new or ongoing discriminatory or protectionist activity at the state or local level.[16]

Stare Decisis Considerations. On the judicial front, the Tier 1 Test regarding textual analysis holds that precedential considerations are equally important. In fact, legal scholars and policymak-

Footnotes:
16. It is worth noting that Congress did reverse course with respect to aviation, trucking, and the railroad industry. For many decades, Congress crafted policies that artificially restricted the growth of interstate commerce in these fields and worked, in many cases, hand in hand with the states to perpetuate a blatantly cartelistic and protectionist system. As a result, prices remained high, service quality suffered, and interstate commerce floundered. When federal officials decided to reverse course in the late 1970s and early 1980s, the deregulatory initiatives they introduced eliminated many state-based barriers to interstate commerce that previously they had endorsed or accepted. This greatly facilitated the development of today's vigorously competitive interstate airline, transportation, and shipping markets.

ers who espouse a textualist vision of constitutional interpretation (especially the textualism of the conservative variant) as described in Chapter 4 would argue that, under the judicial doctrine known as *stare decisis*, great deference should be given to the wisdom of past court decisions and doctrine.

The Abridged Sixth Edition of *Black's Law Dictionary* defines *stare decisis* as "Policy of courts to stand by precedent and not to disturb settled point. Doctrine that, when court has once laid down a principle of law as applicable to a certain state of facts, it will adhere to that principle, and apply it to all future cases, where facts are substantially the same...."[17] *Stare decisis* considerations are important in commercial law and with regard to economic liberty for contradictory reasons:

1. **The precedents are bad** because many of the cases that involved Commerce Clause interpretation and reasoning strayed far from the Founders' original understanding of the nature of interstate commerce and the purpose of the Commerce Clause.

2. **The precedents are good** because many Commerce Clause cases (including those of the so-called Dormant Commerce Clause variant) were faithful to the Founders' vision of the purpose of the Commerce Clause.

The first consideration raises an obvious question: How much precedential value should judges place on past Commerce Clause case law if it is so severely corrupted and at odds with original constitutional understanding? Some textualists, especially some members of the libertarian school of textualist thought, have entertained the idea of getting rid of all bad Commerce Clause case law through a single sweeping decision. The University of Chicago's Richard Epstein has suggested that "The most attractive possibility is to roll back the carpet to the original 1787 position. In essence that means to take all the decisions that are regarded as sacrosanct by everyone...and overrule them one and all, preferably with a single blow."[18]

Despite being quite sympathetic to this cause, some conservatives on the Court and in academia have expressed fear that such a radical step might be too disruptive, since not every case handed down since 1787 has corrupted the original balance of powers and under-

Footnotes:
17. *Black's Law Dictionary*, Abridged 6th Ed. (St. Paul, Minn.: West Publishing Co., 1991), p. 978.
18. Richard A. Epstein, "Constitutional Faith and the Commerce Clause," *Notre Dame Law Review*, Vol. 71, No. 1 (1995), p. 190.

standing of the Commerce Clause. In fact, as noted in the second consideration above, many cases got it right, and therefore it might be a mistake to try to sweep all Commerce Clause jurisprudence off the books with one comprehensive case.

More important, such a move might be dangerous because its effects could reverberate throughout the political and market economy in radical and unforeseen ways. For better or worse, a sizable body of judicial and administrative law has developed in the political marketplace to apply the judicial and legislative judgments of the past. Tossing out all the Commerce Clause decisions would throw this system into disarray, at least initially. Moreover, these laws now act as the ground rules for the conduct of business by many important industry sectors in America. If a single case were to strike all such previous decisions off the books, the results might be harmful to commercial businesses and economic activity in general.

This does not mean, however, that the Court should not strike down corrupt case law that has been put on the books by previous generations if cases come before it that demand reconsideration of past precedents. Rather, it is to add a note of caution that it should be done in a prudent fashion and that great deference should be given to efforts by Congress to address such problems within the legislative arena. In fact, it would be wise for the Court to let Congress take the lead in this process and merely supplement congressional efforts when appropriate. The transitional process will be frustrating and rife with problems, and Congress will be in a better position to deliberate over the pace and nature of the rollback of corrupt statutes and jurisprudence.

Yet, if controversies come before the Court that require rulings on issues involving the proper scope and interpretation of the Commerce Clause, the justices certainly should use such opportunities to defend the Founders' original vision, and possibly overturn constitutionally corrupt Commerce Clause cases in the process. Cases such as *N.L.R.B. v. Jones & Laughlin Steel Co.* (1937),[19] *U.S. v. Darby* (1941),[20] *Wickard v. Filburn* (1942),[21] and *Garcia v. San Antonio Metro. Transit Authority* (1985)[22] are prime candidates for reconsideration by the Court. They should be struck down if new cases emerge that bring into question their constitutional merit.

Footnotes:
19. 301 U.S. 1 (1937).
20. 312 U.S. 100 (1941).
21. 317 U.S. 111 (1942).
22. 469 U.S. 528 (1985).

The Delicate Balance

Again, however, the courts also must take care not to disrupt previous cases and the elements of constitutional jurisprudence that have enhanced the free flow of interstate commerce or have protected important constitutionally held economic rights. Indeed, the courts would be wise to pay greater attention to the rights and liberties protected by the Contract Clause of the Constitution and the Privileges and Immunities Clause of the Fourteenth Amendment in future cases.

In conclusion, as noted in the previous chapter, the judiciary will be forced to deal with many interstate commerce and economic liberty disputes whether they like it or not. As a matter of principle, therefore, when such cases arise, the Supreme Court should not shy away from its constitutional responsibility to safeguard the Founders' federalist model.

It is wrong to claim that such actions represent unwarranted judicial activism, since such a judicial role is essential if the constitutional system of checks and balances is to remain intact and effective. Conservatives in particular should realize that agreement with this argument represents tacit agreement with the Court's false logic in *Garcia*—that only Congress and the federal electoral process can protect the federalist system. As the past five decades have proven, when the Court abdicates its role as guardian of the constitutional restraints on federal overreach, the states have little recourse and lose power and jurisdiction accordingly.

TIER 2 TEST: PRACTICAL INTERPRETORY CONSIDERATIONS REGARDING INTERSTATE COMMERCE

If the Constitution speaks directly to a commercial matter or a dispute involving economic rights and liberties, it seems fairly obvious what the outcome of the dispute should be. But literal textualism is useful only to a certain point. It would be a mistake to read too much into certain words or phrases in the Constitution, but it also would be improper to read too little into them. As Justice Scalia notes in his recent defense of textualism, "A text should not be construed strictly, and it should not be construed leniently; it should be construed reasonably, to contain all that it fairly means."[23]

In no other area of constitutional law is this statement more true than in federalism jurisprudence and Commerce Clause interpretation. Clearly, the regulation of interstate commerce is a literal textual

Footnotes:
23. Scalia, *A Matter of Interpretation: Federal Courts and the Law,* p. 23.

New Federalism Tensions and a Framework for the Future

responsibility assigned to Congress under the Constitution. But what is interstate commerce? What is the true purpose of the Commerce Clause? And what sort of practical considerations must be taken into account when attempting to apply the Framers' original vision of constitutional federalism to modern industries and technologies? These issues are considered as falling within the Tier 2 Test on practical interpretory considerations regarding interstate commerce.

The Purpose of the Commerce Clause. As mentioned throughout this book, the one area of traditional federal responsibility that has been the most controversial, problematic, and frequently abused is the provision in Article 1, Section 8, Clause 3 of the Constitution that allows Congress to "regulate commerce...among the several states...." As the evidence adduced in Chapter 2 illustrates, however, the Commerce Clause has solid historic justification: It is rooted in the Framers' understanding that full nationhood and a vigorous national market could not develop in a system characterized by factionalism and parochial protectionism.

> According to Madison, the Commerce Clause "was intended as a negative and preventative provision against injustice among the States themselves, rather than as a power to be used for positive purposes of the General Government...."

Therefore, there is no doubt that the Commerce Clause qualifies under the Tier 1 Test as a clearly federal power that Congress and the Court have the right to enforce. When states or localities establish barriers to interstate commerce, or are acting in a way that otherwise discourages the free flow of commerce, Congress can act within its constitutionally defined powers to *proscribe* state or local policies that discriminate unfairly against interstate commerce. It is just as clear, however, that the Constitution grants no further power to Congress under the Commerce Clause to take more affirmative or *prescriptive* steps to force states and localities to do anything more than cease their anti-commercial activities. In other words, the Commerce Clause was never intended to become a tool of social engineering that Congress could use to justify the myriad of patently unconstitutional laws and programs it has established this past century. To quote Madison again, the Commerce Clause "was intended as a negative and preventative provision against injustice among the States themselves, rather than as a power to be used for positive purposes of the General Government...."[24]

Footnotes:
24. Letter from James Madison to J. C. Cabell, February 12, 1829, quoted in Raoul Berger, "Judicial Manipulation of the Commerce Clause," *Texas Law Review*, Vol. 74, Issue 4 (March 1996), p. 705.

The Delicate Balance

But while the Commerce Clause clearly finds textual support in the Constitution, it also remains open to ongoing interpretation and debate as scholars and policymakers seek to apply it to modern issues and controversies. It is fortunate, therefore, that certain tests are available to help Congress and the courts understand when authority can be exercised legitimately under the Commerce Clause. These tests attempt to preserve both the delicate balance of dual federalism advocated by the Founders and the early constitutional jurisprudence handed down by the Supreme Court, but do not give credence to modern arguments that virtually any human or economic activity may qualify as interstate commerce.

The effort to devise useful and principled tests is guided by three constitutional imperatives, or core values, that led the Founders to abandon the Articles of Confederation and include the Commerce Clause and other commerce-enhancing measures in the original Constitution:

1. **The prohibition of protectionism.** States or localities should not be allowed to implement statutes or regulations that establish explicit protectionist barriers to the free flow of commerce across interstate boundaries.

2. **The prohibition of discrimination.** States or localities should not be allowed to implement statutes or regulations that unfairly discriminate against the goods or services of out-of-state interests in favor of in-state interests.

3. **The prohibition of extraterritorial jurisdiction.** States or localities should not be allowed to exercise authority beyond their geographical boundaries.

In a sense, these are the only three tests that are required to determine whether federal intervention is justified under the Commerce Clause. The additional tests or considerations listed below are merely tools to help uncover protectionist intent, discriminatory effects, or extraterritorial overreach and then counsel a course of action for federal officials. Once these tests have proven that states or localities are acting in an unconstitutional manner, some limited form of federal intervention can be justified.

Clearly, most economic and social activities do not meet these requirements. Yet a handful of economic activities do qualify for some degree of federal oversight under this framework. The following discussion should help bring about a better understanding of just when such limited oversight or intervention is justified.

New Federalism Tensions and a Framework for the Future

A More Rigorous "Interstate Commerce" Test. The regulation of businesses and commercial activity by state and local governments serves to discourage commerce and competition, and it does so in many ways. For example, every zoning law or land use restriction implemented by city or county planning boards interferes with the efficient operation of local economies.[25] Likewise, the growing multitude of state and local environmental regulations clearly imposes significant costs on industries and individuals within their respective jurisdictions.

In most cases, however, the mere fact that a state or local activity has such anti-competitive consequences is not enough to justify federal intervention to remedy the problem. The key question is whether the activity or industry in question is truly *inter*state in scope. Interstate commerce is literally economic activity between or involving two or more states. Therefore, when states are taxing or regulating commerce that is purely *intra*state in scope, or completely within the confines of one state, Congress does not have the power to intervene. "A finding that a state regulation harms in-state interests should not be sufficient to justify preemption," notes Richard J. Pierce, former Dean of the University of Pittsburgh School of Law.[26] Consumers and businesses that are dissatisfied with their current regulatory arrangements can "vote with their feet" by moving to more hospitable jurisdictions.[27]

Moreover, the "commerce" in interstate commerce is just that—commerce—and not manufacturing, production, or anything else. Again, Chief Justice Melville Weston Fuller's argument in *United States v. E. C. Knight Co.* that "Commerce succeeds to manufacture, and is not a part of it" is just as applicable today as it was in 1895.[28]

Footnotes:

25. See David Bernstein, "Equal Protection for Economic Liberty: Is the Court Ready," Cato Institute *Policy Analysis*, October 5, 1992.; Bernard H. Siegan, *Land Use Without Zoning* (Lexington, Mass.: D. C. Heath, 1972); and Bernard H. Siegan, "Economic Liberties and the Constitution: Protection at the State Level," in James A. Dorn and Henry G. Manne, eds., *Economic Liberties and the Judiciary* (Washington, D.C.: Cato Institute, 1987), pp. 137–150.
26. Richard J. Pierce, Jr., "Regulation, Deregulation, Federalism, and Administrative Law: Agency Power to Preempt State Regulation," *University of Pittsburgh Law Review*, Vol. 46 (Spring 1995), p. 607.
27. Likewise, the mere fact that state or local governments are not living up to a political responsibility that national legislators or regulators feel is important does not justify federal intervention to impose national solutions to parochial problems.
28. Justice Melville Weston Fuller, *United States v. E. C. Knight Co.*, 156 U.S. 1, 12 (1895).

The Delicate Balance

The Court reiterated and strongly reinforced this distinction probably for the last time in its 1918 decision in *Hammer v. Dagenhart*.[29]

And yet, it is often difficult to define clearly what constitutes interstate commerce when the technologies or industries in question exhibit unique characteristics. Consider the wireless electromagnetic spectrum, through which cellular telephone service, broadcast television programming, satellite phone and television programming, taxi dispatches, and emergency broadcast services are provided. When a television signal is broadcast or a cellular call is initiated through the wireless spectrum, portions of that broadcast or phone call may be transmitted from one broadcast transmitter or cellular tower to another. As the broadcast television signals or cellular telephone signals travel from antenna to antenna or tower to tower, they may pass over a number of geographic boundaries. If some of these antennas or towers are located within State A and still others are located in States B, C, D, and so on, do these states not have the right to tax or regulate the broadcast television or cellular telephone call as they wish? Is this *intra*state or *inter*state commerce?

> When considering difficult jurisdictional questions...policymakers would be wise to remember the advice of legal scholar Richard Epstein: "It is...the nature of the transaction, rather than its location, that stamps it as a part of interstate commerce."

Thus far in the history of American telecommunications regulation, states and localities have been precluded from taxing or regulating wireless transmissions. The reasoning of Congress and the Federal Communications Commission concerning this prohibition has been simple: Commercial wireless transmissions, by their nature, defy containment by artificial geographical boundaries. Most wireless transmissions are not just interstate in nature, but often global and extraterrestrial. And even if only one portion or segment of a television broadcast or cellular transmission passes between two intrastate antennas or towers, in many cases, the signal probably originated somewhere outside the jurisdiction in question.

When considering difficult jurisdictional questions such as these, policymakers would be wise to remember the advice of legal scholar Richard Epstein: "It is...the nature of the transaction, rather than its location, that stamps it as a part of interstate commerce."[30] Epstein's

Footnotes:
29. 247 U.S. 251 (1918).
30. Richard A. Epstein, "The Proper Scope of the Commerce Power," *Virginia Law Review*, Vol. 73, No. 8 (November 1987), p. 1403.

New Federalism Tensions and a Framework for the Future

sound rule of thumb is applicable to many fields, including the taxation and regulation of the Internet, financial services and securities regulation, the electrical power sector, navigation and aviation, and many other industries.

Nevertheless, the location of certain types of technologies and industries *will* make a difference in many jurisdictional battles. Continuing with our broadcast and cellular example, even though states and localities can be prohibited from regulating the interstate and global transmissions that pass through broadcast antennas or cellular towers, do they not have the right to determine where the antennas or towers are sited? This is a much more problematic question that has led to acrimonious disputes between state and federal regulators in recent years. State and local regulators argue correctly that siting and zoning issues traditionally have been a local responsibility; federal regulators respond—also correctly—that state and local regulators can adversely affect the integrity and efficient operation of broadcast and cellular systems by artificially limiting the number of antennas or towers that can be constructed or regulating where they can be placed.

Congress attempted to deal with this problem by striking a balance between these competing principles in the Telecommunications Act of 1996. In Title VII, Section 704, Congress specified that "nothing in this Act shall limit or affect the authority of a State or local government or instrumentality thereof over decisions regarding the placement, construction, and modification of personal wireless service facilities." But Title VII then went on to establish a handful of important limitations on this local power. Specifically, local governments "shall not unreasonably discriminate among providers of functionally equivalent services; and shall not prohibit or have the effect of prohibiting the provision of personal wireless services."

Among the other limitations outlined in Section 706 of the Telecommunications Act:

- "A State or local government or instrumentality thereof shall act on any request for authorization to place, construct, or modify personal wireless service facilities within a reasonable period of time after the request is duly filed with such government or instrumentality, taking into account the nature and scope of such request."
- "Any decision by a State or local government or instrumentality thereof to deny a request to place, construct, or modify personal wireless service facilities shall be in writing and supported by substantial evidence contained in a written record."

The Delicate Balance

> - "No State or local government or instrumentality thereof may regulate the placement, construction, and modification of personal wireless service facilities on the basis of the environmental effects of radio frequency emissions to the extent that such facilities comply with the [FCC's] regulations concerning such emissions."
>
> - "Any person adversely affected by any final action or failure to act by a State or local government or any instrumentality thereof that is inconsistent with this subparagraph may, within 30 days after such action or failure to act, commence an action in any court of competent jurisdiction. The court shall hear and decide such action on an expedited basis. Any person adversely affected by an act or failure to act by a State or local government or any instrumentality thereof that is inconsistent with clause (iv) may petition the Commission for relief."

> **As Justice Clarence Thomas has noted in *United States* v. *Lopez*, "Although the precise line between interstate/foreign commerce and purely intrastate commerce was hard to draw, the Court attempted to adhere to such a line for the first 150 years of our Nation."**

The language of the Telecommunications Act suggests that its authors tried to strike a balance by preserving a clear realm of authority for state and local officials while at the same time proscribing regulatory activities that would have negative or discriminatory effects on interstate commerce. Obviously, achieving such a balance is not easy. In fact, these provisions embody the belief of Farber and Hudec that federalism laws and policies "have a certain irreducible messiness in dealing with such fundamental tensions."[31] The important point is that competing goals and values are being balanced to ensure that legitimate local police powers are honored as long as they do not interfere egregiously with the business of cellular companies and consumers engaged in interstate commerce. This probably was the most pragmatic solution available to Congress.

The lesson to be drawn is that disputes over what constitutes interstate commerce are far more complex than ever before. But the fact that preserving the balance of powers between state sovereignty and the maintenance of national commerce may prove more difficult in today's economy does not necessarily mean that such an effort should not be undertaken. As Justice Clarence Thomas has noted in *United States* v. *Lopez*, "Although the precise line between

Footnotes:
31. Farber and Hudec, "Free Trade and the Regulatory State," p. 1438.

WHAT CONSTITUTES INTERSTATE COMMERCE IN THE TECHNOLOGICAL AGE?

Interstate Commerce (Possible Grounds for Federal Oversight)	Not Commerce at All (No Grounds for Federal Oversight)
Flow of electrons through electricity grids across state lines.	Construction of an electrical generation plant.
Transmissions of analog or digital wavelengths and signals through wireless devices.	Design and construction of cellular or any telecommunications devices.
Sale, shipment, and distribution (by plane, truck, train, or ship) of food across state lines.	Production of food and agricultural activity in general.
Electronic commerce over the Internet.	Production of computer hardware or software.
Airline travel and shipping.	Aircraft manufacturing or construction and management of airports.
Sale of financial services on-line.	Establishment of minimum insurance premium standards for fire, home, and auto insurance policies.
Sale of clothes through on-line catalogs or through mail-order services.	Manufacture of clothing or apparel.
Interstate trucking, shipping, and transportation services.	Construction and maintenance of roads and highways.
Environmental externalities of a multi-state nature such as air, ocean, or river pollution.	Environmental problems of a parochial nature such as local air and water standards, land control, species protection, and park and nature preservation.

interstate/foreign commerce and purely intrastate commerce was hard to draw, the Court attempted to adhere to such a line for the first 150 years of our Nation."[32]

The Delicate Balance

Thus, the Court and especially Congress should attempt once again to determine how *intra*state versus *inter*state lines of jurisdictional responsibility can and should be drawn for modern industries and technologies. More specifically, legislators and judges who believe in restoring the Founders' intent with respect to the Commerce Clause must attempt to define as clearly as possible the difference between intrastate and interstate commerce. They must also seek to revive the "commerce versus manufacturing" distinction made in the *E. C. Knight* case a century ago.

The table above presents examples of what constitutes interstate commerce in today's modern economy and corresponding or related activities that would not qualify as interstate commerce, or even as commerce at all. Epstein's sound rule of thumb—that it is the nature of the transaction, rather than its location, that stamps it as a part of interstate commerce—helps to define the difference between the two.

Substantial Interstate Spillovers/Negative Externalities. Another way to gauge whether state-by-state actions or policies will have an adverse effect on interstate commerce is to examine whether they result in "substantial spillover effects." Richard Pierce crafted a Substantial Interstate Spillover Test in a 1984 study for the Administrative Conference of the United States:

> It is in the national interest to permit each state to adopt its own regulatory policy to the extent that such state decisions affect only, or predominately, the interests of state residents. States should not be permitted, however, to make regulatory decisions that create substantial interstate spillovers.... Congress has the power under the Supremacy Clause to limit the ability of each state to adopt regulatory policies that create substantial interstate spillovers.[33]

More specifically, this test asks whether state policies have spawned negative externalities or have had adverse side effects on parties outside their jurisdiction which unjustly burden interstate producers or consumers. As Jacques Leboeuf has noted, "[I]t is clear that the framers intended the federal government to have regulatory authority only in those instances where state regulation generated

Footnotes:
32. Justice Clarence Thomas (concurring opinion), *United States v. Lopez*, 115 S.Ct. 1624 (1995).
33. Richard J. Pierce, *Regulation, Deregulation, Federalism and Administrative Law*, Report to the Administrative Conference of the United States, October 1984, p. 74.

externalities. There is no reason that this understanding cannot be applied to federal enactments today."[34]

In other words, federal officials have the right to protect national commerce and the interests of consumers who are injured by state actions that have negative spillover effects or create negative externalities. For example, several Supreme Court cases dealing with milk or dairy subsidies illustrate how such a Substantial Interstate Spillover Test or Negative Externality Test has been applied in the past:

- In *Baldwin v. G.A.F. Seelig, Inc.* (1935),[35] the Court struck down a New York statute that sought to establish the prices for milk imported from Vermont and other states in order to protect New York milk producers. "New York has no power to project its legislation into Vermont by regulating the price to be paid in that state for milk acquired there," the Court noted. Furthermore, "New York is equally without power to prohibit the introduction within her territory of milk of wholesome quality acquired in Vermont, whether at high prices or low ones." In summary, the Court argued that "Nice distinctions have been made at times between direct and indirect burdens. They are irrelevant when the avowed purpose of the obstruction, as well as its necessary tendency, is to suppress or mitigate the consequences of competition between the states."

- In *Dean Milk Co. v. City of Madison* (1951),[36] the Court struck down an ordinance passed by the city of Madison, Wisconsin, that prohibited all milk sales in the city unless the milk was produced at a municipally approved pasteurization plant within five miles of the city. "Even in the exercise of its unquestioned power to protect the health and safety of its people," the Court noted, "a municipality may not erect an economic barrier protecting a major local industry against competition from without the state, if reasonable nondiscriminatory alternatives, adequate to conserve legitimate local interests, are available." In other words, while state or local governments have the right to enforce their own unique health and safety standards through their police powers, they may not do so in a way that unduly burdens consumers or customers in other states who are attempting to engage in interstate commercial activity.[37]

Footnotes:
34. Jacques Leboeuf, "The Economics of Federalism and the Proper Scope of the Federal Commerce Power," *San Diego Law Review*, Vol. 31 (Summer 1994), p. 607.
35. 294 U.S. 511 (1935).
36. 340 U.S. 349 (1951).

- In the recent case of *West Lynn Creamery v. Healy* (1994),[38] the Court struck down a Massachusetts law which required that out-of-state milk producers pay a special assessment to the state that was then distributed to in-state dairy farmers. "[T]he purpose and effect of the pricing order are to divert market share to Massachusetts dairy farmers," the Court held. "This diversion necessarily injures the dairy farmers in neighboring States."

In these cases, the Court held that because the policies of certain states or municipalities had negative spillover effects on companies or consumers in other states, the laws or regulations in question were unconstitutionally extraterritorial and discriminatory in nature.

In a similar sense, a Substantial Interstate Spillover Effects Test justifies a certain degree of federal oversight of the ongoing process of stranded cost compensation in the electric industry, which is being used by many states to create new protectionist burdens on interstate commerce. Essentially, many large (and usually poorly managed) electric utilities have convinced legislators and regulators in their home states to grant them exorbitant bailouts for any future losses—or stranded costs—that they may incur as a result of electricity deregulation. Almost all these plans to bail out in-state utilities involve the creation of new, discriminatory transitional charges (in other words, taxes) on consumers or potential competitors. The problem is that the effects of these taxes might be felt well beyond the borders of the state that enforces them. States clearly have the right to study the future health of in-state utilities, but they do not have the right to impose discriminatory taxes on out-of-state consumers or competitors to bail out their in-state utilities.

More important, these bailouts, which could total $200 billion to $300 billion or more when the process is complete, are slowly creating a full-blown economic war among the states—a war that threatens the nation's economic vitality. Many state officials view the stranded cost bailout process as a way to assure incumbent utilities

Footnotes:
37. Pierce has noted that "States are adept at imposing facially evenhanded regulatory requirements that purport to serve valid state interests, but whose adverse effects are felt almost entirely by out-of-state interests. The Court attempts to limit state authority to take actions that produce de facto, as well as facial, discrimination against interstate commerce. Thus, it occasionally invalidates a state action that has a clear discriminatory effect even if the stated purpose of the action is not discriminatory." Richard J. Pierce, Jr., "Regulation, Deregulation, Federalism, and Administrative Law: Agency Power to Preempt State Regulation," p. 616.
38. 512 U.S. 186 (1994).

New Federalism Tensions and a Framework for the Future

an advantage over out-of-state competitors. This mentality has forced state policymakers and regulators to consider seriously the arguments by utility companies that the price tag associated with their individual bailouts should be increased to match any bailout packages granted to competitors in neighboring states.

Congress should assume the referee's role in this process to see that the state-by-state electricity bailout war does not spin out of control, with widespread and deleterious interstate spillover effects. The most logical way to referee without trampling on the right of the states to make certain compensatory determinations is for Congress to forbid electrical companies from entering the interstate electricity market if they accept state-granted bailouts. In other words, any electric utility that applied for and received a multibillion-dollar bailout to cover past or future economic losses would be quarantined within its current service jurisdiction. This would ensure that the anti-competitive externalities associated with such bailouts do not spill over into interstate markets. It also would discourage utilities from asking for the money in the first place. Firms that already had accepted some form of bailout, however, would be allowed to compete in interstate markets if they agreed to refund any bailout funds confiscated from consumers on past billing statements.[39]

This sensible compromise may be the best way to balance the rights of the states to make bailout determinations with the right of the federal government to protect the free flow of interstate commerce and economic harmony among the states. Congress should not shirk its constitutionally required duty as protector of America's national marketplace from illegal state-created barriers to interstate competition.[40]

Footnotes:
39. See David J. McCarthy, "Federalism and Electric Industry Restructuring: How to Stop the Trade War Here at Home," presentation at The Heritage Foundation, February 27, 1998.
40. For more information, see Adam D. Thierer, "A Five-Point Checklist for Successful Electricity Deregulation Legislation," Heritage Foundation *Backgrounder* No. 1169, April 13, 1998; *Reply Brief for Petitioner Indianapolis Power & Light Company*, Petition for Review of the Order of the Pennsylvania Public Utility Commission Entered May 22, 1997 at Docket Nos. R–00973877, R–00973877C001 and R–00973877C0002, No. 1597 CD 1997; *The Securitization Swindle*, A White Paper by IPALCO Enterprises, Inc., Indianapolis, Indiana, May 1997, p. 30; and Adam D. Thierer, "Electricity Deregulation: Separating Fact From Fiction in the Debate Over Stranded Cost Recovery," Heritage Foundation *Talking Points* No. 20, March 11, 1997, pp. 12–13.

The Delicate Balance

In sum, the Substantial Spillover Effects Test or Negative Externality Test is best thought of as a standard employed by the Court to determine the balance between the right of the states to regulate commerce and Congress's right to protect the interstate component of commerce. In *Pike v. Bruce Church, Inc.* (1970), for example, the Court established another famous balancing test:

> Where the statute regulates evenhandedly to effectuate a legitimate local public interest, and its effects on interstate commerce are only incidental, it will be upheld unless the burden imposed on such commerce is clearly excessive in relation to the putative local benefits. If a legitimate local purpose is found, then the question becomes one of degree. And the extent of the burden that will be tolerated will of course depend on the nature of the local interest involved, and on whether it could be promoted as well with a lesser impact on interstate activities.[41]

Other cases that employ such balancing tests include *South Carolina State Highway Department v. Barnwell* (1938),[42] *Southern Pacific Co. v. Arizona* (1945),[43] *Bibb v. Navajo Freight Lines, Inc.* (1959),[44] *Hunt v. Washington Apple Advertising Commission* (1977),[45] *Philadelphia v. New Jersey* (1978),[46] *Kassel v. Consolidated Freightways Corp.* (1981),[47] and *Maine v. Taylor* (1986).[48] Summaries of each of these cases may be found in Appendix III.

Again, in these balancing cases, the Court typically has regarded "legitimate local public interests" or police powers as matters that deal with substantial health, safety, or environmental concerns. If states can demonstrate a legitimate and verifiable interest in pursuing such goals to benefit their citizens, and if the resulting impact on interstate commerce will not be excessive, the Court will allow such state actions to stand despite their discriminatory nature.[49] If, however, such a state law or regulation in no way furthers these ends,

Footnotes:
41. *Pike v. Bruce Church, Inc.*, 397 U.S. 137 (1970).
42. 303 U.S. 177 (1938).
43. 325 U.S. 761 (1945).
44. 359 U.S. 520 (1959).
45. 432 U.S. 333 (1977).
46. 437 U.S. 617 (1978).
47. 450 U.S. 662 (1981).
48. 477 U.S. 131 (1986).
49. See *South Carolina State Highway Department v. Barnwell Brothers, Inc.*, 303 U.S. 177 (1938).

the Court has held the policy to be an unconstitutional burden on interstate commerce or economic freedom in general.[50]

A more recent balancing test is found in *United States v. Lopez* (1995). In this decision, Chief Justice Rehnquist established the "three broad categories of activity that Congress may regulate under its commerce power." The second and third criteria are of particular interest:

1. Congress may regulate the use of the channels of interstate commerce.
2. Congress is empowered to regulate and protect the instrumentalities of interstate commerce, or persons or things in interstate commerce, even though the threat may come from intrastate activities.
3. Congress's commerce authority includes the power to regulate those activities having a substantial relation to interstate commerce, i.e., those activities that substantially affect interstate commerce.[51]

Such balancing tests can be useful in gauging the protectionist or discriminatory nature of a state law or regulation. Yet critics have noted that the problem with such balancing tests, including the Substantial Interstate Spillover Effects Test or Negative Externality Test, is that, if taken too far, they become overly broad and easily abused forms of a rather ambiguous "indirect effects" test. Such indirect effects tests on occasion have been used by the Court to expand the reach of the Commerce Clause beyond the Founders' intended limits. Furthermore, judgments regarding what constitute indirect effects, or even substantial impacts, are often quite subjective.

But such concerns about balancing tests may be somewhat misplaced. "Despite what the Court has said," in the words of Donald H. Regan, professor of law and philosophy at the University of Michigan, "it has not been balancing. It has been following a simpler and better-justified course.... [T]he Court has been concerned exclusively with preventing states from engaging in purposeful economic protectionism. Not only is this what the Court has been

Footnotes:
50. This was the case in *Southern Pacific Co. v. Arizona ex. rel. Sullivan*, 325 U.S. 761 (1945); *Bibb v. Navajo Freight Lines*, 359 U.S. 520 (1959); *Raymond Motor Transportation, Inc. v. Rice*, 434 U.S. 42 (1978); and *Kassel v. Consolidated Freightways Corp.*, 450 U.S. 662 (1981).
51. Chief Justice William Rehnquist, *United States v. Lopez*, 115 S. Ct. 1624 (1995).

The Delicate Balance

doing, it is just what the Court should do. This and no more."[52] In other words, most so-called balancing tests, including the Substantial Spillover Effects Test, are merely attempts to gauge the protectionist, discriminatory, or extraterritorial nature of a state or local statute or regulation. Again, these are the core principles that should lie at the heart of all Commerce Clause considerations.

The bottom line, therefore, is that if balancing tests can demonstrate that states or localities have exercised extraterritorial jurisdiction, or have implemented policies that have a clearly discriminatory or protectionist impact on interstate commerce, such tests are useful insofar as they protect and promote the intentions of the Framers. However, these tests would not be legitimate policy tools if they are:

1. Interpreted too loosely or read too broadly;
2. Used to justify intrusive new federal programs or policies;
3. Employed to discourage beneficial state-by-state experimentation; or
4. Used to interfere with the exercise of legitimate state and local police powers.

The task of striking this balance doubtless will continue to be both difficult and controversial.

Technological Complexity and Network Externality Considerations. This final interstate commerce consideration or test attempts to expand upon several of the foregoing tests by asking whether there can be discriminatory, protectionist, or extraterritorial effects associated with state-by-state regulation of sophisticated modern markets or technologies, especially complex, interlocking national networks.

To frame such a Technological Complexity or Network Externality Test, consider again the example of wireless broadcast television and cellular telephone transmission. Because the efficient operation of wireless networks and technologies demands the unfettered coordination of multiple spectrum signals and transmissions, broadcast television and cellular telephone systems would break down under the weight of competing regulatory systems if such competition were allowed to exist. If America had 50 different sets of regulations governing the transmission prices or standards for broadcast and

Footnotes:
52. Donald H. Regan, "The Supreme Court and State Protectionism: Making Sense of the Dormant Commerce Clause," *Michigan Law Review*, Vol. 84 (1986), p. 1092.

cellular networks, it is highly doubtful that innovation and competition could be fostered.

Likewise, electric power companies produce and then distribute power through a complex, interconnected electrical grid nationwide. Although these power providers have immobile production facilities that reside in a variety of different states and localities, the nation's electrical system would not work properly if grid management differed radically from state to state.

Thus, in such network industries, it seems clear that the technologies involved are interstate in scope and that there is a national need to protect interstate competition across these networks from discriminatory or extraterritorial state action. Such regulation will ensure that all American consumers and companies can share in the benefits of an open internal marketplace. Furthermore, when the deregulation of such complex network industries as wireline and wireless telecommunications, the electricity sector, financial services networks, and the transportation and aviation industries is considered, the complex physics of the technologies involved may require some minimal federal oversight to ensure that deregulation can proceed efficiently.

Consider the cases of certain network industries that have been deregulated in the past. Imagine what would have happened if the states had been allowed to deregulate America's aviation industry using separate schedules and plans in the late 1970s. If one state had deregulated the market completely while surrounding states remained closed, it cannot be doubted that the efficient and safe routing of air traffic would have been affected adversely. Furthermore, each state would have sought to protect its own in-state carriers and would have rigged deregulation to ensure the preservation of certain routes and services, regardless of how inefficient they were to operate.

Instead, the federal government, led by congressional Democrats and the Carter Administration, undertook a comprehensive and radical effort that completely deregulated the aviation market on a rapid timetable. The results have been extremely beneficial for consumers. In fact, a recent study by industry analysts Robert Crandall, senior fellow at the Brookings Institution, and Jerry Ellig, senior research fellow at the Center for Market Processes at George Mason University, notes that since 1977, airline deregulation has saved consumers almost $20 billion, has improved overall safety, and has encouraged greater industry innovation.[53] Overall, prices have fallen almost 40 percent since the federal government deregulated the airlines in 1978.[54]

The Delicate Balance

Would deregulation have occurred as smoothly or been as beneficial for consumers if a state-by-state approach had been pursued instead? It is highly unlikely. Many states undoubtedly would have undertaken efforts to preserve inefficient routes and protect local carriers, followed by multibillion-dollar bailouts for state-favored incumbent air carriers. In any event, some degree of federal oversight would have been needed to coordinate interstate air traffic and activity.

Similarly, under the Technological Complexity/Network Externality Test, we can ask how beneficial it would be for the states to exercise exclusive regulatory power over wireless cellular telecommunications standards, satellite transmissions, or even new communications technologies like the Internet. Although many states have considered plans to regulate or tax various forms of telecommunications services that are clearly national or even global in character, Congress has restricted such anti-competitive, unconstitutional efforts.

In fact, Members of Congress have sponsored measures seeking to protect the Internet from state-by-state regulation and taxation for this very reason. The Internet Tax Freedom Act, introduced by Representative Christopher Cox (R–CA) and Senator Ron Wyden (D–OR), for example, restricts the ability of state and local governments to exercise their taxing authority over the Internet, essentially prohibiting America's 30,000 tax jurisdictions from imposing multiple, overlapping, incompatible taxes on Internet commerce.[55] This bill was passed by Congress in October 1998. Likewise, the Internet Protection Act of 1997, introduced by Representatives Richard White (R–WA) and W. J. (Billy) Tauzin (R–LA), would have prohibited federal, state, and local regulation of "the rates, charges, practices, classifications, facilities, or services for or in connection with the provision of Internet information services to customers."[56]

Footnotes:
53. Robert Crandall and Jerry Ellig, *Economic Deregulation and Customer Choice: Lesson for the Electric Industry* (Fairfax, Va.: Center for Market Processes, 1997), pp. 34–47.
54. See Adam D. Thierer, "20th Anniversary of Airline Deregulation: Cause for Celebration, Not Re-regulation," Heritage Foundation *Backgrounder* No. 1173, April 22, 1998.
55. See Adam D. Thierer, "Not Too Late to Stop the Internet Tax Crusade," Heritage Foundation *Executive Memorandum* No. 520, April 3, 1998, and Adam D. Thierer, "Why Congress Must Save the Internet from State and Local Taxation," Heritage Foundation *Executive Memorandum* No. 488, June 23, 1997.

New Federalism Tensions and a Framework for the Future

Congressional action can be justified in these cases because the Internet comprises a complex global network that cannot be taxed or regulated in any sensible, efficient way at the state or local level without inducing deleterious network externalities. Anyone who understands the nature of the Internet should agree that this is the only sensible and realistic way to ensure the continued development of this global medium. As Dan L. Burk, Assistant Professor of Law at Seton Hall University, has argued:

> The potential negative effects of...state regulation on the growth of the Internet extends beyond the boundaries of any of the states, and the effects of state regulation will likewise spill over state borders. Such regulatory leakage implicates constitutional doctrines designed to preserve both the sovereignty of the individual states and the coherence of the United States as a whole. Thus, the prospect of states applying haphazard and uncoordinated multijurisdictional regulation to the Internet's seamless electronic web raises profound questions regarding the relationship between the several states.[57]

Furthermore, relevant Supreme Court decisions in *National Bellas Hess, Inc. v. Illinois Department of Revenue*[58] and *Quill Corp. v. North Dakota*[59] have determined that it is unconstitutional for a state or locality to impose tax-collection obligations on mail-order firms that do not have some sort of "nexus," or physical presence, within the jurisdiction imposing the sales tax. Thus, Congress is well within its power in prohibiting state and local efforts to impose Internet tax collection obligations on out-of-state electronic vendors as well.[60]

Footnotes:
56. See Adam D. Thierer, "What's Next for Telecommunications Deregulation?" Heritage Foundation *Backgrounder* No. 1145, October 28, 1997, pp. 3–6.
57. Dan L. Burk, "How State Regulation of the Internet Violates the Commerce Clause," *Cato Journal*, Vol. 17, No. 2 (Fall 1997), p. 147.
58. 386 U.S. 753 (1967).
59. 504 U.S. 298 (1992).
60. See, generally, Saba Ashraf, "Virtual Taxation: State Taxation of Internet and On-line Sales," *Florida State University Law Review*, Vol. 24, No. 3 (1997); available on Internet site *http://www.law.fsu.edu/lawreview/issues/243/ashrfram.html*. Ashraf concludes that, "Until states persuade Congress to allow them to tax out-of-state vendors based upon their presence on the Internet or on-line, companies are free to sell goods without collecting use tax, as long as they do not otherwise have physical presence in-state."

The Delicate Balance

In a similar manner, the outdated regulatory structure of today's sophisticated financial services industry poses some troubling questions regarding jurisdictional assignments. Increasingly, everything from stocks, bonds, futures, and mutual funds to life, fire, and auto insurance policies is marketed to consumers across America by a multitude of companies. Yet states have varying laws regarding the provision of insurance policies and traditionally have imposed strict limits on the sale of bundled financial services, especially from out-of-state companies.

Undoubtedly, the modern financial services industry, which has become increasingly reliant on the nation's tightly integrated communications infrastructure, including the Internet, has both *intra*state and *inter*state components. After all, banks, credit unions, insurance companies, and other financial institutions reside within the jurisdictional confines of different states and localities. Thus, a good argument can be made that state and local regulators can exercise a certain degree of regulatory authority over these companies. However, appreciating the interstate and indeed global nature of this industry, Congress also can claim jurisdiction over much of the commerce that takes place within America's massive financial services industry.

Furthermore, the increasing integration of previously distinct segments of the financial services industry means that Americans can be offered a bundled, branded package of financial services from a single company of their choice as long as state and local laws do not prohibit such a development. To ensure that state laws cannot interfere with the freedom of companies to offer bundled services to consumers through America's financial services networks, Congress can take steps to prohibit violations of the freedom of contract between these companies and consumers. However, some regulatory tasks probably will remain that could be handled more efficiently and effectively at the state or local level, since such regulation will not have negative spillover effects associated with it and there will be no externalities associated with parochial action.[61]

For example, as noted with respect to automobile insurance regulation, although great benefits might be generated by federal efforts to ensure that consumers have choice when purchasing auto insurance policies, such a federal "auto choice" plan is probably unwarranted regardless of such consumer savings. Insurance oversight traditionally is a state responsibility, and in this case there are no

Footnotes:
61. For more information, see John S. Barry, "Federalism and Financial Services," Heritage Foundation *Backgrounder* No. 1160, May 1, 1998.

negative spillovers or negative network effects associated with state-by-state regulation. Furthermore, it is doubtful that commerce in this field is in any way interstate in nature.

Finally, it is important to note that the deregulation of some network industries might create reciprocity concerns demanding some limited degree of federal attention. For example, if State A is willing to open its markets to competition but the surrounding States B, C, and D are not, a reciprocity concern will be raised. The reciprocity issue arises because firms from States B, C, and D can enter State A to compete, but firms in State A cannot go into those markets and offer services. Reciprocity is a concern in the electricity sector, where state-by-state deregulation has posed problematic reciprocity questions as well as concerns about discriminatory treatment of out-of-state carriers. Language has been included in certain congressional bills aimed at deregulating this industry, either to deal with these concerns or, at a minimum, to ensure that trade in electricity is not artificially hindered by discriminatory treatment at the state level.

As we have seen with respect to other areas, however, the fact that some reciprocity concerns might exist in this field or other industries is not, by itself, necessarily enough to justify wide-scale federal intervention. Congress might be able to deal with these problems simply by giving the states the right to settle reciprocity concerns through bilateral or regional trade agreements, although a better way to break down barriers to interstate competition and consumer choice in most cases would be a multilateral agreement among all the states, either voluntarily negotiated between them or enforced by Congress.

In closing, it is also worth noting that this same model of negative or network externalities can be applied to many environmental issues and jurisdictional disputes that divide American industries and governments. In their brilliant recent exploration of environmental externalities and regulatory authority, Henry N. Butler and Jonathan R. Macey develop a simple "Matching Principle" to determine the most appropriate and efficient level of regulation for various environmental concerns. Simply stated, "The Matching Principle suggests that, in general, the size of the geographic area affected by a specific pollution source should determine the appropriate governmental level for responding to the pollution. There is no need for the regulating jurisdiction to be larger than the regulated activity."[62]

Butler and Macey devised this Matching Principle theory largely by examining the scope of various environmental externalities, and then attempted to establish a sensible balance of powers accordingly. They concluded (1) that most externality problems are created by the lack of well-defined property rights and (2) that, even when existing interstate environmental externalities grant federal authorities some jurisdictional authority under their Matching Principle, this does not justify reckless, command-and-control federal regulation. Instead, they counsel regulatory flexibility and market-based solutions to problems involving environmental externalities of an interstate scope, such as many clean air and water issues:

> [O]ne of the most convincing arguments for federal environmental regulation is the control of interstate externalities. If nontrivial external costs are imposed across state boundaries, then the issue should be addressed by a higher level of government. But the presence of interstate externalities does not imply that they must be corrected by federal regulation that usurps completely the role of local initiatives. Moreover, acceptance of the interstate externalities justification for federal environmental regulation does not necessarily lead one to support a specific type of regulatory response. The current regime of command-and-control regulations is no more justified under this analysis than alternative market-based approaches.... Rather than having federal regulators impose regulations on polluters, the interstate externalities problem can be addressed by reallocating environmental authority in a manner that would force states and state decisionmakers to bear the full costs of their decisions regarding the regulation of pollution.[63]

Footnotes:
62. Henry N. Butler and Jonathan R. Macey, "Externalities and the Matching Principle: The Case for Reallocating Environmental Regulatory Authority," *Yale Law & Public Policy Review / Yale Journal on Regulation*, Symposium Issue, "Constructing a New Federalism: Jurisdictional Competence and Competition," Vol. 14, No. 2 (March 1–2, 1996), p. 25.
63. Butler and Macey, "Externalities and the Matching Principle," p. 42. For a comprehensive assessment of the future of environmental policy and regulation in light of recent Supreme Court federalism jurisprudence, see Jonathan H. Adler, "The Green Aspects of *Printz*: The Revival of Federalism and Its Implications for Environmental Law," *George Mason Law Review*, Vol. 6, No. 3 (Spring 1998), pp. 573–633. Adler addresses and debunks many myths associated with federal versus state efforts to regulate environmental quality and notes (p. 633) that recent federalism cases "offer the opportunity to reawaken state experimentation and revisit the nationalist assumptions underlying contemporary environmental policy."

6

PRACTICAL STEPS TOWARD A REVIVAL OF FEDERALISM

Despite the corruption of the Commerce Clause by the courts and Congress in recent times, abandonment of the Founders' goals and intentions regarding America's federalist system of governance is anything but justified. Even with the added complexity of modern, high-tech industries and technologies that the Framers could not have envisioned, the original model of federalism is every bit as applicable today as it was over 200 years ago. As Richard Epstein has noted, "There has been no basic transformation of the economy that requires, or allows, a parallel transformation in the scope of the commerce clause."[1] The industries and technologies that dominate American commercial life may have undergone remarkable change since the Founding, but the same underlying laws of economics still apply; the original understanding of the Commerce Clause should apply as well.

Ironically, as today's Congress finds itself searching for ways to balance the sometimes conflicting goals of an unfettered national marketplace and state and local sovereignty, it faces many of the same dilemmas that forced the Founders to strike a compromise during the Constitutional Convention over 200 years ago. The framework developed in the previous chapters is intended to assist efforts to strike that proper balance for today's complex industries and technologies, and to do so in a way that both honors the constitutional goals of the Founders and establishes a context within which these issues can be debated sensibly and resolved in a more satisfactory fashion.

Thus far, however, this framework has been somewhat abstract. Policymakers need a concrete, achievable agenda if they are to rein-

Footnotes:
1. Richard A. Epstein, "The Proper Scope of the Commerce Power," *Virginia Law Review*, Vol. 73, No. 8 (November 1987), p. 1397.

The Delicate Balance

vigorate American federalism in the short term. Therefore, this chapter will provide some reform mechanisms that can help restore the Founders' original balance of powers; it also will explore the question of whether more radical, underlying alterations or additions to the Constitution need to be made by a new constitutional convention.

> Ironically, as today's Congress finds itself searching for ways to balance the sometimes conflicting goals of an unfettered national marketplace and state and local sovereignty, it faces many of the same dilemmas that forced the Founders to strike a compromise during the Constitutional Convention over two hundred years ago.

RESTORING THE FOUNDERS' VISION: IS A CONSTITUTIONAL CONVENTION NECESSARY?

A November 1987 conference held by the now-defunct Advisory Commission on Intergovernmental Relations asked, "Is Constitutional Reform Necessary to Reinvigorate Federalism?"[2] Although the conference came to no definite conclusion, it is worth noting that many scholars who take federalism seriously have been asking this question for decades, and arriving at different answers.

Within textualist circles, in particular, the question of how best to restore the proper constitutional balance of powers has long been a subject of debate; again, however, no definitive answer has arisen. Both conservative and libertarian textualists regard any change in the underlying structure of the Constitution, whether through constitutional convention or through constitutional amendment, as a matter of the utmost gravity and something that ought never to be undertaken lightly. A few advocates of reform, however, believe it would be wise to consider convening a meeting to propose and perhaps eventually adopt changes in the American Constitution aimed at restoring the Founders' original model of federalism.

Yet, even when calls for a convention are made with such noble intentions in mind, many textualists argue that re-opening the Constitution through constitutional convention involves as many risks as opportunities. In particular, some fear that the same special interests that have corrupted America's constitutional system throughout this century would work to capture any constitutional reform pro-

---

Footnotes:
2. *Is Constitutional Reform Necessary to Reinvigorate Federalism?* (Washington, D.C.: Advisory Commission on Intergovernmental Relations, M-154, November 1987).

cess, especially one takes the form of a single convention. Consequently, most textualists would agree that a constitutional convention should be convened only in the event that all other avenues of federalism reform have been exhausted.

This is not an easy issue to resolve, and no attempt will be made here to pass judgment on the wisdom of holding a constitutional convention on issues of federalism. Rather, the following discussion will attempt merely to outline what might be considered an agenda for such a convention, or for any conference or meeting on federalism that takes place in future years.

In any convention, conference, or meeting that takes place, federal, state, and local legislators could discuss methods of restoring the proper constitutional balance of powers between these levels of government while also preserving and enhancing America's vigorous interstate commercial marketplace. Optimally, and at a minimum, four objectives should guide any such effort:

1. **Clearly delineate which issues are truly federal in scope.** The first task of any convention or conference on federalism issues would be to re-examine the U.S. Constitution and clearly delineate the few enumerated powers allowed to the federal government. Sections 8, 9, and 10 of Article I establish a fairly unambiguous list of federal powers that remain among the only constitutionally justified tasks for the federal government.

   As the following table illustrates, these responsibilities include national defense and international diplomacy, trade and treaty negotiation, immigration procedures, the monetary system, patent and copyright enforcement, bankruptcy procedures, the protection of certain important constitutional rights or liberties, and the regulation of interstate commerce. Once participants in a constitutional convention on federalism have agreed on this list of legitimate federal responsibilities, they can detail the many unnecessary or unjustifiable powers that the federal government has accrued over the past two centuries.

2. **Propose a radical devolution of all remaining national programs and residual federal powers to the states and localities.** Despite the advisability of terminating or privatizing as many federal programs and powers as possible, a variety of political pressures and interests could make it very difficult for Congress to do so. But even when program elimination or privatization is not possible, devolution may well be quite feasible. In particular, as the table also illustrates, the vast majority of issues involving crime control or prison maintenance, roads and highways, education and schools, zoning and land management, and the environ-

The Delicate Balance

Areas Of Justifiable Federal Jurisdictions	Areas Where the Federal Government Has No Constitutional Right to Act (Devolution Candidates)
▪ National security and defense	▪ Most crime or prison issues
▪ Diplomacy	▪ Roads and highways
▪ Trade and treaty negotiation	▪ Education and schools
▪ Immigration procedures	▪ Medical care
	▪ Child care
▪ Monetary system maintenance	▪ Zoning and land management
▪ Patent and copyright system	▪ Sanitation systems
▪ Bankruptcy procedures	▪ Most environmental issues
▪ Interstate commerce regulation	

ment could be handled more efficiently and effectively by state and local officials. At a minimum, a constitutional convention or conference should identify a group of programs that could be returned to states and localities immediately, and then list other candidates for long-term devolution to the states.[3]

3. Outline areas of commercial activity where jurisdictional responsibility is unclear and discuss how to handle them. The Framers wisely gave the federal government the power to monitor interstate commerce in order to prohibit state-based protectionism and advance the cause of national commercial union. But it also is easy for federal legislators to abuse the commerce power, as they have done throughout this century. Nevertheless, even though the focus of the Commerce Clause power given to Congress should be interpreted more narrowly, in many cases

Footnotes:
3. For a comprehensive list of program elimination or devolution candidates, see Scott A. Hodge, ed., *Balancing America's Budget: Ending the Era of Big Government* (Washington, D.C.: The Heritage Foundation, 1997).

federal policymakers still need to exercise this authority to restrain improper state activities that adversely affect interstate commerce. As Judge Robert Bork has noted:

> The fact that the pendulum has swung too far in the direction of centralization should not produce a knee-jerk hostility to federal power. In many circumstances, federal regulation is necessary and constitutionally legitimate.... Much as some of us may deplore the misuse of [federal] power, we must not fall into the opposite error of resisting its use on all occasions.[4]

Therefore, future meetings or conferences on federalism should concentrate on the need to outline reasonable compromises on the regulation of interstate commerce. Congress should make it clear, and the states should be willing to accept, that there will be times when a small degree of state legislative and regulatory authority will need to be sacrificed to ensure the free flow of commerce across state boundaries.

However, even in cases in which some federal action to this end might be permissible, Congress should concentrate on *pro*scriptive and not *pre*scriptive remedies. That is, federal policymakers should focus on areas of interstate commerce in which state and local action should be clearly prohibited. The national government should not attempt to prescribe how state and local governments should carry out other programs or policies of a purely parochial nature, as Congress has done since the time of the New Deal.

4. Give the states new powers to constrain the future growth of the national government. This action by a constitutional convention or federalism conference would guarantee that once the federal government's powers were scaled back to constitutionally justified levels, they would remain there. Any such package of new state powers should include three specific checks on federal authority:[5]

- A supermajority veto power over federal legislation or regulation to force Congress to reconsider particularly egregious or potentially unconstitutional acts;

- The ability to propose constitutional amendments without having to call for a constitutional convention, a change that

Footnotes:
4. Robert H. Bork, "Federalism and Federal Regulation: The Case of Product Labeling," Washington Legal Foundation, *Critical Legal Issues*, Working Paper Series No. 46, July 1991, p. 4.

would put the states on an equal footing with Congress, which already has this power; and

- The right, when they feel that egregious federal mandates and policies have been imposed on them, to convene their congressional delegations, possibly in annual or semi-annual non-binding meetings of state and federal representatives in the various state capitals to discuss federal policies and programs.

These are merely a few of the many reforms that could be pursued through a constitutional convention or conference on federalism. Other less controversial but no less substantively important reforms (some of which are discussed below) include:

- Term limits for federal officeholders;
- Better use of block grants or vouchers to accomplish socioeconomic goals;
- Comprehensive federal regulatory reform;
- Passage of a balanced budget amendment to rein in federal spending; and
- Strengthening of the Unfunded Mandates Reform Act of 1995.[6]

Footnotes:
5. The American Legislative Exchange Council (ALEC) has drawn up a series of "model bills" that could be used by Congress or state legislatures to pursue these goals. See Charles J. Cooper and David H. Thompson, "The Tenth Amendment: The Promise of Liberty, Strategies to Restore the Balance of Power Between the Federal and State Governments," American Legislative Exchange Council, *The State Factor*, Vol. 22, No. 7 (October 1996), and American Legislative Exchange Council, *Sourcebook of American State Legislation 1995*, Vol. II, January 1995, pp. 275–280.
6. For many other creative ways to rein in federal power, return functions to the states, and avoid political pitfalls along the way, see Douglas Seay and Robert E. Moffit, "Transferring Functions to the States," in Stuart M. Butler and Kim R. Holmes, eds., *Mandate for Leadership IV: Turning Ideas Into Actions* (Washington, D.C.: The Heritage Foundation, 1997), pp. 87–127. See also Douglas Seay and Wesley Smith, "Federalism," in Stuart M. Butler and Kim R. Homes, eds., *Issues '96: The Candidate's Briefing Book* (Washington, D.C.: The Heritage Foundation, 1996), pp. 427–434.

OTHER WAYS TO HELP DETERMINE JURISDICTIONAL RESPONSIBILITY OR EASE FEDERALISM TENSIONS

Beyond these recommendations, a variety of additional tools and proposals could be adopted immediately by various levels of government to help ease many federalism tensions before they develop.

> **CONGRESS:**
> - Revive Executive Order 12612 and codify its principles in statutory form.
> - Implement anti-delegation legislation to curb the pre-emptive power of independent regulatory agencies.
>
> **STATES AND LOCALITIES:**
> - Work together to develop uniform laws when appropriate.
> - Replace potentially discriminatory laws, hidden taxes and regulations, and cross-subsidization mechanisms with transparent, non-discriminatory rules and programs funded through general treasury revenues.
> - Develop voluntary pacts to end or diminish "the economic war between the states."
>
> **ALL UNITS OF GOVERNMENT:**
> - Devise Regulatory Responsibility Matrices to help determine jurisdictional responsibility.

Congress: Revive Executive Order 12612 and codify its principles in statutory form. To guide the process of assessing jurisdictional responsibility and limiting the role of the federal government, Congress would be wise to revive the principles contained in President Reagan's Executive Order 12612, which President Clinton attempted to revoke. (The complete text of the executive order may be found in Appendix IV.)

Eventually, President Clinton's attempt to eviscerate the federalism legacy of the Founders and President Reagan through his own Executive Order 13083 had to be withdrawn because of the intensely adverse reaction it generated, but it remains vital that Congress take steps to ensure that such a blatant betrayal of federalism principles by presidential fiat cannot occur in the future. Congress needs to send an unambiguous message (1) that the principles embodied in E.O. 12612 represent the most accurate articulation of the Founders' original model of American government and (2) that, as a body elected by the American people to represent their interests, it intends to uphold that model.

Congress could accomplish this task by codifying the language of the Reagan executive order to provide permanent guidance to all federal officials on federalism matters. Once these guidelines were given the force of law by Congress, federal agencies would no longer be able to get away with ignoring the objectives established either by E.O. 12612 or by the Constitution.

Codification of E.O. 12612 would place strict guidelines on federal agencies looking to pre-empt state or local activity and would require them to prepare a "Federalism Assessment" for any proposed rule that might have sufficient federalism implications to warrant such substantive review. These Federalism Assessments would be reviewed by the Office of Management and Budget (OMB) and by Congress to ensure that federal agencies were not running roughshod over the Constitution and the autonomy of state and local governments. At a minimum, codification of E.O. 12612 would require that federal officials consult closely with state and local officials before attempting any pre-emptive action.

This codification could take many forms. Congress, for example, could simply take the exact language of the executive order and codify it as law without any significant changes or accompanying statutory language. This approach is embodied in two bills proposed during the late summer of 1998: S. 2445, the Federalism Enforcement Act of 1998, introduced by Senator Fred Thompson (R–TN) and several co-sponsors, and H.R. 4422, the Federalism Act of 1998, introduced by Representative James Moran (D–VA) and several co-sponsors from both parties. Both bills, despite minor differences regarding the inclusion of judicial review language, would codify the language of E.O. 12612 virtually verbatim.

A second option would be to amend the existing congressional statutes that deal with jurisdictional matters, intergovernmental affairs, or regulatory policy making. Two legislative vehicles that could easily be amended to include the federalism guidelines and protections found in E.O. 12612 are already available. They are the Unfunded Mandates Reform Act of 1995 (UMRA)[7] and the Congressional Review Act (CRA), which was implemented as part of the

Footnotes:
7. Unfunded Mandates Reform Act of 1995, Public Law No. 104–4, March 22, 1995.

Small Business Regulatory Enforcement Fairness Act of 1996 (SBREFA).[8]

The Unfunded Mandates Reform Act, one of the first pieces of legislation enacted by the 104th Congress when the Republicans assumed a majority in both houses as a result of the 1994 elections, requires that federal officials attempt to estimate the costs of proposed mandates on the states and creates a mechanism whereby Congress can attempt to minimize these costs or strike down such mandates altogether. The Congressional Review Act provides a mechanism by which Congress can review and disapprove final rules issued by federal regulatory agencies; it also requires that agencies attempt to estimate the costs associated with new rules and provide interpretations or explanations regarding the need for these rules.

The UMRA has been criticized for certain deficiencies, including its lack of coverage for existing statutes and mandates; it also has been largely ignored by Congress.[9] But the UMRA also represents an important existing statutory protection against federal intrusion into state and local matters. It could be improved by the inclusion of E.O. 12612's Federalism Policymaking Criteria within Title II and by the addition of stronger judicial review language within Title IV to make its new and existing requirements more effective. With these improvements, the Unfunded Mandates Reform Act would give Congress and the courts a mechanism they could use to demand strict federalism accountability by federal officials.

The same approach could be taken to amending the Congressional Review Act. As with the UMRA, however, Congress has neglected to use the CRA to rein in over-zealous federal regulators.[10] In fact, it has failed to reject any new rules under the CRA, despite an onslaught of expensive new regulatory proposals by federal agencies. Nonetheless, the CRA has the potential to become an important tool in future congressional efforts to control federal regulatory activity. If it were amended to include E.O. 12612's Federal-

Footnotes:
8. Small Business Regulatory Enforcement Fairness Act of 1996, Public Law No. 104–121, March 29, 1996. The Congressional Review Act is contained in Subtitle E of Title II of the SBREFA.
9. See Angela Antonelli, "Promises Unfulfilled: Unfunded Mandates Reform Act of 1995," *Regulation*, No. 2 (1996), pp. 46–54.
10. See Angela Antonelli, "Needed: Aggressive Implementation of the Congressional Review Act," Heritage Foundation F.Y.I. No. 131, February 19, 1997, and Susan E. Dudley and Angela Antonelli, "Congress and the Clinton OMB: Unwilling Partners in Regulatory Oversight?" *Regulation*, Fall 1997, pp. 17–23.

ism Policymaking Criteria, yet another procedural impediment to federal pre-emption would exist; at the very least, Congress would be additionally obligated to review federal rules for their federalism implications and strike down those that do not abide by the Constitution.

Congress: Implement anti-delegation legislation to curb the pre-emptive power of independent regulatory agencies. Congress should codify the Federalism Policymaking Criteria and the restrictions of E.O. 12612 in a statutory vehicle. Such a law would serve as an important short-term constraint on unjustified federal attempts to impose rules and mandates on the states, localities, and individual Americans.

These efforts, however, should be viewed more as stop-gap measures than as substantive, long-term reform that effectively and permanently restores the proper constitutional balance of powers. As long as federal regulatory agencies and officials are granted broad discretionary powers, as if they were elected lawmakers, they will continue to ignore the UMRA and the CRA. They also will continue to implement cumbersome, intrusive federal regulations and mandates on states, businesses, and individuals.

This should not be surprising. Regulators exist to regulate. They cannot be expected either to surrender power voluntarily or to stop imposing expensive, pre-emptive rules, since it would not be in their best interest to do so. Nor should anyone mistake who is to blame for such activity: It was Congress that delegated broad discretionary powers to the agencies in the first place, and if it would start to take back authority that has been delegated unconstitutionally in the past, the power of federal regulatory agencies and administrative offices would be severely diminished. No longer would federal regulators threaten the original constitutional structure of government as they have throughout this century.

From the time of the New Deal, Congress has justified such delegation as allowing for more scientific lawmaking by administrative experts. Moreover, granting regulators rulemaking authority was seen as a way to conserve valuable time for Congress to debate the heart of the issues, leaving executive branch agencies to fill in the fine print. Although the Court struck down earlier efforts by Congress to delegate authority to these agencies,[11] the judicial branch eventually joined this silent conspiracy to undermine the Constitution and accepted these rationales for delegation.[12]

Footnotes:
11. See, in particular, *A.L.A. Schechter Poultry Corp. v. United States*, 295 U.S. 495 (1935).

Constitutional scholars have found these justifications for delegation wholly deficient.[13] The foremost criticism of delegation is that it conflicts with the Constitution. The language of Article I, Section 1 is clear: "All legislative powers herein granted shall be vested in a Congress of the United States, which shall consist of a Senate and a House of Representatives." Nowhere does the Constitution allow for the exercise of lawmaking powers or functions by non-elected executive branch administrators and bureaucrats.

This leads to another criticism: Delegation violates the principle of separation of powers between the branches of government and cannot be regarded as a better method of serving the public, because it represents a system of governance that is both unaccountable and undemocratic. As Senator Sam Brownback (R–KS) has noted:

> [P]erhaps the most pernicious aspect of delegation is that voters can no longer hold government accountable. Originally designed to be the most accountable branch of government, Congress has grown increasingly irresponsible. The fundamental link between voter and lawmaker has been severed. A handful of broadly written laws has spawned a virtual alphabet soup of government agencies and an overwhelming regulatory burden that undermines the very idea of representative government.[14]

Footnotes:
12. The Supreme Court decision in *J. W. Hampton, Jr., & Co. v. U.S.*, 276 U.S. 394 (1928), is widely cited as a watershed moment in the history of anti-delegation since from that case forward the Court legitimized and accepted congressional efforts to delegate power to administrative bodies. Prior to *J. W. Hampton*, the Court had held firmly to a doctrine of non-delegation of congressional authority to administrative agencies.
13. Pioneering work has been done in this field by Theodore Lowi in his classic work of political science *The End of Liberalism*. See Theodore J. Lowi, "Liberal Jurisprudence: Policy Without Law," in *The End of Liberalism: The Second Republic of the United States* (New York: W. W. Norton & Company, 1969, 1979), pp. 92–126. More recently, a study by New York Law School professor David Schoenbrod has been instrumental in calling attention to the deficiencies of delegation. See David Schoenbrod, *Power Without Responsibility: How Congress Abuses the People Through Delegation* (New Haven, Conn.: Yale University Press, 1993).
14. Senator Sam Brownback, prepared statement on the Congressional Responsibility Act of 1997, presented before the Subcommittee on Commercial and Administrative Law, Committee on the Judiciary, U.S. House of Representatives, September 25, 1997; available on the Internet at http://www.house.gov/judiciary/5128.htm.

This has led Cato Institute scholars David Schoenbrod and Jerry Taylor to refer to the practice of delegation as "the corrosive agent of democracy" and to argue that "delegation does not help secure 'good government;' it helps destroy it."[15]

Congressional action to end the unconstitutional practice of delegating authority to administrative agencies would have important implications for federalism. Such a bold move would minimize the pre-emptive powers of the federal government and hold elected Members of Congress accountable for their actions. With Congress no longer able to blame regulatory agencies and administrators for government overreach, Washington's ability to interfere in state and local matters would be greatly diminished.

Legislation has been introduced in Congress that would advance this anti-delegation agenda. The Congressional Responsibility Act of 1997, introduced in the Senate (S. 433) by Senator Brownback and in the House (H.R. 1036) by Representative J. D. Hayworth (R–AZ), has garnered wide bipartisan support. If eventually implemented, anti-delegation efforts like the Congressional Responsibility Act would represent a significant step back toward accountable, limited government, ending what Representative Hayworth—referring specifically to the practice of delegation—has called "regulation without representation."[16]

States: Work together to develop uniform laws when appropriate. The states should explore ways to diminish jurisdictional tensions by working together to enact harmonious laws and regulations, especially for issues that involve complex commercial activity.

An association already exists to promote this effort. Founded in 1892, the National Conference of Commissioners on Uniform State Laws (NCCUSL) has spent the past 100 years proposing and promoting the adoption of uniform state laws. State commissioners from all 50 states, the District of Columbia, Puerto Rico, and the U.S. Virgin Islands work through this Chicago-based nonprofit association to "promote the principle of uniformity by drafting and proposing specific statutes in areas of the law where uniformity is

Footnotes:
15. David Schoenbrod and Jerry Taylor, "The Delegation of Legislative Powers," in *Cato Handbook for Congress, 105th Congress* (Washington, D.C.: Cato Institute, 1997), p. 47.
16. Representative J. D. Hayworth, prepared statement on the Congressional Responsibility Act of 1997, presented before the Subcommittee on Commercial and Administrative Law, Committee on the Judiciary, U.S. House of Representatives, September 25, 1997; available on the Internet at *http://www.house.gov/hayworth/testimony/1036.htm.*

desirable."[17] The NCCUSL has had great success in the fields of probate law, child custody issues, and business incorporation standards. The states would be wise to expand the scope of its coverage to include uniform policies for the sorts of commercial issues and industries that form the focus of this book.

Such an effort is also the focus of the American Legislative Exchange Council (ALEC), the nation's largest nonpartisan, individual membership association of state legislators. With over 3,000 members from legislatures in all 50 states, ALEC convenes several task forces that issue policy papers on commerce issues, including commerce and economic development in general, energy and electricity, environment and natural resource questions, tax policy, telecommunications and information technology, trade and transportation, and other economic topics.

ALEC's state policymakers and private-sector representatives work through frequent task force meetings to outline "model legislation" or "model bills" for state legislatures on a wide range of economic issues. If adopted by the states, the model legislation in these fields recommended by ALEC could do much to lessen the need for federal intervention to solve interstate commerce disputes.[18]

Finally, state and federal regulators should continue to work through the National Association of Regulatory Utility Commissioners (NARUC) to improve the quality of any regulations still deemed necessary. According to NARUC's own constitution, as amended most recently in November 1996:

> The objectives of the Association shall be the advancement of commission regulation through the study and discussion of subjects concerning the operation and supervision of public utilities and carriers, the promotion of uniformity of regulation of public utilities and carriers by the several commissions, the promotion of coordinated action by the commissions of the several States to protect the common interests of the people with respect to the regulation of public utilities and carriers, and the promotion of cooperation of the commissions of the several States with each other and with the Federal commissions represented in the Association.[19]

Footnotes:
17. National Conference of Commissioners on Uniform State Laws, Internet site: *http://www.law.upenn.edu/library/ulc/brochure.htm*.
18. For more information about the American Legislative Exchange Council and its programs, see their Internet site: http://www.alec.org.

The Delicate Balance

This goal is carried out by several standing committees on such issues as communications, electricity, energy resources and the environment, finance and technology, gas, international relations, and water.

Although regulation at any government level is rarely preferable to decisions made in the marketplace, to the extent that legislators do determine that regulations are necessary, the work of the NCCUSL, ALEC, and NARUC is vital to ensuring that the regulatory process proceeds as efficiently as possible. The uniform state policies suggested by these organizations can help to alleviate many jurisdictional battles or federalism concerns *before* they develop.

States and localities: Replace potentially discriminatory laws, hidden taxes and regulations, and cross-subsidization mechanisms with transparent, non-discriminatory rules and programs funded through general treasury revenues. A comprehensive review of federalism jurisprudence reveals that a significant number of jurisdictional cases and controversies could have been avoided if state or local governments had used more appropriate methods of assisting or furthering their parochial interests.

State or local governments frequently attempt to aid local industries through hidden subsidies, protectionist tax schemes, or discriminatory regulatory policies—often camouflaging them as "health and safety" or "economic development" measures. Many agricultural jurisdictional disputes, for example, involve suits by producers in one state against another state on the grounds that the other state is using hidden, discriminatory taxes to confiscate profits from out-of-state interests and then redistributing the funds to in-state producers to give them an unfair competitive advantage. Likewise, in the transportation sector, states have enacted policies that discriminate against out-of-state carriers to give in-state carriers a leg up on the competition. Such protectionist schemes usually are found unconstitutional by the courts unless some overriding, parochial "police power" interest justifies such discriminatory behavior.

Even though discriminatory policies that unfairly burden interstate commerce or restrict consumer choice should be disallowed by the courts or Congress, federal officials do not necessarily have the right to ban all schemes intended to aid local industries or attract new interests. It is never advisable for any level of government to prop up fledgling industries or promote industrial policies. When

Footnotes:
19. See "Constitution of the National Association of Regulatory Utility Commissioners (As Amended November 20, 1996)," Internet site *http://www.erols.com/naruc/policies.htm*.

state or local officials do decide to do so, however, they should understand that, from a constitutional perspective, there is a right way and a wrong way to assist parochial interests.

The wrong way to aid local interests is through discriminatory and protectionist measures, since they not only hinder interstate commerce, but also breed "an economic war between the states," as Lawrence W. Reed of the Mackinac Center argues.[20] States and localities should move away from the use of hidden taxes, investment credits, tax-exempt municipal bonds, cross-subsidization schemes, and the wide variety of other measures and mechanisms that hide the true costs of government programs from the public.

When states or localities feel compelled to assist in-state interests, the most appropriate way to do so is through direct and visible mechanisms that are funded through general treasury revenues, not hidden taxes or other redistributionist regulatory policies. In other words, if state policymakers want to subsidize an indigenous industry, they should allocate funds within their current fiscal year budget and have an open debate and public vote on whether the state and its taxpayers should be supporting such a subsidization scheme.

This system might still have incidental or indirect effects on interstate commerce, but it would not be facially discriminatory since no out-of-state industries, consumers, or citizens would be asked to pick up the tab for another state's ill-considered industrial policies. Furthermore, such a system would be more accountable to the public and to voters who would be able to determine the wisdom of continuing industrial policies for which they are paying out of their own pockets.

States and localities also should do away with all coercive tax incentives and methods that favor in-state activities over out-of-state activities. Any tax that compels out-of-state producers to pay higher taxes, fees, or penalties to underwrite programs or policies that favor indigenous interests is clearly unconstitutional and should be struck down by federal officials if states and localities fail to eliminate them on their own.[21] State and local officials should concentrate on lowering the tax and regulatory burden on all businesses

Footnotes:
20. Lawrence W. Reed, "Time to End the Economic War Between the States," *Regulation*, Vol. 19, No. 2 (1996), pp. 35–43.
21. For more information, see Walter Hellerstein, "Commerce Clause Restraints on State Tax Incentives," Paper published by the Federal Reserve Bank of Minneapolis for "The Economic War Among the States," a conference held in Washington, D.C., on May 21–22, 1996; available on Internet site *http://woodrow.mpls.frb.fed.us/sylloge/econwar/heller.html*.

equally, both to attract additional investment to their states and to retain existing industry.

Finally, it should go without saying that the authorization, certification, or creation or any sort of public utility monopoly or geographic franchise territory is never justifiable as a method of furthering state and local police powers. Foreclosing the possibility of interstate competition and restricting economic freedom of choice does not serve the public interest; it also is an unconstitutional exercise of authority that should be abandoned.

States: Develop voluntary pacts to end or diminish "the economic war between the states." Besides taking steps to eliminate discriminatory state and local policies, state and local policymakers need to go further and declare a long-overdue truce in the so-called economic war between the states. Lawrence Reed has cogently pointed out just why this "war of industrial policy planners and their economic development bureaucracies" poses a serious threat to the vitality of America's engine of economic growth:

> This war is becoming an exercise in mutually assured destruction, or at least one in which all victories are Pyrrhic ones at best, with the victors losing almost as much as the vanquished. Many governors, state legislators, and policy analysts already understand the destructive nature of such beggar-thy-neighbor practices. They should make a major effort to seek ways to establish economic peace in the Republic.[22]

Reed is correct to point out that "peace in the Republic" is at stake if this war of competing industrial policies continues to escalate. The weapons used in this war include not only the blatantly discriminatory tools described above, but also such business-luring methods and mechanisms as selective tax breaks or tax credits, targeted property tax reductions and other tax abatements, discounted land or buildings, and other forms of direct and indirect subsidies.

To reiterate, if a state is using mechanisms to lure new business investment, and if those mechanisms clearly discriminate against interstate consumers or producers, Congress or the courts can act to strike down methods that burden interstate commerce. But what about other methods and mechanisms that do not facially discriminate against interstate interests? Can Congress or the courts strike down these actions simply because they are so economically inefficient or incidentally affect interstate commerce?

Footnotes:
22. Reed, "Time to End the Economic War Between the States," p. 35.

Practical Steps Toward a Revival of Federalism

The answers to these questions remain unclear; good arguments can be made on both sides of the debate. State and local officials claim that economic development efforts are nothing new and that, despite the potential negative side effects associated with competition for new businesses and jobs, the states should retain the freedom and the right to experiment with different forms of industrial policy.

Critics of current economic development policies counter that these state-by-state industrial policy efforts have spun out of control and are tantamount to a highly inefficient new form of state-by-state protectionism. For example, Melvin L. Burstein and Arthur J. Rolnick of the Minneapolis Federal Reserve Bank have argued that this war of competing industrial policies "interferes with interstate commerce and undermines the national economic union by misallocating resources and causing states to provide too few public goods."[23] Burnstein and Rolnick conclude that the states will be unable or unwilling to end this melee on their own, and that "Only Congress, with its sweeping constitutional powers, particularly under the Commerce Clause, has the ability to end this economic war among the states."[24]

During the 105th Congress, Representative David Minge (D–MN) introduced legislation that would have imposed just such a federal solution. Under H.R. 3044, the Distorting Subsidies Limitation Act of 1997,[25] the ability of states and localities to formulate firm-specific subsidization programs under the guise of economic development would have been significantly limited.

Yet, practically speaking, beyond sensible efforts aimed at weeding out unconstitutional subsidization practices or tax schemes, it may prove very difficult for federal officials to take the more radical step of prohibiting all state and local industrial policy efforts to lure new businesses. "Given national policy trends in favor of devolution, attempts to control the direction of local initiative by senior levels of government would seem politically unpalatable," argues Graham S. Toft, president of the Indianapolis-based Indiana Economic Development Council, Inc.[26]

Footnotes:
23. Melvin L. Burstein and Arthur J. Rolnick, "Congress Should End the Economic War Among the States," *The Region*, Federal Reserve Bank of Minneapolis, March 1995; available on Internet site *http://woodrow.mpls.frb.fed.us/pubs/fedgaz/edi961a.html*.
24. *Ibid.*
25. H.R. 3044, Distorting Subsidies Limitation Act of 1997, 105th Cong., 1st Sess., November 13, 1997.

The Delicate Balance

One reason for this is that it often is difficult to draw a bright line between state efforts that are clearly protectionist or discriminatory and those that are intended simply to improve the general business climate of the state and encourage new investment. After all, if a federal prohibition were established, an attempt by one state to eliminate a group of business regulations or lower a class of corporate taxes might be interpreted by others as an attempt to raise discriminatory or protectionist barriers, which it clearly would not be.

The demarcation between the two might be revealed through an investigation of whether state efforts to attract new jobs or businesses are *narrowly targeted* at specific firms or *generally applied* to all businesses. That is, if a state is initiating policies that have non-discriminatory, across-the-board effects on all businesses (both within and outside the state), then commerce-enhancing policies applied to all firms would withstand federal scrutiny. On the other hand, state efforts to use selective tax breaks, subsidies, or regulatory preferences to attract specific firms or industries would be held impermissible by federal legislators or judges.

Representative Minge would discourage firm- or industry-specific preferences by levying an excise tax on targeted state or local government development subsidies. Under H.R. 3044, the federal government would impose an excise tax on "any person engaged in a trade or business who derives any benefit during such year from any targeted subsidy provided by any State or local governmental unit." Essentially, the federal tax would offset any potential economic benefit a firm might receive from a state or local industrial policy program, thereby reducing the usefulness of that program as a tool of economic development, both for businesses and for state governments.

But what federal agency or legislative body will be keeping its watchful eye on the states to ensure that such inefficient, anti-competitive targeting does not occur? Will the House Commerce Committee and Senate Commerce, Science, and Transportation Committee need to create new subcommittees to oversee the laborious process of monitoring not only all 50 states, but also the many municipalities that increasingly use such mechanisms? Conversely, should broad new powers be delegated to the U.S. Department of

Footnotes:
26. Graham S. Toft, "Doing Battle Over the Incentives War: Improve Accountability But Avoid Federal Noncompete Mandates," Paper published by the Federal Reserve Bank of Minneapolis for "The Economic War Among the States," a conference held in Washington, D.C., on May 21–22, 1996; available on Internet site *http://woodrow.mpls.frb.fed.us/sylloge/econwar/toft.html*.

Commerce to police the states and localities for such behavior? And regardless of who is doing the policing, how would they go about establishing offsetting federal excise taxes, since the costs of many subsidization mechanisms are so difficult to quantify in the first place?

Keeping these constraints in mind, a more pragmatic solution is in order. A better resolution to this problem might be a voluntarily negotiated pact among the states to end the economic war through a multilateral armistice. As Lawrence Reed has suggested, this agreement could take the form of an amendment to state constitutions or, preferably, an amendment to the U.S. Constitution proposed by a majority of the states.

Some critics will argue that anything short of a proposed amendment to the Constitution could prove pointless, since some states might have an incentive to cheat and attempt to attract businesses while others were voluntarily surrendering their right to do so. But state and local officials can negotiate through groups like the National Governors' Association, the National Conference of Mayors, or the National Conference of State Legislators to devise an acceptable multilateral solution that binds all states to forgo further destructive industrial policy efforts without requiring a constitutional amendment. Article I, Section 10, Clause 2 of the Constitution does specify that "No State shall, without the consent of Congress…enter into any Agreement or Compact with another State…." Nevertheless, Congress almost certainly would approve such a beneficial multilateral economic peace treaty.

All units of government: Devise Regulatory Responsibility Matrices to help determine jurisdictional responsibility. A final conceptual tool that policymakers at the federal, state, and local levels can use to define more precisely which level of government has responsibility over a given issue is the Regulatory Responsibility Matrix. Because many of the industries and technologies considered in this volume are so complex and multi-faceted, it goes without saying that jurisdictional responsibility may be split among multiple levels of government.

For example, it would be foolish to argue that the task of telecommunications or electricity deregulation can be accomplished solely by federal officials or by states acting on their own. These industries are massive, and the issues involved in deregulating them are numerous. Therefore, the Regulatory Responsibility Matrix can help policymakers assess jurisdictional responsibility by encouraging them to plot schematically on a matrix which level of government

The Delicate Balance

might be best suited to a specific deregulatory task, and on what timetable it should undertake that task.

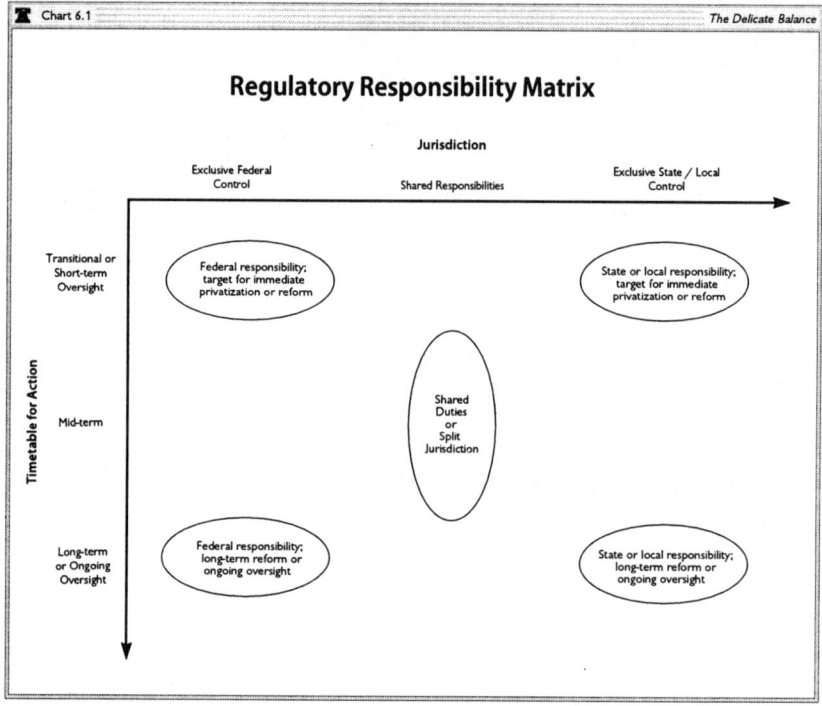

There certainly will be heated debates about how to plot specific issues on such a matrix, but these disputes can serve to breed healthy, ongoing discussions about how best to apply the Framers' original balance of powers to modern industries and issues.

For example, the Telecommunications Regulatory Responsibility Matrix reveals that there is a fairly even split in jurisdictional responsibility over remaining regulatory or deregulatory tasks. Some tasks, such as repeal of protectionist telecommunication trading rules, FCC reform and oversight, and electromagnetic spectrum policy in general, are best administered by federal officials. Other responsibilities, such as universal service subsidization policies intended to assist the poor, schools, and libraries, are more appropriately administered at the state or local level. Many zoning and siting issues within the telecommunications sector also will continue to fall within the purview of the states and localities.

The Electricity Regulatory Responsibility Matrix likewise shows that there are many functions which federal officials will need to

Practical Steps Toward a Revival of Federalism

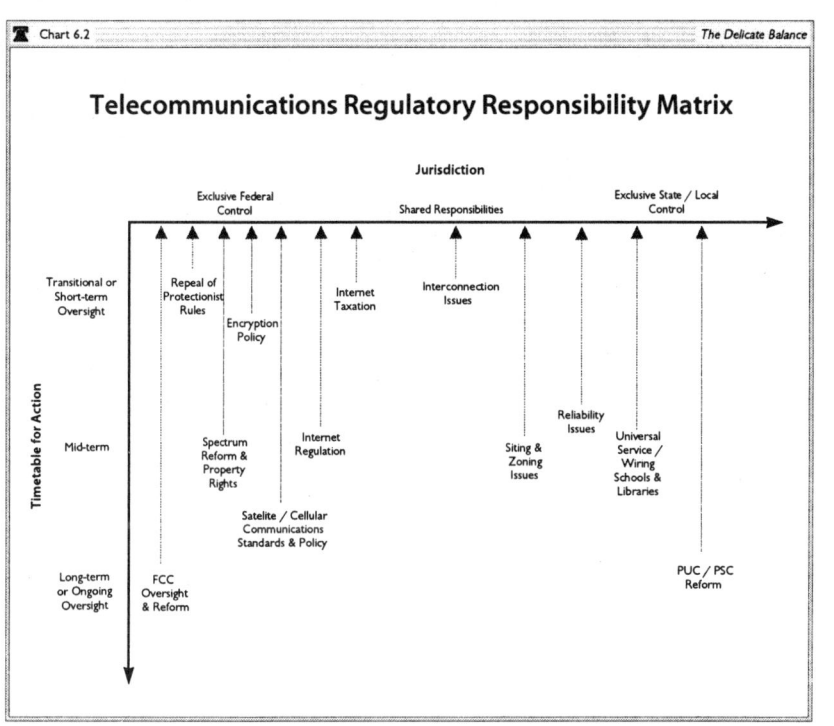

carry out in the short term if the electricity sector is to be fully liberalized. Among these functions are the elimination of unnecessary federal electricity statutes, such as the Public Utility Holding Company Act of 1935 (PUHCA) and the Public Utilities Regulatory Policies Act of 1978 (PURPA); privatization of the Tennessee Valley Authority (TVA) and the federally owned Power Marketing Administrations (PMAs); and the reform and eventual elimination of the Federal Energy Regulatory Commission (FERC). All of these are tasks that the federal government must carry out.

Alternatively, many tasks will remain solely the responsibility of state and local officials. These tasks would include low-income energy assistance, various environmental programs, plant and wire-line siting issues, and reform and eventual elimination of the state's Public Utility Commission (PUC) or Public Service Commission (PSC).

Other deregulatory responsibilities will demand that federal and state officials work together to achieve deregulation on the quickest timetable possible. For example, opening nationwide electricity markets to competition will demand that policymakers at all levels work together to draw up an efficient and effective plan for liberalization. Similarly, stranded cost recovery will be carried out prima-

The Delicate Balance

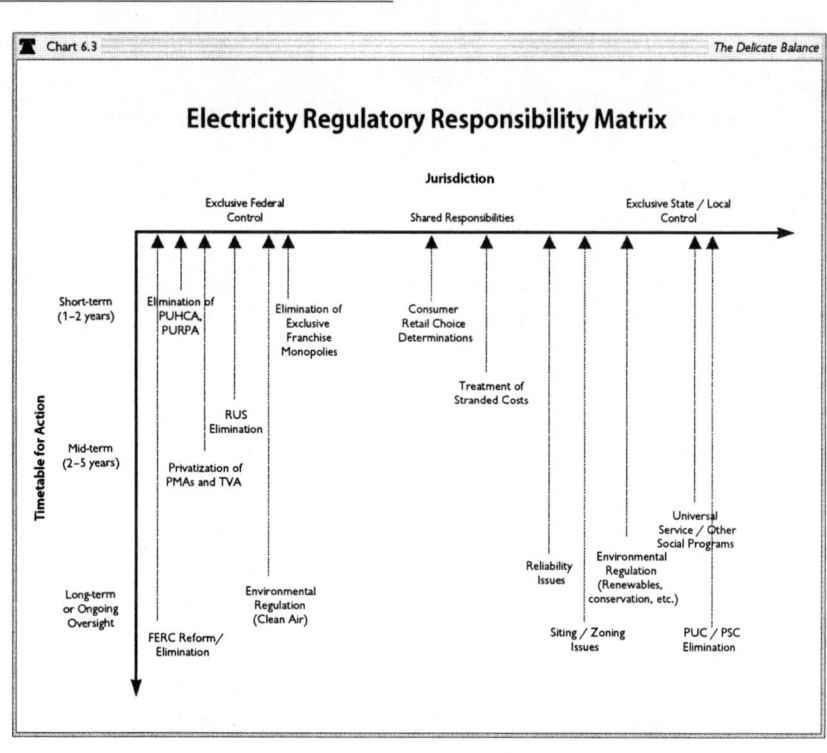

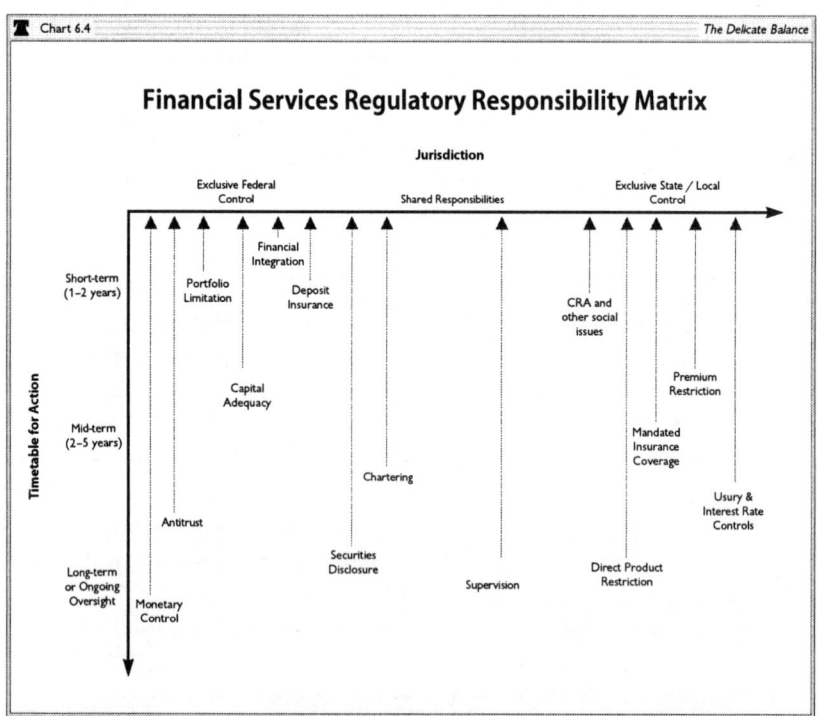

rily at the state level, but Congress can play an important role in the process by ensuring that it remains free of discriminatory or protectionist state rules, regulations, or programs.[27]

The Financial Services Regulatory Responsibility Matrix reveals a similar pattern within that sector. Certain issues, such as monetary policy, antitrust issues, and deposit insurance, remain clearly federal in focus. However, community reinvestment rules, mandated insurance policies, insurance premium policies, and certain types of interest rate regulation probably should remain the province of the states. Shared responsibilities within the financial sector would include the chartering of banks and other firms, securities disclosure policies, and other reporting and supervision policies.[28]

Finally, it is obvious that many environmental problems are simultaneously interstate and intrastate in nature. Federal, regional, state, county, and municipal regulators frequently can claim jurisdiction over a perceived environmental problem. Nevertheless, regulatory responsibility can be assigned better within this field as well.

Federal officials will be required to undertake reform of the Endangered Species Act, the Superfund law, and various federal subsidy programs that have deleterious environmental effects. They also, as noted above, will need to take an affirmative stand on Fifth Amendment protection of private property any time any government attempts to take private property without just compensation. Furthermore, product-labeling policies probably should remain more within the area of federal responsibility so that Americans are not inundated with multiple sets of confusing product safety information.[29]

Clean air and water policies and programs will require a mix of federal, state, and local efforts, depending on the interstate scope of the problem or the externalities generated by the pollution in question.[30] Ongoing endangered species protection efforts, waste disposal policy, wetlands protection, and public lands management would all be handled better by state or local officials. Private solutions involving well-defined property rights and market mecha-

Footnotes:
27. See Adam D. Thierer, "Electricity Deregulation and Federalism: How Congress and the States Can Work Together to Deregulate Successfully," Heritage Foundation *Backgrounder* No. 1125, June 23, 1997.
28. See John S. Barry, "Federalism and Financial Services," Heritage Foundation *Backgrounder* No. 1160, May 1, 1998.
29. See Bork, "Federalism and Federal Regulation: The Case of Product Labeling," and W. Kip Viscusi, *Product-Risk Labeling: A Federal Responsibility* (Washington, D.C.: The AEI Press, 1993).

The Delicate Balance

nisms obviously would be superior to government meddling in any of these cases, however.

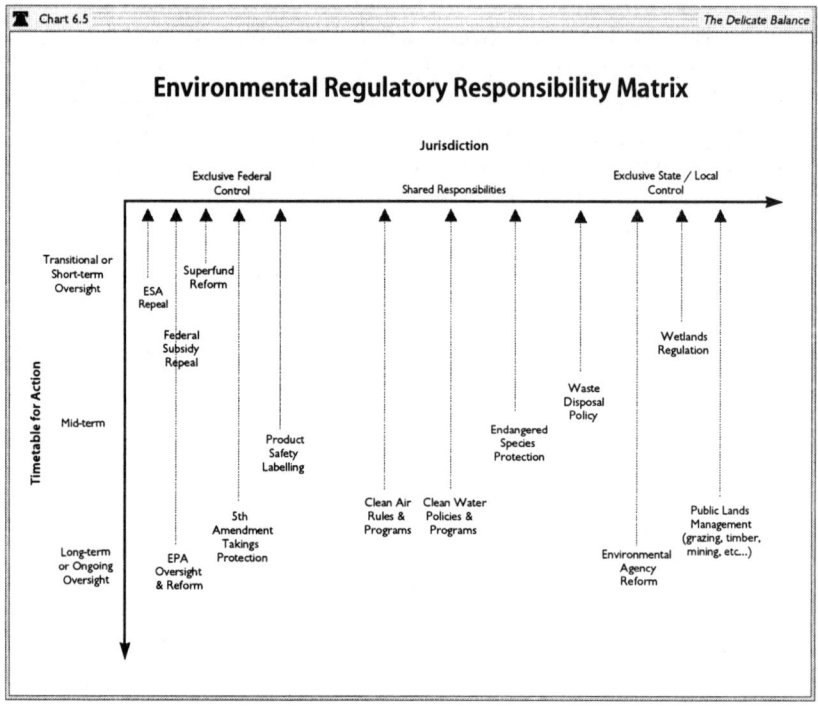

Chart 6.5 — Environmental Regulatory Responsibility Matrix

Two final points should be made with regard to the use of such matrices. First, they are not intended to be exact scientific tools that fix policy issues rigidly in a certain locale on the matrix for all time. The placement of many issues on the matrix inevitably will be a fairly subjective undertaking. Furthermore, either the placement of an issue on the matrix will change over time or (ideally) the issue will disappear from the matrix altogether, as rapidly as possible.

Second, it should be emphasized again that the placement of a certain issue or regulatory responsibility on the matrix should not be seen as an endorsement of government action in that field. Optimally, nothing would appear on these matrices, since private self-regulation is almost always preferable to government regulation at any level. However, some public regulation probably will remain

Footnotes:
30. See Henry N. Butler and Jonathan R. Macey, "Externalities and the Matching Principle: The Case for Reallocating Environmental Regulatory Authority," Yale Law & Public Policy Review / Yale Journal on Regulation, Symposium Issue, "Constructing a New Federalism: Jurisdictional Competence and Competition," Vol. 14, No. 2 (March 1–2, 1996), pp. 23–66.

indefinitely, and other rules will be difficult to eliminate in the short term.

Therefore, these matrices are meant to act as a guide to help establish which level of government is best suited to the administration of a particular regulatory task when that task is deemed necessary. Furthermore, it is hoped that they are used more often than not to assign *deregulatory* responsibilities to various levels of government, allowing market liberalization in high-tech industries to advance on multiple fronts as quickly as possible.

7

FEDERALISM'S FUTURE

In a February 13, 1818, letter to the editor of one of America's first news magazines, *The Weekly Register*, John Adams detailed his thoughts on the greatest accomplishments of the American Revolution and the American Founding. Among them, he noted:

> The Colonies had grown up under Constitutions of Government, so different, there was so great a Variety of Religions, they were composed of so many Nations, their customs, Manners and Habits had so little resemblance, and their Intercourse had been so rare and their Knowledge of each other so imperfect, that to unite them in the Principles of Theory and the same System of Action was certainly a very difficult Enterprize. The compleat Accomplishment of it, in so short a time and by such a simple means, was perhaps a singular Example in the History of Mankind. Thirteen clocks were made to strike together; a perfection of Mechanism which no Artist had ever before effected.[1]

One hundred and eighty years after Adams penned these sentiments, 50 clocks now strike together. Yet it seems reasonable to ask whether they tick together in the same "perfection of Mechanism" which Adams ascribed to the original 13. Is limited constitutional government under a federal republic respected and honored today as it was during Adams's time? Are the autonomy of the individual states and the rights of individual Americans held in the same high regard and esteem as they were during the time of the American Founding? And does commerce flow as freely across geographic borders as the Founders hoped?

Footnotes:
1. John Adams, "What Do We Mean by the American Revolution," February 13, 1818, reprinted in Daniel J. Boorstin, ed., *An American Primer* (New York: Meridian Classics, 1985), p. 249.

The Delicate Balance

Sadly, if the brief history of American federalism recounted in this book is any guide, the answers to these questions are not encouraging. Today, governments at all levels have grown arrogant, power-hungry, and abusive of the rights of the people. Robust commercial markets and activities have arisen, but many industries and technologies remain artificially constrained by burdensome, overlapping sets of needless regulations at the federal, state, and local level.

It is important, therefore, that federal, state, and local policymakers not waste such a great deal of time bickering over jurisdictional responsibility. Instead, they should concentrate on opening up all commercial sectors to competition and consumer choice on the most rapid timetable possible. Again, the goal should be less government at *all levels* and a new commitment to the Framers' intended commercial system, as summarized perhaps most eloquently by the U.S. Supreme Court in its 1949 decision in *H. P. Hood & Sons, Inc. v. DuMond*:

> Our system, fostered by the Commerce Clause, is that every farmer and every craftsman shall be encouraged to produce by the certainty that he will have free access to every market in the Nation, that no home embargoes will withhold his exports, and no foreign state will by customs duties or regulations exclude them. Likewise, every consumer may look to the free competition from every producing area in the Nation to protect him from exploitation by any. Such was the vision of the Founders, such has been the doctrine of this Court which has given it reality.[2]

What makes the American experiment so remarkable is that the Founders' vision embraced, simultaneously and unapologetically, a free, national, capitalistic marketplace *and* the virtues of small, local, decentralized government.

John Adams was correct, therefore, to claim that the "Mechanism" the Framers created through the Declaration and Constitution was a system "which no Artist had ever before effected." The constitutional system of federalism that the Framers formulated is, in the words of Pulitzer Prize-winning journalist Felix Morley, "the distinctively American contribution to political art...."[3] But what would Adams and the rest of the Founders make of their experiment if they could examine it today?

Footnotes:
2. *H. P. Hood & Sons, Inc. v. DuMond* 336 U.S. 525 (1949).
3. Felix Morley, *Freedom and Federalism* (Indianapolis, Ind.: Liberty Press, 1959), p. xxiv.

Federalism's Future

Without doubt, this century has not been kind to the Framers' original vision of federalism. In one sense, it is surprising and somewhat encouraging to see that the basic framework has endured despite the efforts of so many to weaken its foundations. Furthermore, the states, despite their diminished stature throughout this century, by their very existence and perseverance have remained an important check on the growth of the central government in a time that will be remembered as the age of totalitarianism.

If the federalist system as created by the Founders is to act once again as the guarantor of the right of the people to establish the types of communities they desire while also preserving their freedom to benefit from a vibrant national marketplace, a new appreciation of the original delicate balance of powers must be generated.

The genius of the Founders lies in the fact that they did not attempt to box the nation into a single standard of life or code of commercial interaction. They understood that flexibility and creativity would be needed to quell the rise of regional factionalism. The American federal republic would need to balance competing goals and values. "As we rethink federalism," note legal scholars Robert P. Inman and Daniel L. Rubenfield, "we must recognize—as did our Founding Fathers—that the selection of the institutions of federalism necessarily carries with it a balancing of these competing social goals of economic efficiency, political participation, and the protection of individual rights and liberties."[4] As observed by William N. Eskridge, Jr., and John Ferejohn, also students of the Constitution, "A robust federalism must maintain boundaries between state and national authority by protecting the states against invasion by national institutions, by protecting the states from incursions by their neighbors, and by restraining states from transgression on core national/constitutional values."[5]

As we have seen, some legal theorists and policymakers believe more stress should be placed on the autonomy of the individual states and the benefits of local political experimentation. Others argue that an unfettered nationwide marketplace for companies and consumers is of paramount importance. As this book has argued, however, these values are not mutually exclusive.

Footnotes:
4. Robert P. Inman and Daniel L. Rubenfield, "Rethinking Federalism," *Journal of Economic Perspectives*, Vol. 11, No. 4 (Fall 1997), p. 61.
5. William N. Eskridge, Jr., and John Ferejohn, "The Elastic Commerce Clause: A Political Theory of American Federalism," *Vanderbilt Law Review*, Vol. 47 (1994), p. 1359.

The Delicate Balance

American commercial federalism is not a zero-sum game. Both the autonomy of the states and the economic rights of companies and consumers can be enhanced by a judicious balancing of these constitutional imperatives. Through this process, the liberty of all Americans is preserved and protected. As the Supreme Court noted in *Gregory v. Ashcroft*:

> One fairly can dispute whether our federalist system has been quite as successful in checking government abuse as Hamilton promised, but there is no doubt about the design. If this "double security" is to be effective, there must be a proper balance between the States and the Federal Government. These twin powers will act as mutual restraints only if both are credible. In the tension between federal and state power lies the promise of liberty.[6]

Indeed, Steven Calabresi goes so far as to argue that "[F]ederalism is much more important to the liberty and well being of the American people than any other structural feature of our constitutional system...including the separation of powers, the Bill of Rights, and judicial review."[7]

Hence, as it is hoped this analysis has made evident, the Founders established in the Constitution a principled yet flexible framework within which difficult political issues could be resolved peacefully in order to preserve and protect social and economic harmony in the United States of America. In some ways, therefore, their masterpiece will remain forever a work in progress.

The challenge for today's policymakers is to ensure that this enduring work of political art is understood, cherished, and honored as the bulwark of liberty that it was intended to be. Anything less would be an insult to the Founders' eternal vision and most important contribution to modern civilization.

Footnotes:
6. *Gregory v. Ashcroft*, 501 U.S. 452 (1991).
7. Stephan G. Calabresi, "A Government of Limited and Enumerated Powers: In Defense of *United States v. Lopez*," *Michigan Law Review*, Vol. 94 (1995), pp. 754, 756.

APPENDIX I
THE ARTICLES OF CONFEDERATION

Articles of Confederation
November 15, 1777

To all to whom these Presents shall come, we the undersigned Delegates of the States affixed to our Names send greeting.

Articles of Confederation and perpetual Union between the states of New Hampshire, Massachusetts-bay, Rhode Island and Providence Plantations, Connecticut, New York, New Jersey, Pennsylvania, Delaware, Maryland, Virginia, North Carolina, South Carolina, and Georgia.

I. The Stile of this Confederacy shall be "The United States of America".

II. Each state retains its sovereignty, freedom, and independence, and every power, jurisdiction, and right, which is not by this Confederation expressly delegated to the United States, in Congress assembled.

III. The said States hereby severally enter into a firm league of friendship with each other, for their common defence, the security of their liberties, and their mutual and general welfare, binding themselves to assist each other, against all force offered to, or attacks made upon them, or any of them, on account of religion, sovereignty, trade, or any other pretense whatever.

IV. The better to secure and perpetuate mutual friendship and intercourse among the people of the different States in this Union, the free inhabitants of each of these States, paupers, vagabonds, and fugitives from justice excepted, shall be entitled to all privileges and immunities of free citizens in the several States; and the people of each State shall have free ingress and regress to and from any other State, and shall enjoy therein all the privileges of trade and commerce, subject to the same duties, impositions, and restrictions as the inhabitants thereof respectively, provided that such restrictions shall not extend so far as to prevent the removal of property imported into any State, to any other State, of which the owner is an inhabitant; provided also that no imposition, duties or restriction shall be laid by any State, on the property of the United States, or either of them.

The Delicate Balance

If any person guilty of, or charged with, treason, felony, or other high misdemeanor in any State, shall flee from justice, and be found in any of the United States, he shall, upon demand of the Governor or executive power of the State from which he fled, be delivered up and removed to the State having jurisdiction of his offense.

Full faith and credit shall be given in each of these States to the records, acts, and judicial proceedings of the courts and magistrates of every other State.

V. For the most convenient management of the general interests of the United States, delegates shall be annually appointed in such manner as the legislatures of each State shall direct, to meet in Congress on the first Monday in November, in every year, with a power reserved to each State to recall its delegates, or any of them, at any time within the year, and to send others in their stead for the remainder of the year.

No State shall be represented in Congress by less than two, nor more than seven members; and no person shall be capable of being a delegate for more than three years in any term of six years; nor shall any person, being a delegate, be capable of holding any office under the United States, for which he, or another for his benefit, receives any salary, fees or emolument of any kind.

Each State shall maintain its own delegates in a meeting of the States, and while they act as members of the committee of the States.

In determining questions in the United States, in Congress assembled, each State shall have one vote.

Freedom of speech and debate in Congress shall not be impeached or questioned in any court or place out of Congress, and the members of Congress shall be protected in their persons from arrests or imprisonments, during the time of their going to and from, and attendence on Congress, except for treason, felony, or breach of the peace.

VI. No State, without the consent of the United States in Congress assembled, shall send any embassy to, or receive any embassy from, or enter into any conference, agreement, alliance or treaty with any King, Prince or State; nor shall any person holding any office of profit or trust under the United States, or any of them, accept any present, emolument, office or title of any kind whatever from any King, Prince or foreign State; nor shall the United States in Congress assembled, or any of them, grant any title of nobility.

APPENDIX I: The Articles of Confederation

No two or more States shall enter into any treaty, confederation or alliance whatever between them, without the consent of the United States in Congress assembled, specifying accurately the purposes for which the same is to be entered into, and how long it shall continue.

No State shall lay any imposts or duties, which may interfere with any stipulations in treaties, entered into by the United States in Congress assembled, with any King, Prince or State, in pursuance of any treaties already proposed by Congress, to the courts of France and Spain.

No vessel of war shall be kept up in time of peace by any State, except such number only, as shall be deemed necessary by the United States in Congress assembled, for the defence of such State, or its trade; nor shall any body of forces be kept up by any State in time of peace, except such number only, as in the judgement of the United States in Congress assembled, shall be deemed requisite to garrison the forts necessary for the defence of such State; but every State shall always keep up a well-regulated and disciplined militia, sufficiently armed and accoutered, and shall provide and constantly have ready for use, in public stores, a due number of field pieces and tents, and a proper quantity of arms, ammunition and camp equipage.

No State shall engage in any war without the consent of the United States in Congress assembled, unless such State be actually invaded by enemies, or shall have received certain advice of a resolution being formed by some nation of Indians to invade such State, and the danger is so imminent as not to admit of a delay till the United States in Congress assembled can be consulted; nor shall any State grant commissions to any ships or vessels of war, nor letters of marque or reprisal, except it be after a declaration of war by the United States in Congress assembled, and then only against the Kingdom or State and the subjects thereof, against which war has been so declared, and under such regulations as shall be established by the United States in Congress assembled, unless such State be infested by pirates, in which case vessels of war may be fitted out for that occasion, and kept so long as the danger shall continue, or until the United States in Congress assembled shall determine otherwise.

VII. When land forces are raised by any State for the common defence, all officers of or under the rank of colonel, shall be appointed by the legislature of each State respectively, by whom such forces shall be raised, or in such manner as such State shall direct, and all vacancies shall be filled up by the State which first made the appointment.

The Delicate Balance

VIII. All charges of war, and all other expenses that shall be incurred for the common defence or general welfare, and allowed by the United States in Congress assembled, shall be defrayed out of a common treasury, which shall be supplied by the several States in proportion to the value of all land within each State, granted or surveyed for any person, as such land and the buildings and improvements thereon shall be estimated according to such mode as the United States in Congress assembled, shall from time to time direct and appoint.

The taxes for paying that proportion shall be laid and levied by the authority and direction of the legislatures of the several States within the time agreed upon by the United States in Congress assembled.

IX. The United States in Congress assembled, shall have the sole and exclusive right and power of determining on peace and war, except in the cases mentioned in the sixth article—of sending and receiving ambassadors—entering into treaties and alliances, provided that no treaty of commerce shall be made whereby the legislative power of the respective States shall be restrained from imposing such imposts and duties on foreigners, as their own people are subjected to, or from prohibiting the exportation or importation of any species of goods or commodities whatsoever—of establishing rules for deciding in all cases, what captures on land or water shall be legal, and in what manner prizes taken by land or naval forces in the service of the United States shall be divided or appropriated—of granting letters of marque and reprisal in times of peace—appointing courts for the trial of piracies and felonies commited on the high seas and establishing courts for receiving and determining finally appeals in all cases of captures, provided that no member of Congress shall be appointed a judge of any of the said courts.

The United States in Congress assembled shall also be the last resort on appeal in all disputes and differences now subsisting or that hereafter may arise between two or more States concerning boundary, jurisdiction or any other causes whatever; which authority shall always be exercised in the manner following. Whenever the legislative or executive authority or lawful agent of any State in controversy with another shall present a petition to Congress stating the matter in question and praying for a hearing, notice thereof shall be given by order of Congress to the legislative or executive authority of the other State in controversy, and a day assigned for the appearance of the parties by their lawful agents, who shall then be directed to appoint by joint consent, commissioners or judges to constitute a court for hearing and determining the matter in question: but if they cannot agree, Congress shall name three persons out of each of the

APPENDIX I: The Articles of Confederation

United States, and from the list of such persons each party shall alternately strike out one, the petitioners beginning, until the number shall be reduced to thirteen; and from that number not less than seven, nor more than nine names as Congress shall direct, shall in the presence of Congress be drawn out by lot, and the persons whose names shall be so drawn or any five of them, shall be commissioners or judges, to hear and finally determine the controversy, so always as a major part of the judges who shall hear the cause shall agree in the determination: and if either party shall neglect to attend at the day appointed, without showing reasons, which Congress shall judge sufficient, or being present shall refuse to strike, the Congress shall proceed to nominate three persons out of each State, and the secretary of Congress shall strike in behalf of such party absent or refusing; and the judgment and sentence of the court to be appointed, in the manner before prescribed, shall be final and conclusive; and if any of the parties shall refuse to submit to the authority of such court, or to appear or defend their claim or cause, the court shall nevertheless proceed to pronounce sentence, or judgement, which shall in like manner be final and decisive, the judgement or sentence and other proceedings being in either case transmitted to Congress, and lodged among the acts of Congress for the security of the parties concerned: provided that every commissioner, before he sits in judgement, shall take an oath to be administered by one of the judges of the supreme or superior court of the State, where the cause shall be tried, "well and truly to hear and determine the matter in question, according to the best of his judgement, without favor, affection or hope of reward": provided also, that no State shall be deprived of territory for the benefit of the United States.

All controversies concerning the private right of soil claimed under different grants of two or more States, whose jurisdictions as they may respect such lands, and the States which passed such grants are adjusted, the said grants or either of them being at the same time claimed to have originated antecedent to such settlement of jurisdiction, shall on the petition of either party to the Congress of the United States, be finally determined as near as may be in the same manner as is before prescribed for deciding disputes respecting territorial jurisdiction between different States.

The United States in Congress assembled shall also have the sole and exclusive right and power of regulating the alloy and value of coin struck by their own authority, or by that of the respective States—fixing the standards of weights and measures throughout the United States—regulating the trade and managing all affairs with the Indians, not members of any of the States, provided that

The Delicate Balance

the legislative right of any State within its own limits be not infringed or violated—establishing or regulating post offices from one State to another, throughout all the United States, and exacting such postage on the papers passing through the same as may be requisite to defray the expenses of the said office—appointing all officers of the land forces, in the service of the United States, excepting regimental officers—appointing all the officers of the naval forces, and commissioning all officers whatever in the service of the United States—making rules for the government and regulation of the said land and naval forces, and directing their operations.

The United States in Congress assembled shall have authority to appoint a committee, to sit in the recess of Congress, to be denominated "A Committee of the States", and to consist of one delegate from each State; and to appoint such other committees and civil officers as may be necessary for managing the general affairs of the United States under their direction—to appoint one of their members to preside, provided that no person be allowed to serve in the office of president more than one year in any term of three years; to ascertain the necessary sums of money to be raised for the service of the United States, and to appropriate and apply the same for defraying the public expenses—to borrow money, or emit bills on the credit of the United States, transmitting every half-year to the respective States an account of the sums of money so borrowed or emitted—to build and equip a navy—to agree upon the number of land forces, and to make requisitions from each State for its quota, in proportion to the number of white inhabitants in such State; which requisition shall be binding, and thereupon the legislature of each State shall appoint the regimental officers, raise the men and cloath, arm and equip them in a solid-like manner, at the expense of the United States; and the officers and men so cloathed, armed and equipped shall march to the place appointed, and within the time agreed on by the United States in Congress assembled. But if the United States in Congress assembled shall, on consideration of circumstances judge proper that any State should not raise men, or should raise a smaller number of men than the quota thereof, such extra number shall be raised, officered, cloathed, armed and equipped in the same manner as the quota of each State, unless the legislature of such State shall judge that such extra number cannot be safely spread out in the same, in which case they shall raise, officer, cloath, arm and equip as many of such extra number as they judge can be safely spared. And the officers and men so cloathed, armed, and equipped, shall march to the place appointed, and within the time agreed on by the United States in Congress assembled.

APPENDIX I: The Articles of Confederation

The United States in Congress assembled shall never engage in a war, nor grant letters of marque or reprisal in time of peace, nor enter into any treaties or alliances, nor coin money, nor regulate the value thereof, nor ascertain the sums and expenses necessary for the defence and welfare of the United States, or any of them, nor emit bills, nor borrow money on the credit of the United States, nor appropriate money, nor agree upon the number of vessels of war, to be built or purchased, or the number of land or sea forces to be raised, nor appoint a commander in chief of the army or navy, unless nine States assent to the same: nor shall a question on any other point, except for adjourning from day to day be determined, unless by the votes of the majority of the United States in Congress assembled.

The Congress of the United States shall have power to adjourn to any time within the year, and to any place within the United States, so that no period of adjournment be for a longer duration than the space of six months, and shall publish the journal of their proceedings monthly, except such parts thereof relating to treaties, alliances or military operations, as in their judgement require secrecy; and the yeas and nays of the delegates of each State on any question shall be entered on the journal, when it is desired by any delegates of a State, or any of them, at his or their request shall be furnished with a transcript of the said journal, except such parts as are above excepted, to lay before the legislatures of the several States.

X. The Committee of the States, or any nine of them, shall be authorized to execute, in the recess of Congress, such of the powers of Congress as the United States in Congress assembled, by the consent of the nine States, shall from time to time think expedient to vest them with; provided that no power be delegated to the said Committee, for the exercise of which, by the Articles of Confederation, the voice of nine States in the Congress of the United States assembled be requisite.

XI. Canada acceding to this confederation, and adjoining in the measures of the United States, shall be admitted into, and entitled to all the advantages of this Union; but no other colony shall be admitted into the same, unless such admission be agreed to by nine States.

XII. All bills of credit emitted, monies borrowed, and debts contracted by, or under the authority of Congress, before the assembling of the United States, in pursuance of the present confederation, shall be deemed and considered as a charge against the United States, for payment and satisfaction whereof the said United States, and the public faith are hereby solemnly pleged.

The Delicate Balance

> XIII. Every State shall abide by the determination of the United States in Congress assembled, on all questions which by this confederation are submitted to them. And the Articles of this Confederation shall be inviolably observed by every State, and the Union shall be perpetual; nor shall any alteration at any time hereafter be made in any of them; unless such alteration be agreed to in a Congress of the United States, and be afterwards confirmed by the legislatures of every State.

And Whereas it hath pleased the Great Governor of the World to incline the hearts of the legislatures we respectively represent in Congress, to approve of, and to authorize us to ratify the said Articles of Confederation and perpetual Union. Know Ye that we the undersigned delegates, by virtue of the power and authority to us given for that purpose, do by these presents, in the name and in behalf of our respective constituents, fully and entirely ratify and confirm each and every of the said Articles of Confederation and perpetual Union, and all and singular the matters and things therein contained: And we do further solemnly plight and engage the faith of our respective constituents, that they shall abide by the determinations of the United States in Congress assembled, on all questions, which by the said Confederation are submitted to them. And that the Articles thereof shall be inviolably observed by the States we respectively represent, and that the Union shall be perpetual.

In Witness whereof we have hereunto set our hands in Congress. Done at Philadelphia in the State of Pennsylvania the ninth day of July in the Year of our Lord One Thousand Seven Hundred and Seventy-Eight, and in the Third Year of the independence of America.

APPENDIX II
THE CONSTITUTION OF THE UNITED STATES OF AMERICA

We the People of the United States, in Order to form a more perfect Union, establish Justice, insure domestic Tranquillity, provide for the common defence, promote the general Welfare, and secure the Blessings of Liberty to ourselves and our Posterity, do ordain and establish this Constitution for the United States of America.

Article. I.

Section 1.

All legislative Powers herein granted shall be vested in a Congress of the United States, which shall consist of a Senate and House of Representatives.

Section 2.

The House of Representatives shall be composed of Members chosen every second Year by the People of the several States, and the Electors in each State shall have the Qualifications requisite for Electors of the most numerous Branch of the State Legislature.

No Person shall be a Representative who shall not have attained to the age of twenty five Years, and been seven Years a Citizen of the United States, and who shall not, when elected, be an Inhabitant of that State in which he shall be chosen.

Representatives and direct Taxes shall be apportioned among the several States which may be included within this Union, according to their respective Numbers, which shall be determined by adding to the whole Number of free Persons, including those bound to Service for a Term of Years, and excluding Indians not taxed, three fifths of all other Persons. The actual Enumeration shall be made within three Years after the first Meeting of the Congress of the United States, and within every subsequent Term of ten Years, in such Manner as they shall by Law direct. The Number of Representatives shall not exceed one for every thirty Thousand, but each State shall have at Least one Representative; and until such enumeration shall be made, the State

The Delicate Balance

of New Hampshire shall be entitled to chuse three, Massachusetts eight, Rhode-Island and Providence Plantations one, Connecticut five, New-York six, New Jersey four, Pennsylvania eight, Delaware one, Maryland six, Virginia ten, North Carolina five, South Carolina five, and Georgia three.

When vacancies happen in the Representation from any State, the Executive Authority thereof shall issue Writs of Election to fill such Vacancies.

The House of Representatives shall chuse their Speaker and other Officers; and shall have the sole Power of Impeachment.

Section 3.

The Senate of the United States shall be composed of two Senators from each State, chosen by the Legislature thereof, for six Years; and each Senator shall have one Vote.

Immediately after they shall be assembled in Consequence of the first Election, they shall be divided as equally as may be into three Classes. The Seats of the Senators of the first Class shall be vacated at the Expiration of the second Year, of the second Class at the Expiration of the fourth Year, and of the third Class at the Expiration of the sixth Year, so that one third may be chosen every second Year; and if Vacancies happen by Resignation, or otherwise, during the Recess of the Legislature of any State, the Executive thereof may make temporary Appointments until the next Meeting of the Legislature, which shall then fill such Vacancies.

No Person shall be a Senator who shall not have attained to the Age of thirty Years, and been nine Years a Citizen of the United States, and who shall not, when elected, be an Inhabitant of that State for which he shall be chosen.

The Vice President of the United States shall be President of the Senate, but shall have no Vote, unless they be equally divided.

The Senate shall chuse their other Officers, and also a President pro tempore, in the Absence of the Vice President, or when he shall exercise the Office of President of the United States.

The Senate shall have the sole Power to try all Impeachments. When sitting for that Purpose, they shall be on Oath or Affirmation. When the President of the United States is tried, the Chief Justice shall preside: And no Person shall be convicted without the Concurrence of two thirds of the Members present.

Judgment in Cases of Impeachment shall not extend further than to removal from Office, and disqualification to hold and enjoy any

APPENDIX II: The Constitution

Office of honor, Trust or Profit under the United States: but the Party convicted shall nevertheless be liable and subject to Indictment, Trial, Judgment and Punishment, according to Law.

Section 4.

The Times, Places and Manner of holding Elections for Senators and Representatives, shall be prescribed in each State by the Legislature thereof; but the Congress may at any time by Law make or alter such Regulations, except as to the Places of chusing Senators.

The Congress shall assemble at least once in every Year, and such Meeting shall be on the first Monday in December, unless they shall by Law appoint a different Day.

Section 5.

Each House shall be the Judge of the Elections, Returns and Qualifications of its own Members, and a Majority of each shall constitute a Quorum to do Business; but a smaller Number may adjourn from day to day, and may be authorized to compel the Attendance of absent Members, in such Manner, and under such Penalties as each House may provide.

Each House may determine the Rules of its Proceedings, punish its Members for disorderly Behaviour, and, with the Concurrence of two thirds, expel a Member.

Each House shall keep a Journal of its Proceedings, and from time to time publish the same, excepting such Parts as may in their Judgment require Secrecy; and the Yeas and Nays of the Members of either House on any question shall, at the Desire of one fifth of those Present, be entered on the Journal.

Neither House, during the Session of Congress, shall, without the Consent of the other, adjourn for more than three days, nor to any other Place than that in which the two Houses shall be sitting.

Section 6.

The Senators and Representatives shall receive a Compensation for their Services, to be ascertained by Law, and paid out of the Treasury of the United States. They shall in all Cases, except Treason, Felony and Breach of the Peace, be privileged from Arrest during their Attendance at the Session of their respective Houses, and in going to and returning from the same; and for any Speech or Debate in either House, they shall not be questioned in any other Place.

No Senator or Representative shall, during the Time for which he was elected, be appointed to any civil Office under the Authority of the United States, which shall have been created, or the Emolu-

The Delicate Balance

ments whereof shall have been encreased during such time; and no Person holding any Office under the United States, shall be a Member of either House during his Continuance in Office.

Section 7.

All Bills for raising Revenue shall originate in the House of Representatives; but the Senate may propose or concur with amendments as on other Bills.

Every Bill which shall have passed the House of Representatives and the Senate, shall, before it become a law, be presented to the President of the United States: If he approve he shall sign it, but if not he shall return it, with his Objections to that House in which it shall have originated, who shall enter the Objections at large on their Journal, and proceed to reconsider it. If after such Reconsideration two thirds of that House shall agree to pass the Bill, it shall be sent, together with the Objections, to the other House, by which it shall likewise be reconsidered, and if approved by two thirds of that House, it shall become a Law. But in all such Cases the Votes of both Houses shall be determined by Yeas and Nays, and the Names of the Persons voting for and against the Bill shall be entered on the Journal of each House respectively. If any Bill shall not be returned by the President within ten Days (Sundays excepted) after it shall have been presented to him, the Same shall be a Law, in like Manner as if he had signed it, unless the Congress by their Adjournment prevent its Return, in which Case it shall not be a Law. Every Order, Resolution, or Vote to which the Concurrence of the Senate and House of Representatives may be necessary (except on a question of Adjournment) shall be presented to the President of the United States; and before the Same shall take Effect, shall be approved by him, or being disapproved by him, shall be repassed by two thirds of the Senate and House of Representatives, according to the Rules and Limitations prescribed in the Case of a Bill.

Section 8.

The Congress shall have Power To lay and collect Taxes, Duties, Imposts and Excises, to pay the Debts and provide for the common Defence and general Welfare of the United States; but all Duties, Imposts and Excises shall be uniform throughout the United States;

To borrow Money on the credit of the United States;

To regulate Commerce with foreign Nations, and among the several States, and with the Indian Tribes;

To establish an uniform Rule of Naturalization, and uniform Laws on the subject of Bankruptcies throughout the United States;

APPENDIX II: The Constitution

To coin Money, regulate the Value thereof, and of foreign Coin, and fix the Standard of Weights and Measures;

To provide for the Punishment of counterfeiting the Securities and current Coin of the United States;

To establish Post Offices and post Roads;

To promote the Progress of Science and useful Arts, by securing for limited Times to Authors and Inventors the exclusive Right to their respective Writings and Discoveries;

To constitute Tribunals inferior to the supreme Court;

To define and punish Piracies and Felonies committed on the high Seas, and Offences against the Law of Nations;

To declare War, grant Letters of Marque and Reprisal, and make Rules concerning Captures on Land and Water;

To raise and support Armies, but no Appropriation of Money to that Use shall be for a longer Term than two Years;

To provide and maintain a Navy;

To make Rules for the Government and Regulation of the land and naval Forces;

To provide for calling forth the Militia to execute the Laws of the Union, suppress Insurrections and repeal Invasions;

To provide for organizing, arming, and disciplining, the Militia, and for governing such Part of them as may be employed in the Service of the United States, reserving to the States respectively, the Appointment of the Officers, and the Authority of training the Militia according to the discipline prescribed by Congress;

To exercise exclusive Legislation in all Cases whatsoever, over such District (not exceeding ten Miles square) as may, by Cession of Particular States, and the Acceptance of Congress, become the Seat of the Government of the United States, and to exercise like Authority over all Places purchased by the Consent of the Legislature of the State in which the Same shall be, for the Erection of Forts, Magazines, Arsenals, dock-Yards and other needful Buildings;—And

To make all Laws which shall be necessary and proper for carrying into Execution the foregoing Powers and all other Powers vested by this Constitution in the Government of the United States, or in any Department or Officer thereof.

Section 9.

The Migration or Importation of such Persons as any of the States now existing shall think proper to admit, shall not be prohibited by the Congress prior to the Year one thousand eight hundred and eight, but a Tax or duty may be imposed on such Importation, not exceeding ten dollars for each Person.

The Privilege of the Writ of Habeas Corpus shall not be suspended, unless when in Cases of Rebellion or Invasion the public Safety may require it.

No Bill of Attainder or ex post facto Law shall be passed.

No Capitation, or other direct, Tax shall be laid, unless in Proportion to the Census of Enumeration herein before directed to be taken.

No Tax or Duty shall be laid on Articles exported from any State.

No Preference shall be given by any Regulation of Commerce or Revenue to the Ports of one State over those of another: nor shall Vessels bound to, or from, one State, be obliged to enter, clear or pay Duties in another.

No Money shall be drawn from the Treasury, but in Consequence of Appropriations made by Law; and a regular Statement and Account of the Receipts and Expenditures of all public Money shall be published from time to time.

No Title of Nobility shall be granted by the United States: And no Person holding any Office of Profit or Trust under them, shall, without the Consent of the Congress, accept of any present, Emolument, Office, or Title, of any kind whatever, from any King, Prince or foreign State.

Section 10.

No State shall enter into any Treaty, Alliance, or Confederation; grant Letters of Marque and Reprisal; coin Money; emit Bills of Credit; make any Thing but gold and silver Coin a Tender in Payment of Debts; pass any Bill of Attainder, ex post facto Law, or Law impairing the Obligation of Contracts, or grant any Title of Nobility.

No State shall, without the Consent of the Congress, lay any Imposts or Duties on Imports or Exports, except what may be absolutely necessary for executing it's inspection Laws: and the net Produce of all Duties and Imposts, laid by any State on Imports or Exports, shall be for the Use of the Treasury of the United States; and all such Laws shall be subject to the Revision and Controul of the Congress.

APPENDIX II: The Constitution

No State shall, without the Consent of Congress, lay any Duty of Tonnage, keep Troops, or Ships of War in time of Peace, enter into any Agreement or Compact with another State, or with a foreign Power, or engage in War, unless actually invaded, or in such imminent Danger as will not admit of delay.

Article. II

Section 1.

The executive Power shall be vested in a President of the United States of America. He shall hold his Office during the Term of four Years, and, together with the Vice President, chosen for the same Term, be elected, as follows:

Each State shall appoint, in such Manner as the Legislature thereof may direct, a Number of Electors, equal to the whole Number of Senators and Representatives to which the State may be entitled in the Congress: but no Senator or Representative, or Person holding an Office of Trust or Profit under the United States, shall be appointed an Elector.

The Electors shall meet in their respective States, and vote by Ballot for two Persons, of whom one at least shall not be an Inhabitant of the same State with themselves. And they shall make a List of all the Persons voted for, and of the Number of Votes for each; which List they shall sign and certify, and transmit sealed to the Seat of the Government of the United States, directed to the President of the Senate. The President of the Senate shall, in the Presence of the Senate and House of Representatives, open all the Certificates, and the Votes shall then be counted. The Person having the greatest Number of Votes shall be the President, if such Number be a Majority of the whole Number of Electors appointed; and if there be more than one who have such Majority, and have an equal Number of Votes, then the House of Representatives shall immediately chuse by Ballot one of them for President; and if no Person have a Majority, then from the five highest on the List the said House shall in like Manner chuse the President. But in chusing the President, the Votes shall be taken by States, the Representatives from each State having one Vote; a quorum for this Purpose shall consist of a Member or Members from two thirds of the States, and a Majority of all the States shall be necessary to a Choice. In every Case, after the Choice of the President, the Person having the greatest Number of Votes of the Electors shall be the Vice President. But if there should remain two or more who have equal Votes, the Senate shall chuse from them by Ballot the Vice President.

The Delicate Balance

The Congress may determine the Time of chusing the Electors, and the Day on which they shall give their Votes; which Day shall be the same throughout the United States.

No Person except a natural born Citizen, or a Citizen of the United States, at the time of the Adoption of this Constitution, shall be eligible to the Office of President; neither shall any person be eligible to that Office who shall not have attained to the Age of thirty five Years, and been fourteen Years a Resident within the United States.

In Case of the Removal of the President from Office, or of his Death, Resignation, or Inability to discharge the Powers and Duties of the said Office, the Same shall devolve on the Vice President, and the Congress may by Law provide for the Case of Removal, Death, Resignation or Inability, both of the President and Vice President, declaring what Officer shall then act as President, and such Officer shall act accordingly, until the Disability be removed, or a President shall be elected.

The President shall, at stated Times, receive for his Services, a Compensation, which shall neither be encreased nor diminished during the Period for which he shall have been elected, and he shall not receive within that Period any other Emolument from the United States, or any of them.

Before he enter on the Execution of his Office, he shall take the following Oath or Affirmation:—"I do solemnly swear (or affirm) that I will faithfully execute the Office of President of the United States, and will to the best of my Ability, preserve, protect and defend the Constitution of the United States."

Section 2.

The President shall be Commander in Chief of the Army and Navy of the United States, and of the Militia of the several States, when called into the actual Service of the United States; he may require the Opinion, in writing, of the principal Officer in each of the executive Departments, upon any Subject relating to the Duties of their respective Offices, and he shall have Power to Grant Reprieves and Pardons for Offences against the United States, except in Cases of Impeachment.

He shall have Power, by and with the Advice and Consent of the Senate, to make Treaties, provided two thirds of the Senators present concur; and he shall nominate, and by and with the Advice and Consent of the Senate, shall appoint Ambassadors, other public Ministers and Consuls, Judges of the supreme Court, and all other Officers of the United States, whose Appointments are not herein otherwise provided for, and which shall be established by Law: but

APPENDIX II: The Constitution

the Congress may by Law vest the Appointment of such inferior Officers, as they think proper, in the President alone, in the Courts of Law, or in the Heads of Departments.

The President shall have Power to fill up all Vacancies that may happen during the Recess of the Senate, by granting Commissions which shall expire at the End of their next Session.

Section 3.

He shall from time to time give to the Congress Information of the State of the Union, and recommend to their Consideration such Measures as he shall judge necessary and expedient; he may, on extraordinary Occasions, convene both Houses, or either of them, and in Case of Disagreement between them, with Respect to the Time of Adjournment, he may adjourn them to such Time as he shall think proper; he shall receive Ambassadors and other public Ministers; he shall take Care that the Laws be faithfully executed, and shall Commission all the Officers of the United States.

Section 4.

The President, Vice President and all Civil Officers of the United States, shall be removed from Office on Impeachment for and Conviction of, Treason, Bribery, or other high Crimes and Misdemeanors.

Article. III

Section 1.

The judicial Power of the United States, shall be vested in one supreme Court, and in such inferior Courts as the Congress may from time to time ordain and establish. The Judges, both of the supreme and inferior Courts, shall hold their Offices during good Behaviour, and shall, at stated Times, receive for their Services, a Compensation, which shall not be diminished during their Continuance in Office.

Section 2.

The judicial Power shall extend to all Cases, in Law and Equity, arising under this Constitution, the Laws of the United States, and Treaties made, or which shall be made, under their Authority;—to all Cases affecting Ambassadors, other public ministers and Consuls;—to all Cases of admiralty and maritime Jurisdiction;—to Controversies to which the United States shall be a Party;—to Controversies between two or more States;—between a State and Citizens of another State;—between Citizens of different States;—between Citizens of the same State claiming Lands under Grants of different States, and between a State, or the Citizens thereof, and foreign States, Citizens or Subjects.

In all Cases affecting Ambassadors, other public Ministers and Consuls, and those in which a State shall be Party, the supreme Court shall have original Jurisdiction. In all the other Cases before mentioned, the supreme Court shall have appellate Jurisdiction, both as to Law and Fact, with such Exceptions, and under such Regulations as the Congress shall make.

The Trial of all Crimes, except in Cases of Impeachment, shall be by Jury; and such Trial shall be held in the State where the said Crimes shall have been committed; but when not committed within any State, the Trial shall be at such Place or Places as the Congress may by Law have directed.

Section 3.

Treason against the United States, shall consist only in levying War against them, or in adhering to their Enemies, giving them Aid and Comfort. No Person shall be convicted of Treason unless on the Testimony of two Witnesses to the same overt Act, or on Confession in open Court.

The Congress shall have Power to declare the Punishment of Treason, but no Attainder of Treason shall work Corruption of Blood, or Forfeiture except during the Life of the Person attainted.

Article. IV

Section 1.

Full Faith and Credit shall be given in each State to the public Acts, Records, and judicial proceedings of every other State. And the Congress may by general Laws prescribe the Manner in which such Acts, Records and Proceedings shall be proved, and the Effect thereof.

Section 2.

The Citizens of each State shall be entitled to all Privileges and Immunities of Citizens in the several States.

A Person charged in any State with Treason, Felony, or other Crime, who shall flee from Justice, and be found in another State, shall on Demand of the executive Authority of the State from which he fled, be delivered up, to be removed to the State having Jurisdiction of the Crime.

No Person held to Service or Labour in one State, under the Laws thereof, escaping into another, shall, in Consequence of any Law or Regulation therein, be discharged from such Service or Labour, but shall be delivered up on Claim of the Party to whom such Service or Labour may be due.

Section 3.

New States may be admitted by the Congress into this Union; but no new State shall be formed or erected within the Jurisdiction of any other State; nor any State be formed by the Junction of two or more States, or Parts of States, without the Consent of the Legislatures of the States concerned as well as of the Congress.

The Congress shall have Power to dispose of and make all needful Rules and Regulations respecting the Territory or other Property belonging to the United States; and nothing in this Constitution shall be so construed as to Prejudice any Claims of the United States, or of any particular State.

Section 4.

The United States shall guarantee to every State in this Union a Republican Form of Government, and shall protect each of them against Invasion; and on Application of the Legislature, or of the Executive (when the Legislature cannot be convened) against domestic Violence.

Article. V

The Congress, whenever two thirds of both Houses shall deem it necessary, shall propose Amendments to this Constitution, or, on the Application of the Legislatures of two thirds of the several States, shall call a Convention for proposing Amendments, which, in either Case, shall be valid to all Intents and Purposes, as Part of this Constitution, when ratified by the Legislatures of three fourths of the several States, or by Conventions in three fourths thereof, as the one or the other Mode of Ratification may be proposed by the Congress; Provided that no Amendment which may be made prior to the Year One thousand eight hundred and eight shall in any Manner affect the first and fourth Clauses in the Ninth Section of the first Article; and that no State, without its Consent, shall be deprived of its equal Suffrage in the Senate.

The Delicate Balance

Article. VI

All Debts contracted and Engagements entered into, before the Adoption of this Constitution, shall be as valid against the United States under this Constitution, as under the Confederation.

This Constitution, and the Laws of the United States which shall be made in Pursuance thereof; and all Treaties made, or which shall be made, under the Authority of the United States, shall be the supreme Law of the Land; and the Judges in every State shall be bound thereby, any Thing in the Constitution or Laws of any state to the Contrary notwithstanding.

The Senators and Representatives before mentioned, and the Members of the several State Legislatures, and all executive and judicial Officers, both of the United States and of the several States, shall be bound by Oath or Affirmation, to support this Constitution; but no religious Test shall ever be required as a Qualification to any Office or public Trust under the United States.

Article. VII

The Ratification of the Conventions of nine States, shall be sufficient for the Establishment of this Constitution between the States so ratifying the same.

done in Convention by the Unanimous Consent of the States present the Seventeenth Day of September in the Year of our Lord one thousand seven hundred and Eighty seven and of the Independence of the United States of America the Twelfth In witness whereof We have hereunto subscribed our Names,

>G^{o} WASHINGTON—Presidt. and deputy from Virginia
>[Signed also by the deputies of twelve States.]

Delaware

>Geo: Read
>Gunning Bedford jun
>John Dickinson
>Richard Bassett
>Jaco: Broom

Maryland

>James McHenry
>Dan of St ThoS. Jenifer
>Danl Carroll.

APPENDIX II: The Constitution

Virginia
> John Blair—
> James Madison Jr.

North Carolina
> Wm. Blount
> Richd. Dobbs Spaight.
> Hu Williamson

South Carolina
> J. Rutledge
> Charles Cotesworth Pinckney
> Charles Pinckney
> Pierce Butler.

Georgia
> William Few
> Abr Baldwin

New Hampshire
> John Langdon
> Nicholas Gilman

Massachusetts
> Nathaniel Gorham
> Rufus King

Connecticut
> Wm. Saml. Johnson
> Roger Sherman

New York
> Alexander Hamilton

New Jersey
> Wil: Livingston
> David Brearley
> Wm. Paterson
> Jona: Dayton

Pennsylvania
> B Franklin
> Thomas Mifflin
> Robt Morris
> Geo. Clymer
> Thos. FitzSimons

The Delicate Balance

> Jared Ingersoll
> James Wilson.
> Gouv Morris

Attest William Jackson Secretary

The Bill of Rights

(Ratified effective December 15, 1791)

Amendment I

Congress shall make no law respecting an establishment of religion, or prohibiting the free exercise thereof; or abridging the freedom of speech, or of the press; or the right of the people peaceably to assemble, and to petition the Government for a redress of grievances.

Amendment II

A well regulated Militia, being necessary to the security of a free State, the right of the people to keep and bear Arms, shall not be infringed.

Amendment III

No Soldier shall, in time of peace be quartered in any house, without the consent of the Owner, nor in time of war, but in a manner to be prescribed by law.

Amendment IV

The right of the people to be secure in their persons, houses, papers, and effects, against unreasonable searches and seizures, shall not be violated, and no Warrants shall issue, but upon probable cause, supported by Oath or affirmation, and particularly describing the place to be searched, and the persons or things to be seized.

Amendment V

No person shall be held to answer for a capital, or otherwise infamous crime, unless on a presentment or indictment of a Grand Jury, except in cases arising in the land or naval forces, or in the Militia, when in actual service in time of War or public danger; nor shall any person be subject for the same offence to be twice put in jeopardy of life or limb; nor shall be compelled in any criminal case to be a witness against himself, nor be deprived of life, liberty, or property, without due process of law; nor shall private property be taken for public use, without just compensation.

APPENDIX II: The Constitution

Amendment VI

In all criminal prosecutions, the accused shall enjoy the right to a speedy and public trial, by an impartial jury of the State and district wherein the crime shall have been committed, which district shall have been previously ascertained by law, and to be informed of the nature and cause of the accusation; to be confronted with the witnesses against him; to have compulsory process for obtaining witnesses in his favor, and to have the assistance of counsel for his defence.

Amendment VII

In Suits at common law, where the value in controversy shall exceed twenty dollars, the right of trial by jury shall be preserved, and no fact tried by a jury, shall be otherwise re-examined in any Court of the United States, than according to the rules of the common law.

Amendment VIII

Excessive bail shall not be required, nor excessive fines imposed, nor cruel and unusual punishments inflicted.

Amendment IX

The enumeration in the Constitution, of certain rights, shall not be construed to deny or disparage others retained by the people.

Amendment X

The powers not delegated to the United States by the Constitution, nor prohibited by it to the States, are reserved to the States respectively, or to the people.

Additional Amendments

Amendment XI (1798)

The Judicial power of the United States shall not be construed to extend to any suit in law or equity, commenced or prosecuted against one of the United States by Citizens of another State, or by Citizens or Subjects of any Foreign State.

Amendment XII (1804)

The Electors shall meet in their respective states, and vote by ballot for President and Vice-President, one of whom, at least, shall not be an inhabitant of the same state with themselves; they shall name in their ballots the person voted for as President, and in distinct ballots the person voted for as Vice-President, and they shall make distinct lists of all persons voted for as President, and of all persons voted for as Vice-President, and of the number of votes for each, which lists they shall sign and certify, and transmit sealed to the seat of the government of the United States, directed to the President of the Senate;—The President of the Senate shall, in the presence of the Senate and House of Representatives, open all the certificates and the votes shall then be counted;—The person having the greatest number of votes for President, shall be the President, if such number be a majority of the whole number of Electors appointed; and if no person have such majority, then from the persons having the highest numbers not exceeding three on the list of those voted for as President, the House of Representatives shall choose immediately, by ballot, the President. But in choosing the President, the votes shall be taken by states, the representation from each state having one vote; a quorum for this purpose shall consist of a member or members from two-thirds of the states, and a majority of all the states shall be necessary to a choice. And if the House of Representatives shall not choose a President whenever the right of choice shall devolve upon them, before the fourth day of March next following, then the Vice-President shall act as President, as in the case of the death or other constitutional disability of the President. The person having the greatest number of votes as Vice-President, shall be the Vice-President, if such number be a majority of the whole number of Electors appointed, and if no person have a majority, then from the two highest numbers on the list, the Senate shall choose the Vice-President; a quorum for the purpose shall consist of two-thirds of the whole number of Senators, and a majority of the whole number shall be necessary to a choice. But no person constitutionally ineligible to the office of President shall be eligible to that of Vice-President of the United States.

Amendment XIII (1865)

Section 1. Neither slavery nor involuntary servitude, except as a punishment for crime whereof the party shall have been duly convicted, shall exist within the United States, or any place subject to their jurisdiction.

Section 2. Congress shall have power to enforce this article by appropriate legislation.

Amendment XIV (1868)

Section 1. All persons born or naturalized in the United States, and subject to the jurisdiction thereof, are citizens of the United States and of the State wherein they reside. No State shall make or enforce any law which shall abridge the privileges or immunities of citizens of the United States; nor shall any State deprive any person of life, liberty, or property, without due process of law; nor deny to any person within its jurisdiction the equal protection of the laws.

APPENDIX II: The Constitution

Section 2. Representatives shall be apportioned among the several States according to their respective numbers, counting the whole number of persons in each State, excluding Indians not taxed. But when the right to vote at any election for the choice of electors for President and Vice President of the United States, Representatives in Congress, the Executive and judicial officers of a State, or the members of the Legislature thereof, is denied to any of the male inhabitants of such State, being twenty-one years of age, and citizens of the United States, or in any way abridged, except for participation in rebellion, or other crime, the basis of representation therein shall be reduced in the proportion which the number of such male citizens shall bear to the whole number of male citizens twenty-one years of age in such State.

Section 3. No person shall be a Senator or Representative in Congress, or elector of President and Vice President, or hold any office, civil or military, under the United States, or under any State, who, having previously taken an oath, as a member of Congress, or as an officer of the United States, or as a member of any State legislature, or as an executive or judicial officer of any State, to support the Constitution of the United States, shall have engaged in insurrection or rebellion against the same, or given aid or comfort to the enemies thereof. But Congress may by a vote of two-thirds of each House, remove such disability.

Section 4. The validity of the public debt of the United States, authorized by law, including debts incurred for payment of pensions and bounties for services in suppressing insurrection or rebellion, shall not be questioned. But neither the United States nor any State shall assume or pay any debt or obligation incurred in aid of insurrection or rebellion against the United States, or any claim for the loss or emancipation of any slave; but all such debts, obligations and claims shall be held illegal and void.

Section 5. The Congress shall have power to enforce, by appropriate legislation, the provisions of this article.

Amendment XV (1870)

Section 1. The right of citizens of the United States to vote shall not be denied or abridged by the United States or by any State on account of race, color, or previous condition of servitude.

Section 2. The Congress shall have power to enforce this article by appropriate legislation.

The Delicate Balance

Amendment XVI (1913)

The Congress shall have power to lay and collect taxes on incomes, from whatever source derived, without apportionment among the several States, and without regard to any census of enumeration.

Amendment XVII (1913)

The Senate of the United States shall be composed of two Senators from each State, elected by the people thereof, for six years; and each Senator shall have one vote. The electors in each State shall have the qualifications requisite for electors of the most numerous branch of the State legislatures.

When vacancies happen in the representation of any State in the Senate, the executive authority of such State shall issue writs of election to fill such vacancies: *Provided*, That the legislature of any State may empower the executive thereof to make temporary appointments until the people fill the vacancies by election as the legislature may direct.

This amendment shall not be so construed as to affect the election or term of any Senator chosen before it becomes valid as part of the Constitution.

Amendment XVIII (1919)

Section 1. After one year from the ratification of this article the manufacture, sale, or transportation of intoxicating liquors within, the importation thereof into, or the exportation thereof from the United States and all territory subject to the jurisdiction thereof for beverage purposes is hereby prohibited.

Section 2. The Congress and the several States shall have concurrent power to enforce this article by appropriate legislation.

Section 3. This article shall be inoperative unless it shall have been ratified as an amendment to the Constitution by the legislatures of the several States, as provided in the Constitution, within seven years from the date of the submission hereof to the States by the Congress.

Amendment XIX (1920)

The right of citizens of the United States to vote shall not be denied or abridged by the United States or by any State on account of sex.

Congress shall have power to enforce this article by appropriate legislation.

Amendment XX (1933)

Section 1. The terms of the President and Vice President shall end at noon on the 20th day of January, and the terms of Senators and Representatives at noon on the 3d day of January, of the years in which such terms would have ended if this article had not been ratified; and the terms of their successors shall then begin.

Section 2. The Congress shall assemble at least once in every year, and such meeting shall begin at noon on the 3d day of January, unless they shall by law appoint a different day.

Section 3. If, at the time fixed for the beginning of the term of the President, the President elect shall have died, the Vice President elect shall become President. If a President shall not have been chosen before the time fixed for the beginning of his term, or if the President elect shall have failed to qualify, then the Vice President elect shall act as President until a President shall have qualified; and the Congress may by law provide for the case wherein neither a President elect nor a Vice President elect shall have qualified, declaring who shall then act as President, or the manner in which one who is to act shall be selected, and such person shall act accordingly until a President or Vice President shall have qualified.

Section 4. The Congress may by law provide for the case of the death of any of the persons from whom the House of Representatives may choose a President whenever the right of choice shall have devolved upon them, and for the case of the death of any of the persons from whom the Senate may choose a Vice President whenever the right of choice shall have devolved upon them.

Section 5. Sections 1 and 2 shall take effect on the 15th day of October following the ratification of this article.

Section 6. This article shall be inoperative unless it shall have been ratified as an amendment to the Constitution by the legislatures of three-fourths of the several States within seven years from the date of its submission.

Amendment XXI (1933)

Section 1. The eighteenth article of amendment to the Constitution of the United States is hereby repealed.

Section 2. The transportation or importation into any State, Territory, or possession of the United States for delivery or use therein of intoxicating liquors, in violation of the laws thereof, is hereby prohibited.

The Delicate Balance

Section 3. This article shall be inoperative unless it shall have been ratified as an amendment to the Constitution by conventions in the several States, as provided in the Constitution, within seven years from the date of the submission hereof to the States by the Congress.

Amendment XXII (1951)

Section 1. No person shall be elected to the office of the President more than twice, and no person who has held the office of President, or acted as President, for more than two years of a term to which some other person was elected President shall be elected to the office of the President more than once. But this Article shall not apply to any person holding the office of President when this Article was proposed by the Congress, and shall not prevent any person who may be holding the office of President, or acting as President, during the term within which this Article becomes operative from holding the office of President or acting as President during the remainder of such term.

Section 2. This article shall be inoperative unless it shall have been ratified as an amendment to the Constitution by the legislatures of three-fourths of the several States within seven years from the date of its submission to the States by the Congress.

Amendment XXIII (1961)

Section 1. The District constituting the seat of government of the United States shall appoint in such manner as the Congress may direct:

A number of electors of President and Vice President equal to the whole number of Senators and Representatives in Congress to which the District would be entitled if it were a State, but in no event more than the least populous State; they shall be in addition to those appointed by the States, but they shall be considered, for the purposes of the election of President and Vice President, to be electors appointed by a State; and they shall meet in the District and perform such duties as provided by the twelfth article of amendment.

Section 2. The Congress shall have power to enforce this article by appropriate legislation.

Amendment XXIV (1964)

Section 1. The right of citizens of the United States to vote in any primary or other election for President or Vice President, for electors for President or Vice President, or for Senator or Representative in

Congress, shall not be denied or abridged by the United States or any State by reason of failure to pay any poll tax or other tax.

Section 2. The Congress shall have power to enforce this article by appropriate legislation.

Amendment XXV (1967)

Section 1. In case of the removal of the President from office or of his death or resignation, the Vice President shall become President.

Section 2. Whenever there is a vacancy in the office of the Vice President, the President shall nominate a Vice President who shall take office upon confirmation by a majority vote of both Houses of Congress.

Section 3. Whenever the President transmits to the President pro tempore of the Senate and the Speaker of the House of Representatives his written declaration that he is unable to discharge the powers and duties of his office, and until he transmits to them a written declaration to the contrary, such powers and duties shall be discharged by the Vice President as Acting President.

Section 4. Whenever the Vice President and a majority of either the principal officers of the executive departments or of such other body as Congress may by law provide, transmit to the President pro tempore of the Senate and the Speaker of the House of Representatives their written declaration that the President is unable to discharge the powers and duties of his office, the Vice President shall immediately assume the powers and duties of the office as Acting President.

Thereafter, when the President transmits to the President pro tempore of the Senate and the Speaker of the House of Representatives his written declaration that no inability exists, he shall resume the powers and duties of his office unless the Vice President and a majority of either the principal officers of the executive department or of such other body as Congress may by law provide, transmit within four days to the President pro tempore of the Senate and the Speaker of the House of Representatives their written declaration that the President is unable to discharge the powers and duties of his office. Thereupon Congress shall decide the issue, assembling within forty-eight hours for that purpose if not in session. If the Congress, within twenty-one days after receipt of the latter written declaration, or, if Congress is not in session, within twenty-one days after Congress is required to assemble, determines by two-thirds vote of both Houses that the President is unable to discharge the powers and duties of his office, the Vice President shall continue to discharge the same as Acting President; otherwise, the President shall resume the powers and duties of his office.

Amendment XXVI (1971)

Section 1. The right of citizens of the United States, who are 18 years of age or older, to vote, shall not be denied or abridged by the United States or any state on account of age.

Section 2. The Congress shall have the power to enforce this article by appropriate legislation.

Amendment XXVII (1992)

No law varying the compensation for the services of the Senators and Representatives shall take effect until an election of Representatives shall have intervened.

APPENDIX III
Chronology and Summary of Important Supreme Court Cases Dealing with Federalism, Interstate Commerce, and Economic Liberty

1798 – *Calder* v. *Bull* (3 Dall. 3 U.S. 386). By a vote of 4 to 0, the Court held that the prohibition on *ex post facto* laws found in Article I, Section 10 of the Constitution did not apply to a Connecticut statute that retroactively overturned a dispute over a will. The Court reasoned that the *ex post facto* clause was intended to apply only to criminal legislation and edicts, not other types of legislation.

Surprisingly, however, the Court also used the case to make bold pronouncements on the reach of government power in general. In fact, *Calder* is widely regarded as a progenitor of future substantive due process jurisprudence because of Judge Samuel Chase's strong defense of limitations on the power of legislatures through social compact theory. Chase employed Lockean natural law theory to argue that certain inalienable individual rights could not be violated by governments even when explicit textual support for such rights could not be found. "I cannot subscribe to the omnipotence of a State Legislature," noted Chase, "or that it is absolute and without controul.... An Act of the Legislature (for I cannot call it a law) contrary to the great first principles of the social compact, cannot be considered a rightful exercise of legislative authority." Specifically, Chase argued that "The legislature [cannot] change innocence into guilt [or] violate the right of an antecedent lawful private contract; of the right to private property. To maintain that our Federal, or State, Legislatures possess such powers, if they had not been expressly restrained, would, in my opinion, be a political heresy, altogether inadmissible in our free republican governments."

1819 – *McCulloch* v. *Maryland* (4 Wheat. 17 U.S. 316). By a vote of 7 to 0, the Court upheld the constitutionality of the Second Bank

The Delicate Balance

of the United States, which Congress had created in 1816. The constitutional challenge arose after Maryland attempted to lay taxes on the Bank. In this landmark decision, Chief Justice John Marshall held that the federal government possessed certain implied powers (specifically, through the Necessary and Proper Clause) to carry out its constitutionally defined functions (in this case, to coin money, collect taxes, etc.). *McCulloch v. Maryland* is considered one of the most important, albeit controversial, Supreme Court cases because it rejected arguments that the Constitution could be interpreted strictly at all times and because it justified a broader, looser interpretation of federal powers when necessary to achieve a constitutional imperative. Furthermore, the decision reaffirmed the Supremacy Clause as a guarantee against state efforts to tax or regulate federal entities or federal jurisdictional issues.

1824 – *Gibbons v. Ogden* (9 Wheat. 22 U.S. 1). *Gibbons* was the first and most important Supreme Court case dealing directly with the reach of the Commerce Clause. By a vote of 6 to 0, the Court struck down a New York law granting a monopoly to the use of the Hudson River by a steamboat operator. Chief Justice Marshall authored the Court's unanimous decision, which held that where state laws came into conflict with each other or with national laws, federal action is required to settle the matter.

Marshall reasoned that if the Commerce Clause was to have its intended effect—the restriction of state-based protectionism and discrimination—the scope and definition of the Commerce Clause would have to be construed more broadly to include more than simple goods transported across state boundaries. It would have to include other activities and entities, such as steamboats and the individuals they transported, often referred to as the "instrumentalities of commerce."

1827 – *Brown v. Maryland* (12 Wheat. 25 U.S. 419). By a vote of 6 to 1, the Court held that states could not tax foreign goods in their "original package" until the goods became "commingled" with other products or property within a state. Marshall argued that such taxes, if allowed to stand, would violate Congress's power to regulate foreign and interstate commerce, as well as Article 1, Section 10, Clause 2 of the Constitution, which forbids states from "lay[ing] any Imposts or Duties on Imports or Exports...." *Brown* was watered down in subsequent cases such as *Woodruff v. Parham*, 8 Wall. (75 U.S.) 123 (1869), and *Low v. Austin*, 80 U.S. (12 Wheat.) 419 (1872), and essentially overturned in *Michelin Tire Corporation v. Wages*, 423 U.S. 276

APPENDIX III: Chronology and Summary

(1976), which upheld a Georgia property tax on imported tires held in storage.

1829 – Willson v. Blackbird Creek Marsh Co. (2 Pet. 27 U.S. 245). By a 6 to 0 vote, the Court upheld a Delaware statute that permitted the construction of a dam across a navigable creek even though the waterway had been used for interstate commerce. *Blackbird Creek Marsh Co.* is important because (1) it marked the first time the Marshall court placed substantive limits on the federal government's power to regulate interstate commerce and (2) it was one of the first cases to develop "dormant commerce clause" theory. That is, Marshall ruled for the Court that the Delaware statute was not offensive to Congress's power to protect interstate commerce, especially since Congress had not legislated on or spoken to the issue at hand. Furthermore, the Court gave credence to "state police power" doctrine by arguing that construction of the dam represented a legitimate public safety measure, meaning the state could infringe on interstate commerce. "Measures calculated to [protect public health and safety], provided they do not come in collision with the powers of the general government, are undoubtedly within those which are reserved to the states," ruled Marshall.

1829 – Weston v. Charleston (2 Pet. 27 U.S. 449). By a vote of 4 to 2, the Court struck down a Charleston, South Carolina. law that attempted to tax federal debt certificates. The Court held that such a state or municipal tax would violate the federal government's authority and ability under Article 1, Section 8, Clause 2 "To borrow Money on the credit of the United States."

1837 – New York v. Miln (11 Pet. 36 U.S. 102). By a vote of 6 to 1, the Court ruled that the Commerce Clause was not applicable to persons being transported via ships, merely to goods. The Court ruled that as part of each state's "police power," states could monitor the manifest of ships passing through their jurisdictions. The Court's decision in *Miln*, which probably was influenced by slavery questions of the time, was struck down a century later in *Edwards v. California*, 314 U.S. 160 (1941).

1847 – The License Cases (5 How. 46 U.S. 504). By a vote of 9 to 0, the Court upheld Massachusetts, Rhode Island, and New Hampshire laws which required licenses to sell alcoholic beverages within their jurisdictions on police power grounds. Alcohol distributors in other states had claimed that these licensing laws discriminated against interstate trade in alcohol. In a

The Delicate Balance

series of separate opinions, the Court unanimously disagreed. As Chief Justice Roger Brooke Taney noted in his opinion:

> The controlling and supreme power over commerce with foreign nations and the several States is undoubtedly conferred upon Congress. Yet, in my judgment, the State may nevertheless, for the safety or convenience of trade, or for the protection of the health of its citizens, make regulations of commerce for its own ports and harbours, and for its own territory; and such regulations are valid unless they come in conflict with a law of Congress."

The three cases that were grouped together and decided in *The License Cases* were *Thurlow v. Massachusetts*, *Fletcher v. Rhode Island*, and *Peirce v. New Hampshire*.

1849 – *The Passenger Cases* (7 How. 48 U.S. 283). By a vote of 5 to 4, the Court struck down New York and Massachusetts taxes on ship passengers entering the states, even though the taxes were intended to defray the costs of administering medical examinations or hospitalization costs for new immigrants with contagious diseases. Not surprisingly, the case yielded several contentious opinions, especially because it was influenced by potential slavery implications. *The Passenger Cases* were *Smith v. Turner* and *Norris v. Boston*.

1851 – *Cooley v. Board of Wardens of the Port of Philadelphia* (12 How. 53 U.S. 299). By a vote of 6 to 2, the Court upheld a Pennsylvania law which regulated vessels entering or exiting the port of Philadelphia on the grounds that the matter was local in nature. The Pennsylvania statute requited that any ship entering the port of Philadelphia must employ a local pilot to guide the ship through the port or pay a fine or fee to the government to help fund a retirement system for Pennsylvania ship pilots or widows and dependents of deceased pilots.

The Court argued that while such a law could stand, other laws and issues that were clearly national in scope would demand federal attention. This approach has come to be known as the "*Cooley* Doctrine of selective exclusiveness." That is, in select commercial areas where the subject matter in question demands national attention or uniformity, Congress has exclusive jurisdiction to legislate if it desires to do so. However, when the commercial subject matter is clearly local in character, or when Congress has not addressed the subject at hand, the states are free to legislate. Hence, the subject at hand in

APPENDIX III: Chronology and Summary

Cooley (pilotage regulation) was viewed by the Court as a purely local matter that did not require national attention. The distinction between issues that demanded "national uniformity" and those that where "purely local" remained unclear, however. *Cooley* was the most important Commerce Clause-related decision of the Taney era and the most important Supreme Court Commerce Clause decision of the 19th century next to *Gibbons v. Ogden*.

1852 – *Genesee Chief v. Fitzhugh* (12 How. 53 U.S. 443). By a vote of 8 to 1, the Court ruled that federal jurisdiction over commerce on the seas extended to disputes on interior waterways—in this case, the Great Lakes. This decision, which upheld an 1845 congressional statute expanding federal jurisdiction in the field, encouraged the expansion of water-borne commerce on inland lakes and rivers by applying to navigation and maritime transactions uniform standards which previously had been applied only to commerce on the high seas. By overruling this earlier precedent, *Genesee Chief* showed that the Court was willing to abandon judicial precedent when new technologies (in this case, the steamboat) had made previous standards irrelevant or commercially unworkable.

1873 – *Slaughter-House Cases* (16 Wall. 83 U.S. 36). By a vote of 5 to 4, the Court upheld a Louisiana statute granting a monopoly to a private slaughterhouse company in the New Orleans area. The Court claimed the state grant of monopoly to a single company did not violate other butchers' Fourteenth Amendment economic rights to engage freely in business in the New Orleans area. This decision greatly limited the scope of such Fourteenth Amendment protections as the Privileges and Immunities Clause by narrowly interpreting the substantive due process protections of economic freedom embodied in the Amendment and the Constitution. The majority argued that the Fourteenth Amendment was intended primarily to protect the rights of freed slaves, not all citizens attempting to engage in a trade or occupation.

The majority reasoned that state and local officials should be granted generous regulatory leeway when formulating public policies to promote the health, welfare, safety, and public morality of their communities. These "police powers" where viewed by the majority as being exempt from federal pre-emption even when constitutionally protected rights may be at stake. This led the minority, especially Justice Stephan J. Field, to issue vigorous dissents lamenting the fact that the Court had not taken steps to preserve what Field called "the right of free labor, one of the most sacred and imprescriptible rights of man…." To this day, not surprisingly, *Slaughter-House* remains one of the Court's most controversial decisions.

1875 – ***Welton v. State of Missouri*** **(91 U.S. 275).** In a unanimous decision, the Court held a Missouri statute unconstitutional because it prohibited out-of-state vendors from offering products to Missouri consumers without a license but imposed no similar burden on indigenous vendors. The Court held that a state could not discriminate against interstate commerce in this manner and went on to articulate a more sophisticated definition of interstate commerce while expounding on the nature and extent of Congress's power under the Commerce Clause. Justice Field noted for the Court:

> Commerce is a term of the largest import. It comprehends intercourse for the purposes of trade in any and all its forms, including the transportation, purchase, sale, and exchange of commodities between the citizens of our country and the citizens or subjects of other countries, and between the citizens of different States. The power to regulate it embraces all the instruments by which such commerce may be conducted. So far as some of these instruments are concerned, and some subjects which are local in their operation, it has been held that the States may provide regulations until Congress acts with reference to them; but where the subject to which the power applies is national in its character, or of such a nature as to admit of uniformity of regulation, the power is exclusive of all State authority…. The fact that Congress has not seen fit to prescribe any specific rules to govern inter-State commerce does not affect the question. Its inaction on the subject…is equivalent to a declaration that inter-State commerce shall be free and untrammelled.

1885 – ***Barbier v. Connolly*** **(113 U.S. 27).** In a very concise decision dealing with the reach of municipal police powers, the Court upheld a San Francisco statute that placed restrictions on all-night laundries since such activities might pose a fire hazard to nearby citizens. In his brief decision for the Court, Justice Stephan Field clearly articulated why this type of regu-

APPENDIX III: Chronology and Summary

lation represented a legitimate use of state and local police powers while other types of restrictions might not:

> But neither the [Fourteenth] amendment—broad and comprehensive as it is—nor any other amendment, was designed to interfere with the power of the state, sometimes termed its police power, to prescribe regulations to promote the health, peace, morals, education, and good order of the people, and to legislate so as to increase the industries of the state, develop its resources, and add to its wealth and prosperity. From the very necessities of society, legislation of a special character, having these objects in view, must often be had in certain districts, such as for draining marshes and irrigating arid plains. Special burdens are often necessary for general benefits—for supplying water, preventing fires, lighting districts, cleaning streets, opening parks, and many other objects. Regulations for these purposes may press with more or less weight upon one than upon another, but they are designed, not to impose unequal or unnecessary restrictions upon any one, but to promote, with as little individual inconvenience as possible, the general good.

1887 – *Munn v. Illinois* (94 U.S. 113). By a vote of 7 to 2, the Court upheld an Illinois statute regulating the maximum price that owners of grain elevators could charge customers for storage of grain. Private grain elevator owners argued that the Court should strike down the statute since it violated their Fourteenth Amendment substantive due process rights and also interfered with the free flow of interstate commerce. Instead of upholding the right of grain elevators to contract freely with customers and arrange prices voluntarily, however, the Court ruled that, in the words of Chief Justice Morrison Waite, the business of grain elevator storage was "affected with the public interest" since "Property [becomes] clothed with the public interest when used in a manner to make it of public consequence, and affect the community at large."

Munn was important because it cast further doubt on what protections were extended to industry and commerce under the Constitution and the Fourteenth Amendment. Furthermore, although *Munn*, like the *Slaughter-House* decision, could be interpreted as the Court's reaffirmation of the right of state and local governments to exercise police powers over industry and commerce, these two cases facilitated the 20th century's massive expansion of regulatory activity at all levels of government.

1887 – *Mugler* v. *Kansas* (123 U.S. 623). By a vote of 8 to 1, the Court upheld a Kansas statute prohibiting the manufacture or sale of alcohol without a license. *Mugler*, however, also signaled a new-found willingness to utilize a "reasonableness standard" when reviewing future police power cases to evaluate the legitimacy of certain state or local actions. The key test would be whether the state or local statute in question bore a "real or substantial relation" to an effort to "protect the public health, the public morals, or the public safety...." As Justice John Marshall Harlan elaborated for the majority:

> It does not at all follow that every statute enacted ostensibly for the promotion of these ends is to be accepted as a legitimate exertion of the police powers of the state. There are, of necessity, limits beyond which legislation cannot rightfully go. While every possible presumption is to be indulged in favor of the validity of a statute, the courts must obey the Constitution rather than the law-making department of government, and must, upon their own responsibility, determine whether, in any particular case, these limits have been passed.

1895 – *United States* v. *E. C. Knight Co.* (156 U.S. 1). By a vote of 8 to 1, the Court ruled that the federal government did not have authority under the Sherman Antirust Act of 1890 to regulate the sugar trust since the activities of the trust did not fall within the scope of interstate commerce and did not have a direct effect on interstate commerce. The Court argued that a showing that such activities had an indirect effect on interstate commerce could not justify federal regulation. More important, the Court argued that a distinction needed to be drawn between commerce and manufacturing, which were two separate activities in the eyes of the Court, with federal authorities having no control over the latter activity. In the words of Chief Justice Melville Weston Fuller, "Commerce succeeds to manufacture, and is not a part of it." Whatever potential effect *E. C. Knight* may have had on the expansion of national regulatory power remains a mystery since the decision was nullified when

APPENDIX III: Chronology and Summary

the Court employed more expansive readings of the Commerce Power to justify federal antitrust actions in *Addyston Pipe & Steel Co. v. United States*, 175 U.S. 211 (1899); *Northern Securities Co. v. United States*, 193 U.S. 197 (1904); and *Swift & Co. v. United States*, 196 U.S. 375 (1905). Likewise, as mentioned below, the Court's decision in the *Shreveport Rate Case*, 234 U.S. 342 (1914), signaled the abandonment of any such "direct" versus "indirect" effects test by the Court as was present in *E. C. Knight*.

1897 – *Allgeyer v. Louisiana* (165 U.S. 578). By a vote of 9 to 0, the Court invalidated a Louisiana statute that made it illegal for citizens of the state to enter into insurance contracts through the mail with out-of-state insurance companies. *Allgeyer* is historically important because it marked the Court's first attempt to articulate a "liberty or freedom of contract" rationale for overturning a state statute. Relying on the Contract Clause of the Constitution and the Due Process Clause of the Fourteenth Amendment, the Court argued that, "In the privilege of pursuing an ordinary calling or trade, and of acquiring, holding, and selling property, must be embraced the right to make all proper contracts in relation thereto.... The mere fact that a citizen may be within the limits of a particular state does not prevent his making a contract outside its limits while he himself remains within it."

1903 – *Champion v. Ames* (188 U.S. 321). By a vote of 5 to 4, the Court upheld a congressional statute, the Federal Lottery Act of 1895, which had prohibited the interstate shipment or transportation of lottery tickets. Also known as the "lottery case," *Champion v. Ames* marked the emergence of a national police power rationale for federal regulation of interstate commerce even though no general federal police powers are enumerated within the Constitution. The Court's contentious and confusing majority opinion in *Champion* refused "to justify any attempt to lay down a rule for determining in advance the validity of every statute that may be enacted under the commerce clause." Instead, the majority simply declared that the transportation of lottery tickets could be considered interstate commerce and subjected to congressional limitations.

1905 – *Swift & Co. v. United States* (196 U.S. 375). By a vote of 9 to 0, the Court upheld a federal antitrust suit against the Beef Trust and continued to move away from the *E. C. Knight* "manufacturing vs. commerce" test for gauging the legitimacy of federal intervention via the Commerce Clause. Instead, Oliver

The Delicate Balance

Wendell Holmes noted for the Court that "[C]ommerce among the states is not a legal conception, but a practical one, drawn from the course of business." Moreover, Justice Oliver Wendell Holmes argued, since commodities such as beef might eventually enter the "current of commerce," their manufacture could be regulated under the federal Commerce Power.

1905 – *Lochner v. New York* (198 U.S. 45). By a vote of 5 to 4, the Court struck down a New York State statute limiting the number of hours an employee could work during a day or week. In what remains a highly controversial decision, the majority held that the substantive due process protections of the Fourteenth Amendment were being violated by the statute since the liberty of employers and employees to contract freely was being infringed. As Justice Rufus Peckham noted for the majority:

> It is a question of which of two powers or rights shall prevail, the power of the state to legislate or the right of the individual to liberty of person and freedom of contract. The mere assertion that the subject relates though but in a remote degree, to the public health, does not necessarily render the enactment valid. The act must have a more direct relation, as a means to an end, and the end itself must be appropriate and legitimate, before an act can be held to be valid which interferes with the general right of an individual to be free in his person and in his power to contract in relation to his own labor.

In his famous and oft-quoted dissent, Justice Oliver Wendell Holmes argued that a new constitutional right was being invented and that a particular economic theory was being advanced by the Court against the legislature's wishes. As Homes noted, "[A] constitution is not intended to embody a particular economic theory, whether of paternalism…or of laissez faire."

1908 – *Muller v. Oregon* (208 U.S. 412). By a vote of 9 to 0, the Court upheld an Oregon statute regulating the maximum number of hours per week that women could work in factories and laundries. The *Muller* decision cast doubt on the *Lochner* paradigm of protection of liberty of contract and marked an early departure from substantive due process jurisprudence by the courts. The Court justified this move away from *Lochner* by arguing that women deserved special consideration and protection in the workplace.

APPENDIX III: Chronology and Summary

1908 – *Adair* v. *United States* (208 U.S. 161). By a vote of 7 to 2, the Court struck down a federal law (the Erdman Act of 1898) that prohibited "yellow dog contracts." Yellow dog contracts were contracts drawn up by employers that required employees to agree not to join a union while employed with the company. As in *Lochner*, the Court held that the statute interfered with the substantive due process protections of the Fifth and Fourteenth Amendments since "it arbitrarily sanctions an illegal invasion of the personal liberty as well as the right of property of the defendant." The Court further held that such regulation could not be upheld under Congress's Commerce Clause power since there was no logical connection between union membership and interstate commerce. As Justice Harlan argued for the Court:

> [A]ny rule prescribed for the conduct of interstate commerce, in order to be within the competency of Congress under its power to regulate commerce among the states, must have some real or substantial relation to or connection with the commerce regulated. But what possible legal or logical connection is there between an employee's membership in a labor organization and the carrying on of interstate commerce?

1914 – *Shreveport Rate Case* (234 U.S. 342). By a vote of 7 to 2, the Court held that the Interstate Commerce Commission had the right to set *intra*state railroad rates for a carrier that also engaged in *inter*state commerce over interstate routes. Justice Charles Evans Hughes argued for the Court that:

> [Congress's] authority, extending to these interstate carriers as instruments of interstate commerce, necessarily embraces the right to control their operations in all matters having such a close and substantial relation to interstate traffic that the control is essential or appropriate to the security of that traffic, to the efficiency of the interstate service, and to the maintenance of conditions under which interstate commerce may be conducted upon fair terms and without molestation or hindrance.... Wherever the interstate and intrastate transactions of carriers are so related that the government of the one involves the control of the other, it is Congress, and not the state, that is entitled to prescribe the

The Delicate Balance

> final and dominant rule, for otherwise Congress would be denied the exercise of its constitutional authority, and the state, and not the nation, would be supreme within the national field.

While *Shreveport* can be and has been used to justify federal regulatory activity, its effect on economic freedom remains unclear since it can be cited as justification for federal actions that restrict or prohibit discriminatory state activities or negatively burden interstate commerce.

1915 – *Coppage* v. *Kansas* (236 U.S. 1). By a vote of 6 to 3, the Court struck down a Kansas statute prohibiting yellow dog contracts. Borrowing the logic of *Adair* v. *U.S.*, which struck down a federal effort to regulate yellow dog contracts between employers and employees, the Court held that the Kansas statute was an unconstitutional restriction of the freedom of contract. Once again, the due process protections of the Fifth and Fourteenth Amendments were cited as justification for holding the statute unconstitutional.

1918 – *Hammer* v. *Dagenhart* (247 U.S. 251). By a vote of 5 to 4, the Court struck down a federal child labor law that attempted to ban the interstate transportation of goods that may have been manufactured using child labor. Also known as the "child labor case," *Hammer* v. *Dagenhart* revived the manufacturing–commerce distinction first established in *U.S.* v. *E. C. Knight Co.* to strike down the federal statute as an unwarranted intrusion on the rights of the states. As Justice William Rufus Day argued for the Court:

> The grant of power of Congress over the subject of interstate commerce was to enable it to regulate commerce, and not to give it authority to control the states in the exercise of the police power over local trade and manufacture. The grant of authority over a purely federal matter was not intended to destroy the local powers always existing and carefully reserved to the states in the Tenth Amendment to the Constitution. Police regulations relating to the internal trade and affairs of the states have been uniformly recognized as within such control.

1922 – *Stafford* v. *Wallace* (258 U.S. 495). The Court upheld a federal statute (the Packers and Stockyards Act of 1921) regulating supposed unfair business practices in the wholesale meat market. Despite the *intra*state nature of the meat packing industry, the Court upheld Congress's right to regulate the industry since such activities were part of the flow of *inter*state commerce. Lifting language from its previous decision in *Swift & Co. v. United States*, the Court likewise argued that the *intra*state facilities in question were integral to the flow or stream of *inter*state commerce and that Congress consequently could exercise its Commerce Power to regulate accordingly.

1923 – *Adkins v. Children's Hospital* **(261 U.S. 525).** By a vote of 5 to 3, the Court struck down a federal statute that attempted to impose a minimum wage for women in the District of Columbia. In *Adkins*, the Court returned to the logic of *Lochner* and even went so far as to abandon special distinctions or consideration for women, such as those found in *Muller v. Oregon*. Justice George Sutherland argued for the majority that "There is, of course, no such thing as absolute freedom of contract. It is subject to a great variety of restraints. But freedom of contract is, nonetheless, the general rule and restraint the exception, and the exercise of legislative authority to abridge it can be justified only by the existence of exceptional circumstances."

1932 – *New State Ice Co. v. Liebmann* **(285 U.S. 262).** By a vote of 6 to 2, the Court struck down an Oklahoma statute that attempted to regulate the ice industry as a public utility under the *Munn v. Illinois* public interest rationale. The Court's decision in *New State Ice Co.* did not overrule *Munn*, however. It only added murkiness to the Court's ongoing articulation of what constituted legitimate regulation of businesses that were "clothed with the public interest." Nevertheless, *New State Ice Co.* did provide a passionate defense of Fourteenth Amendment rights to engage in private business free of unnecessary state impediments. As Justice George Sutherland argued for the majority:

> The principle is imbedded in our constitutional system that there are certain essentials of liberty with which the state is not entitled to dispense in the interest of experiments.... [A] regulation which has the effect of denying or unreasonably curtailing the common right to engage in a lawful private business...cannot be upheld consistent with the Fourteenth Amendment.

1934 – *Nebbia v. New York* **(291 U.S. 502).** By a vote of 5 to 4, the Court upheld the constitutionality of a New York statute that fixed the minimum prices for milk throughout the state. In

Nebbia, the emerging New Deal Court began to abandon substantive due process jurisprudence by denying that milk producers could claim protection from such economic regulation under the Fourteenth Amendment. As Justice Owen Roberts argued for the majority:

> So far as the requirement of due process is concerned, and in the absence of other constitutional restriction, a state is free to adopt whatever economic policy may reasonably be deemed to promote public welfare, and to enforce that policy by legislation adopted to its purpose. The courts are without authority either to declare such a policy, or, when it is declared by the legislature, to override it.

1935 – *Baldwin v. G.A.F. Seelig, Inc.* (294 U.S. 511). In *Baldwin*, the Court struck down a New York statute that attempted to establish the prices for milk imported from Vermont and other states in order to protect New York milk producers. "New York has no power to project its legislation into Vermont by regulating the price to be paid in that state for milk acquired there," the Court noted. Moreover, "New York is equally without power to prohibit the introduction within their territory of milk of wholesome quality acquired in Vermont, whether at high prices or low ones." In summary, the Court argued that "Nice distinctions have been made at times between direct and indirect burdens. They are irrelevant when the avowed purpose of the obstruction, as well as its necessary tendency, is to suppress or mitigate the consequences of competition between the states."

1935 – *A.L.A. Schechter Poultry Corp. v. United States* (295 U.S. 495). By a vote of 9 to 0, the Court ruled that President Roosevelt's National Industrial Recovery Act was unconstitutional. Thought of as the centerpiece of FDR's New Deal economic recovery program, the NIRA spawned a complex array of "industrial codes"—roughly 750 within two years of the Act's passage—that regulated a wide range of business and trade practices including work hours, wages, prices, and labor practices. The government defended these corporatist efforts on the grounds that the Great Depression constituted a national economic emergency or crisis that justified such radical federal intervention into the affairs of industry.

The Court rejected the government's reasoning and struck down the NIRA as unconstitutional because (1) the Act was based on a loose reading of the Commerce Clause and the General Welfare Clause and (2) it represented an unconstitutional delegation of lawmaking authority from the legislative branch to the executive branch. Also known as the "sick chicken case," *Schechter* represented one of the Court's last efforts to strike down New Deal programs and large national programs in general on either of these two grounds.

1936 – *Carter* **v.** *Carter Coal Co.* **(298 U.S. 238).** By a vote of 5 to 4, the Court held unconstitutional the Bituminous Coal Conservation Act of 1935, which was intended to regulate business practices, wages, prices, and labor activities in the coal industry. In what was to become its last great effort to draw a firm distinction between direct and indirect interstate commerce, the Court argued that the process of mining and producing coal was a purely intrastate activity that did not have any direct effect on interstate commerce. Furthermore, whatever incidental indirect effects the production of coal within a given locale might have on interstate commerce were held not to justify the sort of federal intervention under the Commerce Clause envisioned in the Coal Conservation Act.

As part of his critique of the Act, Justice George Sutherland provided a lengthy and passionate defense of federalism and the Tenth Amendment that stands as a classic statement of the need for strict textual construction of the Founders' constitutional vision of federalism:

> Every journey to a forbidden end begins with the first step; and the danger of such a step by the federal government in the direction of taking over the powers of the states is that the end of the journey may find the states so despoiled of their powers, or—what may amount to the same thing—so relieved of the responsibilities which possession of the powers necessarily enjoins, as to reduce them to little more than geographical subdivisions of the national domain. It is safe to say that if, when the Constitution was under consideration, it had been thought that any such danger lurked behind its plain words, it would never have been ratified.

The *Carter* decision, in conjunction with *Schechter* the previous year, gave rise to President Roosevelt's court-packing effort to expand the number of judges on the Court so that he could appoint justices favorable to his ideological vision of national corporatism. Although this effort ultimately failed, it encouraged many of the justices to step down, allowing FDR's vision to become reality as the Court abandoned or disregarded any serious constitutional constraints on federal intervention in subsequent cases.

1937 – *West Coast Hotel Co. v. Parrish* **(300 U.S. 379).** By a vote of 5 to 4, the Court upheld a Washington State law which established minimum wage regulations for women. In *West Coast Hotel*, the Court overruled *Adkins v. Children's Hospital* and held that, since the Constitution did not contain explicit literal protections for freedom of contract, government restriction of or interference with the right to contract freely was not unconstitutional.

1937 – *N.L.R.B. v. Jones & Laughlin Steel Co.* **(301 U.S. 1).** By a vote of 5 to 4, the Court upheld the constitutionality of the National Labor Relations Act, which guaranteed the right of workers to organize into unions at their place of work and enter into collective bargaining with their employers. *N.L.R.B. v. Jones & Laughlin* was a watershed moment in constitutional interpretation because it represented the first of many victories for President Franklin Roosevelt and his supporters, who called for a broad or loose reading of the Constitution to justify a generous expansion of federal involvement in the economy. Specifically, it dispensed with any notion that freedom of contract between employers and employees was a two-way street that should be free of government intervention or interference. Equally important, the decision signaled the complete abandonment of traditional efforts to gauge the interstate nature of the commerce in question and held instead that Congress could regulate virtually any intrastate activity that remotely affected interstate commerce.

1938 – *South Carolina State Highway Department v. Barnwell* **(303 U.S. 177).** The Court upheld a South Carolina statute regulating the width and weight of trucks on the state's highways even though the policy had an incidental effect on interstate commerce. The Court's reasoning was summarized by Justice Harlan Fiske Stone:

> [S]o long as the state action does not discriminate, the burden is one which the Constitution permits because it is an inseparable incident of the exercise of legislative authority, which, under the Constitution, has been left to the states. Congress, in the exercise of its plenary

power to regulate interstate commerce, may determine whether the burdens imposed on it by state regulation, otherwise permissible, are too great, and may, by legislation designed to secure uniformity or in other respects to protect the national interest in the commerce, curtail to some extent the state's regulatory power. But that is a legislative, not a judicial function, to be performed in the light of congressional judgment of what is appropriate regulation of interstate commerce, and the extent to which, in that field, state power and local interests should be required to yield to the national authority and interest.

1941 – *U.S. v. Darby* (312 U.S. 100). By a vote of 9 to 0, the Court held that the Fair Labor Standards Act of 1938 was constitutional. The FLSA established a system of minimum wage standards and maximum hour restrictions on industries and businesses whose goods entered the stream of interstate commerce. In order to rule the Act constitutional, the Court in *Darby* was forced to overrule *Hammer v. Dagenhart* and abandon the distinction made in that case between manufacturing and commerce. The new and significantly broader *Darby* standard was as follows:

> The power of Congress over interstate commerce is not confined to the regulation of commerce among the states. It extends to those activities intrastate which so affect interstate commerce or the exercise of the power of Congress over it as to make regulation of them appropriate means to the attainment of a legitimate end, the exercise of the granted power of Congress to regulate interstate commerce.

1942 – *Wickard v. Filburn* (317 U.S. 111). By a vote of 9 to 0, the Court upheld the constitutionality of the Agricultural Adjustment Act of 1938, which, among other things, established production quotas for agricultural output on individual farms. In *Wickard*, the Court went so far as to argue that wheat grown on a farm for personal consumption, and never intended to enter the stream of interstate commerce or even local commerce, could still be regulated by federal officials under the Commerce Clause. "[E]ven if [the] activity be local and though it may not be regarded as commerce," the Court argued, "it may still, whatever its nature, be reached by Congress if it exerts a substantial economic effect on interstate commerce and this irrespective of whether such effect is what might at some earlier time have been defined as 'direct' or indirect'." The Court essentially continued the line of reasoning found in *Darby* and went even further to abandon any type of substantive test or restriction on Congress's ability to regulate intrastate or parochial affairs. Thus, *Wickard* is a landmark decision because it de-legitimized both the "direct versus indirect" test and the "manufacturing versus commerce" distinction.

1945 – *Southern Pacific Co. v. Arizona* **(325 U.S. 761).** This decision involves a classic balancing case that required the Court to weigh the state's authority to exercise police power functions against the adverse effects such regulations might have on interstate commerce. In *Southern Pacific*, the Court held that the Arizona Train Limit Law of 1912 was unconstitutional because it demanded that the lengths of passenger and freight trains be substantially shorter than what was considered the national norm. Since the overwhelming volume of train traffic in Arizona was interstate in nature, and because the Court could find no overriding police power justification for such regulations, the Arizona statute was held to be an impermissible burden on interstate commerce.

1949 – *H. P. Hood & Sons, Inc. v. DuMond* **(336 U.S. 525).** This was another balancing case in which the Court held that it was unconstitutional for the New York Commission of Agriculture to deny an out-of-state milk producer a license to market milk in the state without a sound police power rationale for doing so. "The distinction between the power of the State to shelter its people from menaces to their health or safety and from fraud," Justice Robert H. Jackson noted for the Court, "even when those dangers emanate from interstate commerce, and its lack of power to retard, burden or constrict the flow of such commerce for their economic advantage, is one deeply rooted in both our history and our law." As part of a long and eloquent commentary on the nature of America's open market philosophy on internal trade, Jackson summarized that:

> Our system, fostered by the Commerce Clause, is that every farmer and every craftsman shall be encourage to produce by the certainty that he will have free access to every market in the Nation, that no home embargoes will withhold his exports, and no foreign state will by customs

APPENDIX III: Chronology and Summary

duties or regulations exclude them. Likewise, every consumer may look to the free competition from every producing area in the Nation to protect him from exploitation by any. Such was the vision of the Founders, such has been the doctrine of this Court which has given it reality.

1951 – *Dean Milk Co. v. City of Madison* (340 U.S. 349). In yet another balancing case, the Court struck down an ordinance passed by the city of Madison, Wisconsin, that prohibited all milk sales in the city unless the milk was produced at a municipally approved pasteurization plant within five miles of the city. "Even in the exercise of its unquestioned power to protect the health and safety of its people," the Court noted, "a municipality may not erect an economic barrier protecting a major local industry against competition from without the state, if reasonable nondiscriminatory alternatives, adequate to conserve legitimate local interests, are available." In other words, while state or local governments have the right to enforce their own unique health and safety standards through their police powers, they may not do so in a way that unduly burdens consumers or customers in other states attempting to engage in interstate commercial activity.

1959 – *Bibb v. Navajo Freight Lines, Inc.* (359 U.S. 520). In *Bibb*, another balancing case involving transportation regulation, the Court ruled unanimously that an Illinois law regulating the specifications of mudflaps or splash guards on trucks and trailers was unconstitutional. The Illinois regulation essentially required that, before entering the state, truck operators install mudflaps on their trucks that were unique, almost every other state having accepted the use of conventional or straight mudflaps. In effect, therefore, the Illinois standard, if upheld, would have become the *de facto* national standard. The Court ruled that, although it was implemented in an effort to protect public safety, the Illinois regulation posed such a substantial burden on interstate highway commerce and conflicted so completely with well-established national standards for this industry that it represented a constitutionally impermissible burden on interstate commerce.

1970 – *Pike v. Bruce Church* (397 U.S. 137). This decision involving another classic balancing case struck down an Arizona statute which required that Arizona cantaloupe producers package their produce at packing plants located within the state and in containers approved by the state which were marked as being from Arizona. The Court's conclusion, which is still controversial today, was that the statute posed an unreasonable restraint on interstate commerce in this sector and violated the spirit of the Commerce Clause in general. Perhaps the most famous balancing decision ever penned by the Court, *Pike* is noteworthy because it contains the following oft-repeated general rule:

> Where the statute regulates evenhandedly to effectuate a legitimate local public interest, and its effects on interstate commerce are only incidental, it will be upheld unless the burden imposed on such commerce is clearly excessive in relation to the putative local benefits. If a legitimate local purpose is found, then the question becomes one of degree. And the extent of the burden that will be tolerated will of course depend on the nature of the local interest involved, and on whether it could be promoted as well with a lesser impact on interstate activities.

1976 – *A&P Tea Co. v. Cottrell* (424 U.S. 366). In a unanimous decision, the Court struck down a Mississippi law which provided that milk from other states could be sold in Mississippi only if those states accepted Mississippi milk on a reciprocal basis. When a Louisiana milk producer was denied a permit to sell its milk in Mississippi simply because Louisiana officials had not negotiated a reciprocal agreement with Mississippi, the vendor sued Mississippi, arguing that the law unduly burdened interstate commerce and was therefore unconstitutional. The Court agreed, stressing the benefits of free and open trade among the states and denying Mississippi's contention that such a measure represented a justifiable exercise of its police power.

1976 – *National League of Cities v. Usery* (426 U.S. 833). By a vote of 5 to 4, the Court held that an effort by Congress to extend the application of minimum wage regulations under the Fair Labor Standards Act to employees of state and local governments constituted an unconstitutional intrusion on "traditional aspects of state sovereignty." In direct opposition to much previous post-New Deal jurisprudence on federalism matters, the Court cited the restrictions imposed on Congress by the Tenth Amendment and ruled that there exist constitutional limitations on congressional efforts to exercise authority

APPENDIX III: Chronology and Summary

over the "States as States." Justice William Rehnquist noted for the Court that:

> We have repeatedly recognized that there are attributes of sovereignty attaching to every state government which may not be impaired by Congress, not because Congress may lack an affirmative grant of legislative authority to reach the matter, but because the Constitution prohibits it from exercising the authority in that manner.

National League of Cities proved to be only a fleeting victory for states and localities, however, as the Court again reversed itself less than a decade later in *Garcia v. San Antonio Municipal Transit Authority*.

1977 – Hunt v. Washington Apple Advertising Commission (432 U.S. 333). In another balancing case involving agricultural trade, the Court held unconstitutional a North Carolina statute which required that any apples sold within the state had to be marked by USDA grade only and not be labeled as being of any other grade or quality (in this case, Washington State grades). Because North Carolina was the only state to impose such advertising or marketing restrictions, its regulatory requirements posed significant burdens on all out-of-state apple marketers who would have been forced to produce special packages or labels simply to market their products to consumers in North Carolina.

The Court held in *Hunt v. Washington Apple* that such a regulation was not a valid exercise of state or local police powers since the North Carolina law clearly discriminated against interstate commerce and "offer[ed] the North Carolina apple industry the very sort of protection against competing out-of-state producers that the Commerce Clause was designed to prohibit." The Court concluded by nothing that "When discrimination against commerce of the type we have found is demonstrated, the burden falls on the State to justify it both in terms of the local benefits flowing from the statute and the unavailability of nondiscriminatory alternatives adequate to preserve the local interests at stake."

1978 – Philadelphia v. New Jersey (437 U.S. 617). In a controversial balancing case involving the transportation and storage of solid or liquid waste, the Court struck down, as an unconstitutional burden on interstate commerce, a New Jersey law which prohibited the importation of such wastes from outside the state. The Court ruled that even the transportation and disposal of potentially harmful waste products could be considered "commerce" and therefore fall within the reach of the Commerce Clause when such products were shipped between states. Once the transportation and storage of waste from out-of-state vendors was accepted as interstate commerce, state efforts to prohibit such activity was found to be protectionist or discriminatory, and therefore unconstitutional. Significantly, the Court ruled that it did not matter whether New Jersey intended the statute to have such protectionist or discriminatory effects; the effects themselves were enough to justify striking down the law as unconstitutional. "[T]he evil of protectionism can reside in legislative means as well as legislative ends," the Court held.

1981 – Kassel v. *Consolidated Freightways Corp.* (450 U.S. 662). By a vote of 6 to 3, the Court held that an Iowa statute prohibiting trucks or trailers more than 60 feet in length from operating on the state's highways represented an impermissible burden on interstate commerce. Echoing its 1959 ruling in *Bibb v. Navajo Freight Lines, Inc.* regarding the regulation of truck and trailer mudflaps, the Court held in *Kassel* that while great deference should be given to state and local officials in regulating "matters traditionally of local concern," this must be tempered by a weighing of the importance of such parochial goals against other important constitutional principles. To that end, the Court held that "[T]he incantation of a purpose to promote the public health or safety does not insulate a state law from Commerce Clause attack. Regulations designed for that salutary purpose nevertheless may further the purpose so marginally, and interfere with commerce so substantially, as to be invalid under the Commerce Clause."

1985 – *Garcia v. San Antonio Metro. Transit Authority* (469 U.S. 528). By a vote of 5 to 4, the Court overturned *National League of Cities v. Usery* by holding that the minimum wage and maximum hour regulations of the Fair Labor Standards Act were applicable to state and local government employees. *Garcia* represented the logical culmination of the Court's post-New Deal federalism jurisprudence since it represented a complete abandonment of any judicial check on national power relative to the states. Instead, the majority argued that federalism and the interests of the states were protected better by Congress and the national electoral system instead of the Tenth Amendment and other constitutional restrictions on federal power.

APPENDIX III: Chronology and Summary

1991 – *Gregory v. Ashcroft* (501 U.S. 452). In another federalism case dealing with the reach of congressional powers over traditional state functions, the Court returned to the logic of *National League of Cities* v. *Usery* by arguing that certain aspects of state autonomy or sovereignty were inviolable. Specifically, the Court ruled in *Gregory* that the Age Discrimination in Employment Act of 1967 did not cover state and locally elected judges who might be subject to mandatory retirement laws. Justice Sandra Day O'Connor used *Gregory* to revive and provide a passionate defense of the more traditional understanding of federalism, limited federal authority, and separation of powers that the Court had rejected in *Garcia v. San Antonio*.

1992 – *New York v. United States* (505 U.S. 144). In a complex case, the Court ruled that elements of the Low-Level Radioactive Waste Policy Amendments of 1985 represented an unconstitutional intrusion by the federal government into traditional state matters. The Court held that "even where Congress has the authority under the Constitution to pass laws requiring or prohibiting certain acts, it lacks the power directly to compel the States to require of prohibit those acts." Justice Sandra Day O'Connor went further, noting that the "States are not mere political subdivisions of the United States. State governments are neither regional offices nor administrative agencies of the Federal Government. The positions occupied by state officials appear nowhere on the Federal Government's most detailed organizational chart."

1994 – *West Lynn Creamery v. Healy* (512 U.S. 186). By a vote of 7 to 2, the Court struck down a Massachusetts law requiring out-of-state milk producers to pay a special assessment to the state which was then distributed to in-state dairy farmers as a subsidy. "[T]he purpose and effect of the pricing order are to divert market share to Massachusetts dairy farmers. This diversion necessarily injures the dairy farmers in neighboring States," the Court held. The Court ruled that the Massachusetts statute was discriminatory and protectionist in both intent and effect, and thus a clear violation of the Commerce Clause.

1995 – *U.S. v. Lopez* (U.S. 93–1260). In what quickly came to be considered one of the Court's most important federalism cases since the New Deal, *Lopez* expanded on the line of reasoning contained in *Gregory v. Ashcroft* and *New York v. United States* by holding that the Gun-Free School Zones Act of 1990 represented an unconstitutional federal intrusion within a field traditionally regulated at the state or local level. More important,

The Delicate Balance

the Court provided a strict reading of "interstate commerce" and noted that the issue at hand—regulation of handguns within school zones—could not be considered commerce in any sense of the word, and therefore was beyond the reach of the Commerce Clause. *Lopez*, however, stopped short of overruling previous Court decisions that had opened the door for such a loose interpretation of the Commerce Clause.

1997 – *Printz* v. *United States* (U.S. 95–1478). In a logical extension of the *Lopez* decision, the Court ruled in *Printz* that the Brady Handgun Violence Prevention Act of 1993 was unconstitutional because it commanded state and local officials to carry out a federal regulatory program—in this case, background checks prior to gun purchases. The Court reiterated its judgment in *New York* v. *United States* by noting that:

> The Federal Government may neither issue directives requiring the States to address particular problems, nor command the States' officers, or those of their political subdivisions, to administer or enforce a federal regulatory program. It matters not whether policymaking is involved, and no case by case weighing of the burdens or benefits is necessary; such commands are fundamentally incompatible with our constitutional system of dual sovereignty.

APPENDIX IV
EXECUTIVE ORDER 12612
ON "FEDERALISM"

October 26, 1987

By the authority vested in me as President by the Constitution and laws of the United States of America, and in order to restore the division of government responsibilities between the national government and the States that was intended by the Framers of the Constitution and to ensure that the principles of federalism established by the Framers guide the Executive departments and agencies in the formulation and implementation of policies, it is hereby ordered as follows:

Section 1: *Definitions*. For purposes of this Order:

(a) "Policies that have federalism implications" refers to regulations, legislative comments or proposed legislation, and other policy statements or actions that have substantial direct effects on the States, on the relationship between the national government and the States, or on the distribution of power and responsibilities among the various levels of government.

(b) "State" or "States" refer to the States of the United States of America, individually or collectively, and where relevant, to State governments, including units of local government and other political subdivisions established by the States.

Section 2: *Fundamental Federalism Principles*. In formulating and implementing policies that have federalism implications, Executive departments and agencies shall be guided by the following fundamental federalism principles:

(a) Federalism is rooted in the knowledge that our political liberties are best assured by limiting the size and scope of the national government.

(b) The people and the States created the national government when they delegated to it those enumerated governmental powers relating to matters beyond the competence of the individual States. All other sovereign powers, save those expressly prohibited the States by the Constitution, are reserved to the States or to the people.

(c) The constitutional relationship among sovereign governments, State and national, is formalized in and protected by the Tenth Amendment to the Constitution.

(d) The people of the States are free, subject only to restrictions in the Constitution itself or in constitutionally authorized Acts of Congress, to define the moral, political, and legal character of their lives.

(e) In most areas of government concern, the States uniquely possess the constitutional authority, the resources, and the competence to discern the sentiments of the people, and to govern accordingly. In Thomas Jefferson's words, the States are "the most competent administrations for our domestic concerns and the surest bulwarks against antirepublican tendencies."

(f) The nature of our constitutional system encourages a healthy diversity in the public policies adopted by the people of the several States according to their own conditions, needs, and desires. In the search for enlightened public policy, individual States and communities are free to experiment with a variety of approaches to public issues.

(g) Acts of the national government—whether legislative, executive, or judicial in nature—that exceed the enumerated powers of that government under the Constitution violate the principle of federalism established by the Framers.

(h) Policies of the national government should recognize the responsibility of—and should encourage opportunities for—individuals, families, neighborhoods, local governments, and private associations to achieve their personal, social, and economic objectives through cooperative effort.

(i) In the absence of clear constitutional or statutory authority, the presumption of sovereignty should rest with the individual States. Uncertainties regarding the legitimate authority of the national government should be resolved against regulation at the national level.

Section 3: *Federalism Policymaking Criteria.* In addition to the fundamental federalism principles set forth in section 2, Executive departments and agencies shall adhere, to the extent permitted by law, to the following criteria when formulating and implementing policies that have federalism implications:

(a) There should be strict adherence to constitutional principles. Executive departments and agencies should closely examine the constitutional and statutory authority supporting any Federal action that would limit the policymaking discretion of the States, and should carefully assess the necessity for such action. To the extent

APPENDIX IV: Executive Order 12612 on "Federalism"

practicable, the States should be consulted before any such action is implemented. Executive Order No. 12372 ("Intergovernmental Review of Federal Programs") remains in effect for the programs and activities to which it is applicable.

(b) Federal action limiting the policymaking discretion of the States should be taken only where constitutional authority for the action is clear and certain and the national activity is necessitated by the presence of a problem of national scope. For purposes of this Order:

> (1) It is important to recognize the distinction between problems of national scope (which may justify Federal action) and problems that are merely common to the States (which will not justify Federal action because individual States, acting individually or together, can effectively deal with them).
>
> (2) Constitutional authority for federal action is clear and certain only when authority for the action may be found in a specific provision of the Constitution, there is no provision in the Constitution prohibiting Federal action, and the action does not encroach upon authority reserved to the States.

(c) With respect to national policies administered by the States, the national government should grant the States the maximum administrative discretion possible. Intrusive, Federal oversight of State administration is neither necessary or desirable.

(d) When undertaking to formulate and implement policies that have federalism implications, Executive departments and agencies shall:

> (1) Encourage States to develop their own policies to achieve program objectives and to work with appropriate officials in other States.
>
> (2) Refrain, to the maximum extent possible, from establishing uniform, national standards for programs and, when possible, defer to the States to establish standards.
>
> (3) When national standards are required, consult with appropriate officials and organizations representing the States in developing those standards.

Section 4: *Special Requirements for Preemption.*

(a) To the extent permitted by law, Executive departments and agencies shall construe, in regulations and otherwise, a Federal statute to preempt State law only when the statute contains an express preemption provision or there is some other firm and palpable evidence compelling the conclusion that the Congress intended preemption of State law, or when the exercise of State authority directly conflicts with the exercise of Federal authority under the Federal statute.

(b) Where a federal statute does not preempt State law (as addressed in subsection (a) of this section), Executive departments and agencies shall construe any authorization in the statute for the issuance of regulations as authorizing preemption of State law by rule-making only when the statute expressly authorizes issuance of preemptive regulations or there is some other firm and palpable evidence compelling the conclusion that the Congress intended to delegate to the department or agency the authority to issue regulations preempting State law.

(c) Any regulatory preemption of State law shall be restricted to the minimum level necessary to achieve the objectives of the statute pursuant to which the regulations are promulgated.

(d) As soon as an Executive department or agency foresees the possibility of a conflict between State law and Federally protected interests within its area of regulatory responsibility, the department or agency shall consult, to the extent practicable, with appropriate officials and organizations representing the States in an effort to avoid such a conflict.

(e) When an Executive department or agency proposes to act through adjudication or rule-making to preempt State law, the department or agency shall provide all affected States notice and an opportunity for appropriate participation in the proceedings.

Section 5: *Special Requirements for Legislative Proposals.* Executive departments and agencies shall not submit to the Congress legislation that would:

(a) Directly regulate the States in ways that would interfere with functions essential to the States' separate and independent existence or operate to directly displace the States' freedom to structure integral operations in areas of traditional government functions;

(b) Attach to Federal grants conditions that are not directly related to the purpose of the grant; or,

(c) Preempt State law, unless preemption is consistent with the fundamental federalism principles set forth in section 2, and unless a clearly legitimate national purpose, consistent with the federalism policymaking criteria set forth in section 3, cannot otherwise be met.

APPENDIX IV: Executive Order 12612 on "Federalism"

Section 6: *Agency Implementation.*

(a) The head of each Executive department and agency shall designate an official to be responsible for ensuring the implementation of this Order.

(b) In addition to whatever other actions the designated official may take to ensure implementation of this Order, the designated official shall determine which proposed policies have sufficient federalism implications to warrant the preparation of a Federalism Assessment. With respect to each such policy for which an affirmative determination is made, a Federalism Assessment, as described in subsection (c) of this section, shall be prepared. The department or agency head shall consider any such Assessment in all decisions involved in promulgating and implementing the policy.

(c) Each Federalism Assessment shall accompany any submission concerning the policy that is made to the Office of Management and Budget pursuant to Executive Order No. 12291 or OMB Circular No. A-19, and shall:

- (1) Contain the designated official's certification that the policy has been assessed in light of the principles, criteria, and requirements stated in sections 2 through 5 of this Order;
- (2) Identify any provision or element of the policy that is inconsistent with the principles, criteria, and requirements stated in sections 2 through 5 of this Order;
- (3) Identify the extent to which the policy imposes additional costs or burdens on the States, including the likely source of funding for the States and the ability of the States to fulfill the purposes of the policy; and
- (4) Identify the extent to which the policy would affect the States' ability to discharge traditional State government functions, or other aspects of State sovereignty.

Section 7: *Government-wide Federalism Coordination and Review.*

(a) In implementing Executive Order Nos. 12291 and 12498 and OMB Circular No. A-19, the Office of Management and Budget, to the extent permitted by law and consistent with the provisions of those authorities, shall take action to ensure that the policies of the Executive departments and agencies are consistent with the principles, criteria, and requirements stated in sections 2 through 5 of this Order.

(b) In submissions to the Office of Management and Budget pursuant to Executive Order No. 12291 and OMB Circular No. A-19,

The Delicate Balance

Executive departments and agencies shall identify proposed regulatory and statutory provisions that have significant federalism implications and shall address any substantial federalism concerns. Where the departments or agencies deem it appropriate, substantial federalism concerns should also be addressed in notices of proposed rule-making and messages transmitting legislative proposals to Congress.

Section 8: *Judicial Review.* This Order is intended only to improve the internal management of the Executive branch, and is not intended to create any right or benefit, substantive or procedural, enforceable at law by a party against the United States, its agencies, its officers, or any person.

Ronald Reagan
The White House
October 26, 1987

APPENDIX V
EXECUTIVE ORDER 13083
ON "FEDERALISM"

May 14, 1998
(revoked August 5, 1998)

By the authority vested in me as President by the Constitution and the laws of the United States of America, and in order to guarantee the division of governmental responsibilities, embodied in the Constitution, between the Federal Government and the States that was intended by the Framers and application of those principles by the Executive departments and agencies in the formulation and implementation of policies, it is hereby ordered as follows:

Section 1: *Definitions.* For purposes of this order:

(a) "State" or "States" refer to the States of the United States of America, individually or collectively, and, where relevant, to State governments, including units of local government and other political subdivisions established by the States.

(b) "Policies that have federalism implications" refers to Federal regulations, proposed legislation, and other policy statements or actions that have substantial direct effects on the States or on the relationship, or the distribution of power and responsibilities, between the Federal Government and the States.

(c) "Agency" means any authority of the United States that is an "agency" under 44 U.S.C. 3502(1), other than those considered to be independent regulatory agencies, as defined in 44 U.S.C. 3502(5).

Section 2: *Fundamental Federalism Principles.* In formulating and implementing policies that have federalism implications, agencies shall be guided by the following fundamental federalism principles:

(a) The structure of government established by the Constitution is premised upon a system of checks and balances.

(b) The Constitution created a Federal Government of supreme, but limited, powers. The sovereign powers not granted to the Federal

The Delicate Balance

Government are reserved to the people or to the States, unless prohibited to the States by the Constitution.

(c) Federalism reflects the principle that dividing power between the Federal Government and the States serves to protect individual liberty. Preserving State authority provides an essential balance to the power of the Federal Government, while preserving the supremacy of Federal law provides an essential balance to the power of the States.

(d) The people of the States are at liberty, subject only to the limitations in the Constitution itself or in Federal law, to define the moral, political, and legal character of their lives.

(e) Our constitutional system encourages a healthy diversity in the public policies adopted by the people of the several States according to their own conditions, needs, and desires. States and local governments are often uniquely situated to discern the sentiments of the people and to govern accordingly.

(f) Effective public policy is often achieved when there is competition among the several States in the fashioning of different approaches to public policy issues. The search for enlightened public policy is often furthered when individual States and local governments are free to experiment with a variety of approaches to public issues. Uniform, national approaches to public policy problems can inhibit the creation of effective solutions to those problems.

(g) Policies of the Federal Government should recognize the responsibility of—and should encourage opportunities for—States, local governments, private associations, neighborhoods, families, and individuals to achieve personal, social, environmental, and economic objectives through cooperative effort.

Section 3: *Federalism Policymaking Criteria.* In addition to adhering to the fundamental federalism principles set forth in section 2 of this order, agencies shall adhere, to the extent permitted by law, to the following criteria when formulating and implementing policies that have federalism implications:

(a) There should be strict adherence to constitutional principles. Agencies should closely examine the constitutional and statutory authority supporting any Federal action that would limit the policymaking discretion of States and local governments, and should carefully assess the necessity for such action.

(b) Agencies may limit the policymaking discretion of States and local governments only after determining that there is constitutional and legal authority for the action.

APPENDIX V: Executive Order 13083 on "Federalism"

(c) With respect to Federal statutes and regulations administered by States and local governments, the Federal Government should grant States and local governments the maximum administrative discretion possible. Any Federal oversight of such State and local administration should not unnecessarily intrude on State and local discretion.

(d) It is important to recognize the distinction between matters of national or multi-state scope (which may justify Federal action) and matters that are merely common to the States (which may not justify Federal action because individual States, acting individually or together, may effectively deal with them). Matters of national or multi-state scope that justify Federal action may arise in a variety of circumstances, including:

  (1) When the matter to be addressed by Federal action occurs interstate as opposed to being contained within one State's boundaries.

  (2) When the source of the matter to be addressed occurs in a State different from the State (or States) where a significant amount of the harm occurs.

  (3) When there is a need for uniform national standards.

  (4) When decentralization increases the costs of government thus imposing additional burdens on the taxpayer.

  (5) When States have not adequately protected individual rights and liberties.

  (6) When States would be reluctant to impose necessary regulations because of fears that regulated business activity will relocate to other States.

  (7) When placing regulatory authority at the State or local level would undermine regulatory goals because high costs or demands for specialized expertise will effectively place the regulatory matter beyond the resources of State authorities.

  (8) When the matter relates to Federally owned or managed property or natural resources, trust obligations, or international obligations.

  (9) When the matter to be regulated significantly or uniquely affects Indian tribal governments.

Section 4: *Consultation.*

(a) Each agency shall have an effective process to permit elected officials and other representatives of State and local governments to provide meaningful and timely input in the development of regulatory policies that have federalism implications.

(b) To the extent practicable and permitted by law, no agency shall promulgate any regulation that is not required by statute, that has federalism implications, and that imposes substantial direct compliance costs on States and local governments, unless:

(1) funds necessary to pay the direct costs incurred by the State or local government in complying with the regulation are provided by the Federal Government; or

(2) the agency, prior to the formal promulgation of the regulation,

(A) in a separately identified portion of the preamble to the regulation as it is to be issued in the Federal Register, provides to the Director of the Office of Management and Budget a description of the extent of the agency's prior consultation with representatives of affected States and local governments, a summary of the nature of their concerns, and the agency's position supporting the need to issue the regulation; and

(B) makes available to the Director of the Office of Management and Budget any written communications submitted to the agency by States or local governments.

Section 5: *Increasing Flexibility for State and Local Waivers.*

(a) Agencies shall review the processes under which States and local governments apply for waivers of statutory and regulatory requirements and take appropriate steps to streamline those processes.

(b) Each agency shall, to the extent practicable and permitted by law, consider any application by a State or local government for a waiver of statutory or regulatory requirements in connection with any program administered by that agency with a general view toward increasing opportunities for utilizing flexible policy approaches at the State or local level in cases in which the proposed waiver is consistent with applicable Federal policy objectives and is otherwise appropriate.

(c) Each agency shall, to the extent practicable and permitted by law, render a decision upon a complete application for a waiver within 120 days of receipt of such application by the agency. If the application for a waiver is not granted, the agency shall provide the applicant with timely written notice of the decision and the reasons therefore.

APPENDIX V: Executive Order 13083 on "Federalism"

(d) This section applies only to statutory or regulatory requirements that are discretionary and subject to waiver by the agency.

Section 6: *Independent Agencies.* Independent regulatory agencies are encouraged to comply with the provisions of this order.

Section 7: *General Provisions.*

(a) This order is intended only to improve the internal management of the executive branch and is not intended to, and does not, create any right or benefit, substantive or procedural, enforceable at law or equity by a party against the United States, its agencies or instrumentalities, its officers or employees, or any other person.

(b) This order shall supplement but not supersede the requirements contained in Executive Order 12866 ("Regulatory Planning and Review"), Executive Order 12988 ("Civil Justice Reform"), and OMB Circular A-19.

(c) Executive Order 12612 of October 26, 1987, and Executive Order 12875 of October 26, 1993, are revoked.

(d) The consultation and waiver provisions in sections 4 and 5 of this order shall complement the Executive order entitled, "Consultation and Coordination with Indian Tribal Governments," being issued on this day.

(e) This order shall be effective 90 days after the date of this order.

WILLIAM J. CLINTON
THE WHITE HOUSE,
May 14, 1998

SELECTED BIBLIOGRAPHY

Adams, John. "What Do We Mean by the American Revolution." February 13, 1818. In *An American Primer*, edited by Daniel J. Boorstin. New York, N.Y.: Meridian Classics, 1985.

Adler, Jonathan H. "The Green Aspects of *Printz*: The Revival of Federalism and Its Implications for Environmental Law." *George Mason Law Review*, Vol. 6, No. 3 (Spring 1998): 573–633.

American Legislative Exchange Council. *Sourcebook of American State Legislation 1995*, Vol. II (January 1995): 275–280.

Annett, Alex F. "How Congress Can End the 'Regulatory Limbo' Blocking Property Owners' Access to Justice." Heritage Foundation *F.Y.I.* No. 154, October 1, 1997.

———. "How Congress Can Enhance Property Owners' Access to Justice." Heritage Foundation *Executive Memorandum* No. 492, September 12, 1997.

———. "Justice Delayed Is Justice Denied: How Congress Can Increase Property Owners' Access to Justice." Heritage Foundation *F.Y.I.* No. 158, October 31, 1997.

Antonelli, Angela. "Needed: Aggressive Implementation of the Congressional Review Act." Heritage Foundation *F.Y.I.* No. 131, February 19, 1997.

———. "Promises Unfulfilled: Unfunded Mandates Reform Act of 1995." *Regulation*, No. 2 (1996): 46–54.

———. "Regulation: Demanding Accountability and Common Sense." In *Issues '98: The Candidate's Briefing Book*, edited by Stuart M. Butler and Kim R. Holmes. Washington, D.C.: The Heritage Foundation, 1998.

———— and Susan E. Dudley. "Congress and the Clinton OMB: Unwilling Partners in Regulatory Oversight?" *Regulation* (Fall 1997): 17–23.

"Are There Unenumerated Constitutional Rights?" The Seventh Annual National Federalist Society Symposium on Law and Public Policy, 1988. *Harvard Journal of Law and Public Policy*, Vol. 12, No. 1 (Winter 1989).

Arkes, Hadley. *Beyond the Constitution.* Princeton, N.J.: Princeton University Press, 1990.

————. *The Return of George Sutherland: Restoring a Jurisprudence of Natural Rights.* Princeton, N.J.: Princeton University Press, 1994.

Ashraf, Saba. "Virtual Taxation: State Taxation of Internet and On-Line Sales." *Florida State University Law Review*, Vol. 24, No. 3 (1997).

Barnett, Randy E., ed. *The Rights Retained by the People: The History and Meaning of the Ninth Amendment.* Fairfax, Va.: George Mason University Press, 1989.

Barry, John S. "Federalism and Financial Services." Heritage Foundation *Backgrounder* No. 1160, May 1, 1998.

Beales, J. Howard, and Timothy J. Muris. *State and Federal Regulation of National Advertising.* Washington, D.C.: The AEI Press, 1993.

Beer, Samuel H. *To Make a Nation: The Rediscovery of American Federalism.* Cambridge, Mass.: Harvard University Press, 1993.

Berger, Raoul. *Federalism: The Founders' Design.* Norman, Okla.: University of Oklahoma Press, 1987.

————. "Judicial Manipulation of the Commerce Clause." *Texas Law Review*, Vol. 74, Issue 4 (March 1996): 695–717.

Bernstein, David. "Equal Protection for Economic Liberty: Is the Court Ready?" Cato Institute *Policy Analysis*, October 5, 1992.

Black's Law Dictionary. Abridged 6th ed. St. Paul, Minn.: West Publishing Co., 1991.

Bolick, Clint. *Grassroots Tyranny: The Limits of Federalism.* Washington, D.C.: Cato Institute, 1993.

Boorstin, Daniel J., ed. *An American Primer.* New York, N.Y.: Meridian Classics, 1985.

Selected Bibliography

Bork, Robert H. "Federalism and Federal Regulation: The Case of Product Labeling." Washington Legal Foundation *Critical Legal Issues*, Working Paper Series No. 46, July 1991.

———. *The Tempting of America: The Political Seduction of the Law.* New York, N.Y.: Simon & Schuster, Inc., 1990.

Buchanan, James M. "Federalism and Individual Sovereignty." *The Cato Journal*, Vol. 15, Nos. 2–3 (Fall/Winter 1995/96).

Burk, Dan L. "How State Regulation of the Internet Violates the Commerce Clause." *The Cato Journal*, Vol. 17, No. 2 (Fall 1997): 147–161.

Burstein, Melvin L., and Arthur J. Rolnick. "Congress Should End the Economic War Among the States." *The Region*. Federal Reserve Bank of Minneapolis (March 1995).

Bush, President George. "Federalism Executive Order." Memorandum to the Heads of Executive Departments and Agencies, February 16, 1990.

Butler, Henry N., and Jonathan R. Macey. "Externalities and the Matching Principle: The Case for Reallocating Environmental Regulatory Authority." In *Yale Law & Public Policy Review / Yale Journal on Regulation*, Symposium Issue, "Constructing a New Federalism: Jurisdictional Competence and Competition," Vol. 14, No. 2 (March 1–2, 1996): 23–66.

Butler, Henry N., and Larry E. Ribstein. *The Corporation and the Constitution.* Washington, D.C.: The AEI Press, 1995.

Calabresi, Stephan G. "A Government of Limited and Enumerated Powers: In Defense of *United States* v. *Lopez*." *Michigan Law Review*, Vol. 94 (1995): 752–831.

Carroll, Stephan, Allan Abrahamse, and Mary Vaiana. *The Costs of Excess Medical Claims for Automobile Personal Injuries.* Santa Monica, Cal.: Rand Institute, 1995.

Carson, Clarence B. *A Basic History of the United States, Volume 2: The Beginning of the Republic 1775–1825.* Wadley, Ala.: American Textbook Committee, 1984. 6th ed., January 1991.

Chemerinsky, Erwin. "Rehabilitating Federalism." *Michigan Law Review*, Vol. 92, No. 6 (May 1994): 1333–1346.

Clinton, President William J. "Suspension of Executive Order 13083." White House Office of the Press Secretary, August 5, 1998.

———. Executive Order No. 13083, "Federalism," May 14, 1998. *Federal Register*, Vol. 63, No. 96 (May 19, 1998): 27651–27655.

Cole, Richard L., and Delbert A. Taebel. "The New Federalism: Promises, Programs, and Performance." *Publius: The Journal of Federalism*, Vol. 16, No. 1 (Winter 1986): 3–10.

Cooper, Charles J., and David H. Thompson. "The Tenth Amendment: The Promise of Liberty, Strategies to Restore the Balance of Power Between the Federal and State Governments." In American Legislative Exchange Council, *The State Factor*, Vol. 22, No. 7 (October 1996).

Crandall, Robert, and Jerry Ellig. *Economic Deregulation and Customer Choice: Lesson for the Electric Industry.* Fairfax, Va.: Center for Market Processes, 1997.

DeBow, Michael. "Codifying the Dormant Commerce Clause." *Public Interest Law Review*, Vol. 69 (1995): 69–86.

Detlefsen, Robert R. "Escaping the Tort-Based Auto Accident Compensation System: The Federal Auto Choice Reform Act of 1997." Citizens for a Sound Economy *Issue Analysis* No. 72, June 1, 1998.

Elkins, Stanley, and Eric McKitrick. *The Age of Federalism: The Early American Republic, 1788–1800.* New York, N.Y.: Oxford University Press, 1993.

Entman, Robert, and Charles Firestone. *The Communications Devolution: Federal, State, and Local Relations in Telecommunications Competition and Regulation.* Report of the Tenth Annual Aspen Institute Conference on Telecommunications Policy, Aspen, Colo., August 6–10, 1995.

Epstein, Richard A. "Constitutional Faith and the Commerce Clause." *Notre Dame Law Review*, Vol. 71, No. 1 (1995): 167–191.

———. "The Proper Scope of the Commerce Power." *Virginia Law Review*, Vol. 73, No. 8 (November 1987): 1387–1455.

———. *Takings: Private Property and the Power of Eminent Domain.* Cambridge, Mass.: Harvard University Press, 1985.

———. "Toward a Revitalization of the Contract Clause." *University of Chicago Law Review*, Vol. 51 (Summer 1984): 703–751.

Eskridge, William N., Jr., and John Ferejohn. "The Elastic Commerce Clause: A Political Theory of American Federalism." *Vanderbilt Law Review*, Vol. 47 (1994): 1355–1400.

Selected Bibliography

Farber, Daniel A., and Robert E. Hudec. "Free Trade and the Regulatory State: A GATT's Eye View of the Dormant Commerce Clause." *Vanderbilt Law Review*, Vol. 47 (1994): 1401–1440.

Ferejohn, John, and Barry R. Weingast. *The New Federalism: Can the States Be Trusted?* Stanford, Cal.: Hoover Institution Press, 1997.

Fiske, John. *The Critical Period of American History.* New York, N.Y.: Houghton Mifflin, 1888, 1916.

Forte, David F. "Conservatism and the Rehnquist Court." Heritage Foundation *Lecture* No. 438, June 12, 1992.

Friedman, Lawrence M. *A History of American Law.* 2nd ed. New York, N.Y.: Simon & Schuster, 1973, 1985.

Gavora, Carrie J. "Back to the Drawing Board: Why Tax Reform Is the Key to Health Care Reform." Heritage Foundation *Backgrounder* No. 1189, June 9, 1998.

Gellhorn, Ernest, and Richard J. Pierce, Jr. *Regulated Industries in a Nutshell.* St. Paul, Minn.: West Publishing Co., 1987.

Gingrich, Representative Newt, Representative Dick Armey, and the House Republicans. *Contract With America.* Washington, D.C.: Times Books, Random House, 1994.

Goldwin, Robert A., and William A. Schambra. *How Capitalistic Is the Constitution?* Washington, D.C.: American Enterprise Institute for Public Policy Research, 1982.

Graglia, Lino A. "The Supreme Court and the American Common Market." In *Regulation, Federalism, and Interstate Commerce*, edited by A. Dan Tarlock. Cambridge, Mass.: Oelgeschlager, Gunn & Hain Publishers, Inc., 1981.

Gray, C. Boyden. "Regulation and Federalism." *Yale Journal of Regulation*, Vol. 1, No. 1 (1983): 93–110.

Gunther, Gerald. *Constitutional Law.* 12th ed. Westbury, N.Y.: Foundation Press, Inc., 1991.

Hall, Kermit L., ed. *The Oxford Companion to the Supreme Court of the United States.* New York, N.Y.: Oxford University Press, 1992.

Hall, Kermit L., William M. Wiecek, and Paul Finkelman, eds. *American Legal History: Cases and Materials.* New York, N.Y.: Oxford University Press, 1996.

Hawkins, Robert B., Jr., ed. *American Federalism: A New Partnership for the Republic.* San Francisco, Cal.: Institute for Contemporary Studies, 1982.

Hellerstein, Walter. "Commerce Clause Restraints on State Tax Incentives." Paper published by the Federal Reserve Bank of Minneapolis for a conference on "The Economic War Among the States," Washington, D.C., May 21–22, 1996.

Higgs, Robert. *Crisis and Leviathan: Critical Episodes in the Growth of American Government*. San Francisco, Cal.: Pacific Research Institute for Public Policy, 1989.

Hodge, Scott A., ed. *Balancing America's Budget: Ending the Era of Big Government*. Washington, D.C.: The Heritage Foundation, 1997.

Hunter, Lawrence A., and Ronald J. Oakerson. "An Intellectual Crisis in American Federalism: The Meaning of *Garcia*." In *Federalism and the Constitution: A Symposium on Garcia*. Washington, D.C.: Advisory Commission on Intergovernmental Relations, July 1987.

Inman, Robert P., and Daniel L. Rubenfield. "Rethinking Federalism." *Journal of Economic Perspectives*, Vol. 11, No. 4 (Fall 1997): 43–64.

Is Constitutional Reform Necessary to Reinvigorate Federalism? Washington, D.C.: Advisory Commission on Intergovernmental Relations, M–154, November 1987.

Johnson, Paul. *A History of the American People*. New York, N.Y.: Harper Collins Publishers, 1997.

Kitch, Edmund W. "Regulation and the American Common Market." In *Regulation, Federalism, and Interstate Commerce*, edited by A. Dan Tarlock. Cambridge, Mass.: Oelgeschlager, Gunn & Hain Publishers, Inc., 1981.

Leboeuf, Jacques. "The Economics of Federalism and the Proper Scope of the Federal Commerce Power." *San Diego Law Review*, Vol. 31 (Summer 1994): 555–616.

Levy, Leonard W. *Essays on the Making of the Constitution*. 2nd ed. New York, N.Y.: Oxford University Press, 1969, 1987.

Liner, E. Blaine. *A Decade of Devolution: Perspectives on State–Local Relations*. Washington, D.C.: The Urban Institute Press, 1989.

Lowi, Theodore J. *The End of Liberalism: The Second Republic of the United States*. New York, N.Y.: W. W. Norton & Company, 1969, 1979.

Macedo, Stephan. *The New Right vs. The Constitution*. Washington, D.C.: Cato Institute, 1987.

Selected Bibliography

Maltz, Earl M. "Individual Rights and State Autonomy." *Harvard Journal of Law and Public Policy*, Vol. 12, No. 1 (Winter 1989).

McCarthy, David J. "Federalism and Electric Industry Restructuring: How to Stop the Trade War Here at Home." Presentation at The Heritage Foundation, February 27, 1998.

McLaughlin, Andrew. *A Constitutional History of the United States*. In *Essays on the Making of the Constitution*, edited by Leonard W. Levy. New York, N.Y.: Oxford University Press, 1969, 1987.

Meese, Edwin III. "Address Before the D.C. Chapter of the Federalist Society Lawyers Division," November 15, 1985. In *Report to the Attorney General, Original Meaning Jurisprudence: A Sourcebook*, March 12, 1987.

Merritt, Deborah Jones. "Commerce!" *Michigan Law Review*, Vol. 94, No. 3 (December 1995): 674–751.

———. "The Guarantee Clause and State Autonomy: Federalism for a Third Century." *Columbia Law Review*, Vol. 88 (January 1988): 1–78.

Miller, Dan. *Auto Choice: Impact on the Cities and the Poor*. Joint Economic Committee, U.S. Congress, March 1998.

———. *Auto Choice: Relief for Businesses & Consumers*. Joint Economic Committee, U.S. Congress, July 1998.

Miller, James III, Office of Management and Budget. "Implementation of Executive Order No. 12612, Federalism." Memorandum for the Heads of Executive Departments and Agencies, December 16, 1987.

Miniter, Richard. "Small Towns, Big Government." *The American Enterprise* (November/December 1997): 32–33.

Morley, Felix. *Freedom and Federalism*. Indianapolis, Ind.: Liberty Press, 1959.

Nelson, William E. *The Fourteenth Amendment: From Political Principle to Judicial Doctrine*. Cambridge, Mass.: Harvard University Press, 1988.

O'Connell, Jeffrey, Stephen Carroll, Michael Horowitz, Allan Abrahamse, and Daniel Kaiser. "The Costs of Consumer Choice for Auto Insurance in States Without No-Fault Insurance." *Maryland Law Review*, Vol. 54, No. 2 (1995): 281–351.

O'Connell, Jeffrey, Stephen Carroll, Michael Horowitz, and Allan Abrahamse. "Consumer Choice in the Auto Insurance Market." *Maryland Law Review*, Vol. 52, No. 4 (1993): 1016–1062.

Ogg, Frederic A., and P. Orman Ray. *Essentials of American Government*. 6th ed. New York, N.Y.: Appleton–Century–Crofts, Inc., 1932, 1950.

Ostrom, Vincent. *The Meaning of American Federalism: Constituting a Self-Governing Society*. San Francisco, Cal.: ICS Press, 1991.

Pierce, Richard J. "Regulation, Deregulation, Federalism, and Administrative Law: Agency Power to Preempt State Regulation." *University of Pittsburgh Law Review*, Vol. 46 (Spring 1995): 607–671.

———. *Regulation, Deregulation, Federalism and Administrative Law*. Report to the Administrative Conference of the United States, October 1984.

Pilon, Roger. "Freedom, Responsibility, and the Constitution: On Recovering Our Founding Principles." In David Boaz and Edward H. Crane, eds. *Market Liberalism: A Paradigm for the 21st Century*. Washington, D.C.: Cato Institute, 1993.

Powell, H. Jefferson. "Enumerated Means and Unlimited Ends." *Michigan Law Review*, Vol. 94, No. 3 (December 1995): 651–673.

Prentice, Ezra Parmalee, and John G. Egan. *The Commerce Clause of the Federal Constitution*. Chicago, Ill.: Callaghan and Company, 1898.

Presser, Stephan B. "Uniform Standards for Securities Fraud Suits Are Consistent With Federalism." Washington Legal Foundation *Legal Backgrounder*, Vol. 12, No. 38 (October 24, 1997).

Reagan, President Ronald. Executive Order No. 12612, "Federalism," October 26, 1987. *Federal Register*, Vol. 52, No. 210 (October 30, 1987): 41685–41688.

———. *First Inaugural Address*. Washington, D.C., January 20, 1981.

Redish, Martin H., and Shane V. Nugent, "The Dormant Commerce Clause and the Constitutional Balance of Federalism." *Duke Law Journal*, No. 4 (1987): 569–617.

Reed, Lawrence W. "Time to End the Economic War Between the States." *Regulation*, Vol. 19, No. 2 (1996): 35–43.

Regan, Donald H. "How to Think About the Federal Commerce Power and Incidentally Rewrite *United States v. Lopez*." *Michigan Law Review*, Vol. 94, No. 3 (December 1995): 554–614.

Selected Bibliography

———. "The Supreme Court and State Protectionism: Making Sense of the Dormant Commerce Clause." *Michigan Law Review*, Vol. 84 (1986): 1091–1287.

Reply Brief for Petitioner Indianapolis Power & Light Company. Petition for Review of the Order of the Pennsylvania Public Utility Commission Entered May 22, 1997 at Docket Nos. R–00973877, R–00973877C001, and R–00973877C0002, No. 1597 CD 1997.

Romano, Roberta. *The Genius of American Corporate Law.* Washington, D.C.: The AEI Press, 1993.

Rossiter, Clinton, ed. *The Federalist Papers.* New York, N.Y.: NAL Penguin, 1961.

Scalia, Antonin. *A Matter of Interpretation: Federal Courts and the Law.* Princeton, N.J.: Princeton University Press, 1997.

Scheiber, Harry N. *Federalism and the Judicial Mind: Essays on American Constitutional Law and Politics.* Berkeley, Cal.: Institute of Governmental Studies Press, 1992.

———. "Police Power." In *The Oxford Companion to the Supreme Court of the United States*, edited by Kermit L. Hall. New York, N.Y.: Oxford University Press, 1992.

Schmahmann, David, and James Finch. "The Unconstitutionality of State and Local Enactments in the United States Restricting Ties with Burma (Myanmar)." *Vanderbilt Journal of Transnational Law*, Vol. 30, No. 2 (March 1997): 175–207.

Schoenbrod, David. *Power Without Responsibility: How Congress Abuses the People Through Delegation.* New Haven, Conn.: Yale University Press, 1993.

——— and Jerry Taylor. "The Delegation of Legislative Powers." In *Cato Handbook for Congress, 105th Congress.* Washington, D.C.: Cato Institute, 1997.

Schram, Stanford F., and Carol S. Weissert. "The State of American Federalism: 1996–1997." *Publius: The Journal of Federalism*, Vol. 27, No. 2 (Spring 1997): 1–31.

Schriver, Melinda L., and Grace-Marie Arnett. "Uninsured Rates Rise Dramatically in States with Strictest Health Insurance Regulations." Heritage Foundation *Backgrounder* No. 1211, August 14, 1998.

Schuck, Peter H. "Introduction: Some Reflections on the Federalism Debate." In *Yale Law & Public Policy Review / Yale Journal on Regulation*, Symposium Issue, "Constructing a New Federalism:

Jurisdictional Competence and Competition," Vol. 14, No. 2 (March 1–2, 1996): 1–22.

Seay, Douglas, and Robert E. Moffit. "Transferring Functions to the States." In *Mandate for Leadership IV: Turning Ideas Into Actions*, edited by Stuart M. Butler and Kim R. Holmes. Washington, D.C.: The Heritage Foundation, 1997.

Seay, Douglas, and Wesley Smith. "Federalism." In *Issues '96: The Candidate's Briefing Book*, edited by Stuart M. Butler and Kim R. Holmes. Washington, D.C.: The Heritage Foundation, 1996.

The Securitization Swindle. A White Paper by IPALCO Enterprises, Inc., Indianapolis, Indiana, May 1997.

Shaviro, Daniel. *Federalism in Taxation: The Case for Greater Uniformity*. Washington, D.C.: The AEI Press, 1993.

Shenk, Joshua Wolf. "Washington's Counter-Devolutionaries." *U.S. News & World Report*, November 24, 1997.

Siegan, Bernard H. "The Economic Constitution in Historic Perspective." In *Constitutional Economics: Containing the Economic Powers of Government*, edited by Richard B. McKenzie. Lexington, Mass.: Lexington Books, 1984.

———. "Economic Liberties and the Constitution: Protection at the State Level." In *Economic Liberties and the Judiciary*, edited by James A. Dorn and Henry G. Manne. Washington, D.C.: Cato Institute, 1987.

———. *Land Use Without Zoning*. Lexington, Mass.: D. C. Heath, 1972.

The Status of Federalism in America: A Report of the Working Group on Federalism of the Domestic Policy Council, November 1986.

Tarlock, A. Dan, ed. *Regulation, Federalism, and Interstate Commerce*. Cambridge, Mass.: Oelgeschlager, Gunn & Hain Publishers, Inc., 1981.

Teske, Paul, ed. *American Regulatory Federalism and Telecommunications Infrastructure*. Hillsdale, N.J.: Lawrence Erlbaum Associates, 1995.

Thierer, Adam D. "A Five-Point Checklist for Successful Electricity Deregulation Legislation." Heritage Foundation *Backgrounder* No. 1169, April 13, 1998.

———. "Electricity Deregulation and Federalism: How Congress and the States Can Work Together to Deregulate Successfully." Heritage Foundation *Backgrounder* No. 1125, June 23, 1997.

Selected Bibliography

———. "Electricity Deregulation: Separating Fact from Fiction in the Debate over Stranded Cost Recovery." Heritage Foundation *Talking Points* No. 20, March 11, 1997.

———. "Federal Power Forward Creep." *The Washington Times*, July 28, 1998, A16.

———. "Not Too Late to Stop the Internet Tax Crusade." Heritage Foundation *Executive Memorandum* No. 520, April 3, 1998.

———. "President Clinton's Sellout of Federalism." Heritage Foundation *Executive Memorandum* No. 536, June 25, 1998.

———. "20th Anniversary of Airline Deregulation: Cause for Celebration, Not Re-Regulation." Heritage Foundation *Backgrounder* No. 1173, April 22, 1998.

———. "What's Next for Telecommunications Deregulation?" Heritage Foundation *Backgrounder* No. 1145, October 28, 1997.

———. "Why Congress Must Save the Internet from State and Local Taxation." Heritage Foundation *Executive Memorandum* No. 488, June 23, 1997.

Toft, Graham S. "Doing Battle over the Incentives War: Improve Accountability But Avoid Federal Noncompete Mandates." Paper published by the Federal Reserve Bank of Minneapolis for a conference on "The Economic War Among the States," Washington, D.C., May 21–22, 1996.

Viscusi, W. Kip. *Product-Risk Labeling: A Federal Responsibility*. Washington, D.C.: The AEI Press, 1993.

Wechsler, Herbert. "The Political Safeguards of Federalism: The Role of the States in the Composition and Selection of the National Government." *Columbia Law Review*, Vol. 54, No. 4 (April 1954): 543–560.

Williams, Jerre S. *Constitutional Law in a Nutshell*. St. Paul, Minn.: West Publishing Co., 1979.

Willkie, Wendell L. II, and Alden F. Abbott. "Who Should Regulate Business? Assessing the Federal–State Balance of Power." Washington Legal Foundation *Critical Legal Issues*, Working Paper Series No. 48, August 1992.

Wilson, Vincent, Jr. *The Book of the Founding Fathers*. Brookeville, Md.: American History Research Associates, 1974.

Wolfe, Christopher. "The Contemporary Supreme Court and Federalism: Symposium Discussion." In *Federalism and the Constitu-*

tion: A Symposium on Garcia. Washington, D.C.: Advisory Commission on Intergovernmental Relations, July 1987.

Wood, Gordon S. *The Radicalism of the American Revolution.* New York, N.Y.: Alfred A. Knopf, 1992.

Zimmerman, Joseph F. *Contemporary American Federalism: The Growth of National Power.* Westport, Conn.: Praeger Publishers, 1992.

———. *Interstate Relations: The Neglected Dimension of Federalism.* Westport, Conn.: Praeger Publishers, 1996.

INDEX

A

A&P Tea Co. v. Cottrell (1976), 198
Abbott, Alden F., 87, 88
Abrahamse, Allan, 94
Adair v. United States (1908), 188, 190
Adams, John, 145, 146
Addyston Pipe & Steel Co. v. United States (1899), 186
Adkins v. Children's Hospital (1923), 33, 70, 191, 194
Adler, Jonathan H., 118
Administrative Conference of the United States, 106
Advisory Commission on Intergovernmental Relations, 120
Age Discrimination in Employment Act of 1967, 201
agricultural activity, 105, 132
Agricultural Adjustment Act of 1938, 195
airlines, airline industry, airline deregulation, 1, 13, 94, 95, 103, 105, 113
A.L.A. Schechter Poultry Corp. v. United States (1935), 128, 192
alcoholic beverages, 181
Alex C. Walker Educational and Charitable Foundation, vi
Allgeyer v. Louisiana (1897), 33, 187
amendments to the Constitution (new), 21
American Legislative Exchange Council, 124, 131, 132
American Revolution, 145
    see also Founding Fathers
Annett, Alexander F., vi, 90
antitrust issues, 141
Antonelli, Angela, vi, 6, 127
apples, 199
Arizona, 110, 111, 196, 197
Arizona Train Limit Law of 1912, 196
Arkes, Hadley, 24, 61
Armey, Representative Richard (Dick), 93
Articles of Confederation, 2, 15, 16, 54, 56, 57, 59, 100
    text of, *see* Appendix I, 149–156
Ashraf, Saba, 115
"auto choice" proposals, 93, 94, 95, 116
    Auto Choice Reform Act, 93, 94

auto insurance industry, 83, 95, 105, 116
autonomy of the states, 4
    see also federalism, state-based protectionism, state government

B

balance of powers, ii, 12, 55, 96, 104, 107
    see also federalism
balanced budget amendment, 124
balancing cases, tests, 58, 64, 72, 75, 110, 111, 147, 196, 197, 198, 199
Baldwin v. G.A.F. Seelig, Inc. (1935), 107, 192
Bank of Augusta v. Earle (1839), 27
Bank Holding Company Act, 92
banking, 92
    see also financial services industry
bankruptcy, Bankruptcy Clause, 20, 49, 86, 88, 121, 122, 160
Barbier v. Connolly (1885), 69, 184
barriers to trade, 95, 99, 100, 109
    see also trade
Barry, John S., vi, 116, 141
Beef Trust, 187
Bendix Autolite Corp. v. Midwesco Enterprises (1988), 57, 58, 61
Berger, Raoul, 26, 36, 37, 50, 54, 99
Bernstein, David, 35
Bibb v. Navajo Freight Lines, Inc. (1959), 110, 111, 196, 200
Bill of Rights, 29, 30, 73, 147, 170
Bituminous Coal Conservation Act of 1935, 193
Blackmun, Justice Harry, 39, 56
block grants, 41, 45, 124
Bolick, Clint, 66, 67
Boorstin, Daniel J., 145
Bork, Judge Robert H., 51, 73, 76, 87, 88, 123, 141
Bradley, Judge Joseph P., 65
Brady Handgun Violence Prevention Act of 1993, 202
broad constructionism, broad constructionists, 3, 10, 11, 47, 48–51, 53, 62
    see also federalism
Brookings Institution, 113
Brownback, Senator Sam, 129, 130
Brown v. Maryland (1827), 25, 180
Burk, Dan L., 115
Burma (Myanmar), 85
Burstein, Melvin L., 135
Bush, President George, 41

Index

business incorporation standards, 131
Butler, Henry N., 117, 142
Butler, Justice Pierce, 36
Butler, Stuart M., vi, 55

C

Calabresi, Stephan, 8, 55, 67, 147
Calder v. Bull (1798), 179
California, 89
capitalism, capitalist marketplace, 23, 28, 50, 146
Carroll, Stephan, 94
Carson, Clarence B., 16
Carter Administration, 113
Carter v. Carter Coal Co. (1936), 193
Cato Institute, v, 9, 35, 50, 130
cellular telephone service, 102, 103, 112, 114
Center for Individual Rights, v
Center for Market Processes, 113
centralized government, iv, 49, 123
Champion v. Ames (1903), 187
Chase, Judge Samuel, 179
checks and balances, i, 36, 43, 52, 55, 68, 78, 98
Chicago, 130
child care, 122
child custody, 131
child labor laws, 190
Citizens Access to Justice Act, 7, 89
Citizens for a Sound Economy, 93
City of Boerne v. Flores (1997), 45
civil rights, 68, 69, 89
Clinton, President William J., i, 43, 44, 45, 125
    see also Executive Order 13083
clothing and apparel, 105
coal industry, 193
Code of Federal Regulations, 6
coinage / currency powers, 16, 20, 49, 153, 161
Cole, Richard L., 41
colonies, 145
    see also Founding Fathers
commerce, 26, 32, 81, 100, 146
    vs. manufacturing, 36, 106, 186, 187, 190, 195, 196
    see interstate commerce, trade
Commerce Clause, 14, 19, 24, 25, 26, 27, 28, 35, 37, 38, 39, 46, 50, 51, 54, 57, 59, 69, 81–82, 84, 85, 86–87, 90, 96–100, 106, 160, 180, 181, 184, 186, 187–188, 189, 192, 193, 198

    definition of, 19
    and Dormant Commerce Clause, 57, 58, 96
    and "indirect effects" test, 38, 39, 111, 193, 195
    purpose of, 99
commercial federalism, 24, 147
Committee on the Judiciary, 129
common law, 78
communications, 132
communities, 71–72
compensation, just, *see* just compensation
competition, *i*, 8, 146
    see also capitalism
computer industry, 105
Congress, 7, 9, 51, 57, 61, 85, 87, 90, 95, 97, 98, 99, 103, 109, 111, 119, 121, 125, 126, 190, 194, 198, 199, 200, 201, 149, 150, 151, 152, 153, 154, 155, 156
    and agency oversight, 91
    and anti-delegation legislation, 128–130
    and the Congressional Responsibility Act, 130
    and the Congressional Review Act, 127
    104th, 127
    105th, *iii*, 5, 6, 7, 135
    limits to power, 15
    tests of jurisdiction, 84–118
Congressional Responsibility Act of 1997, 130
Congressional Review Act, 126, 127, 128
Connecticut, 179
conservatives, 8, 10, 66, 98
    and libertarians, 4, 34
    and constitutional interpretation, 34, 87
    and textualism, 4, 53, 61, 96
    see also textualism
Constitution
    amendments to (new), 21
    Article I, 19, 20, 61, 85, 99, 121, 129, 137, 179, 180, 181, 157
    Article II, 86, 163
    Article III, 59, 165
    Article IV, 20, 22, 59, 63, 165
    Article VI, 20, 86, 88, 166
    Bankruptcy Clause, 20
    Bill of Rights, 29, 30, 73, 147, 140
    checks and balances, 36, 43
    Coinage Clause, *see* coinage / currency powers

Index

Commerce Clause, *see* Commerce Clause, Dormant Commerce Clause
Contract Clause, *see* Contract Clause
and the Constitutional Rights Test, 84, 87–90
and a new convention to amend it, *see* constitutional convention
and the delicate balance of powers, iv, 23, 25, 52, 100
and differing interpretations / visions, 51, 96
Due Process Clause, *see* Due Process Clause
and enumerated federal powers, iii, 52, 55, 85, 88, 91, 187
Equal Protection Clause, 9, 63, 89
ex post facto, *see ex post facto* laws
Fifth Amendment, *see* Fifth Amendment
first principles, ii, iv, 7
Fourteenth Amendment, *see* Fourteenth Amendment
framework for federalism, ii, iv, 13, 18, 59
Guarantee Clause, 22
interpretation of, 4, 5–12, 49, 52, 96, 100
and literal reading of, 48, 180
    see also strict textual analysis
"living," 48
Ninth Amendment, *see* Ninth Amendment
patents and copyrights, 20, 88
privileges and immunities, *see* Privileges and Immunities Clause
Seventeenth Amendment, *see* Seventeenth Amendment
Supremacy Clause, *see* Supremacy Clause
"supreme law of the land," 88
Takings Clause, *see* Takings Clause
Tenth Amendment, *see* Tenth Amendment
text of, *see* Appendix II, 157–178
two-tiered test for federal involvement, 13, 84–118
see also economic liberty
see also federalism, Framers
Constitutional Caucus, 45
constitutional convention
    Constitutional Convention, 15, 16, 17, 19, 77, 119
    and wisdom of calling another one, 14, 120–121, 123, 124
Constitutional Rights Test, 84, 87–90
consumer choice, 132, 146
Contract Clause, 9, 20, 65, 69, 70, 75, 98, 187
Contract With America, 5, 6
Cooley Doctrine of selective exclusiveness, 27, 182
Cooley v. Board of Wardens of the Port of Philadelphia (1851), 27, 28, 58, 87–88, 182, 183

Cooper, Charles J., 124
Coppage v. Kansas (1915), 190
copyrights, 49
courts, 10, 74, 90, 96
    and judicial activism, 98
    see also Supreme Court
Cox, Representative Christopher, 114
Crandall, Robert, 113
credit unions, 116
crime, 12, 121, 179
    see also prisons
"current of commerce," 188, 195

D

Day, Justice William Rufus, 190
Dean Milk Co. v. City of Madison (1951), 107, 196
DeBow, Michael, 61
Declaration of Independence, 63, 146
defense, *see* national defense
Delaware, 181
delegation of authority, 67, 128–130, 192
delicate balance, *see* Constitution, federalism
democracy, 130
Democrats, 113
Department of Commerce, 87, 137
deposit insurance, 141
deregulation, v, 4, 10, 14, 53, 83, 95, 108, 109, 113, 114, 137, 138, 143
    see also industries, regulation
Detlefsen, Robert R., 93
devolution, 4, 5, 42, 53, 56, 62, 63, 121–122, 135
Distorting Subsidies Limitation Act of 1997, 135
District of Columbia, 130, 191
Domestic Policy Working Group on Federalism, 2, 4
Dormant Commerce Clause, 58–61, 96, 112, 181
Dorn, James A., 29, 101
dual sovereignty, 23, 28, 38, 46, 76, 99, 202
Dudley, Susan E., 127
due process, 29, 34, 69, 73, 190, 192
    substantive, 28, 30, 31, 33, 34, 64, 65, 75, 179, 183, 185, 188, 189, 191
Due Process Clause, 9, 29, 63, 75, 89, 170, 187
Dunlop, Becky Norton, vi
duties, 20, 85, 180, 149, 160, 162, 163

E

economic development, 132, 135
economic due process, *see* substantive due process
    see also economic freedom
economic factionalism, 134
economic freedom / liberty / rights, 4, 8, 9, 10, 11, 12, 13, 14, 19, 29, 30, 31, 34, 37, 53, 56, 59, 61, 64, 65, 67, 70, 73, 75, 77, 84–118, 94, 96, 134, 183, 190
    barriers to, *see* tariffs
economic war among the states, 133–137
economy, changes in, 119
education policy, 122
Edwards v. California (1941), 181
Egan, John G., 26, 81
Ehrlich, Walter, 28
electoral system, 39, 200
electricity industry, 1, 7, 12, 13, 81, 91–92, 95, 103, 105, 109, 113, 132, 139
    and federal deregulation efforts, 7, 10, 137
    and Electricity Regulatory Responsibility Matrix, 140
    and stranded cost recovery, 108, 139
electronic transactions, 7, 105
Ellig, Jerry, 113
embargoes, *see* trade
emergency broadcast services, 102
Endangered Species Act, 141
energy, 132
    and energy assistance, 139
enumerated powers, i, 19, 21, 23, 36, 49, 52, 55, 72, 85, 86, 88, 91, 187, 203, 204
environmental and natural resource concerns, 105, 122, 141, 142
    externalities, 105, 118, 143
    and Matching Principle, 117–118, 142
    policies, standards, regulations, 83, 101, 110, 139, 141
Environmental Protection Agency, 91
Epstein, Richard A., 17, 37, 38, 65, 70, 96, 102, 106, 119
Equal Protection Clause, 9, 29, 63, 89
Erdman Act of 1898, 188
Eskridge, William N., 26, 147
executive branch, 16, 85, 87
executive orders, 41
    Executive Order 12291, 207
    Executive Order 12372, 205
    Executive Order 12498, 207

Executive Order 12612 (1987), *ii, iii,* 41, 42, 43, 45, 87, 125, 126, 127, 128, 213
    text of, *see* Appendix IV, 203–208
Executive Order 12866, 213
Executive Order 12875, 213
Executive Order 13083 (1998), *i, ii, iii, iv,* 43, 44, 45, 125
    hearing on, *iii,* 44
    suspension of, *iv,* 44, 45
    text of, *see* Appendix V, 209–213
exports, *see* trade
ex post facto laws, 20, 65, 77, 88, 90, 179
    see also retroactive laws
externalities
    see network externalities
    see also environmental and natural resource concerns
extraterritorial jurisdiction, *see* jurisdictional disputes

F

factionalism, 16, 147
    see also protectionism
factories, 188
Fair Labor Standards Act of 1938, 195, 198, 200
Farber, Daniel A., 57, 78, 84, 104
farms, farmers, 195, 196, 201
    see also agricultural activity
Federal Communications Commission (FCC), 91, 102, 104
Federal Energy Regulatory Commission (FERC), 139
federal government, *i*
    enumerated powers, *see* enumerated powers
    checks or limits on, *iv,* 23
    devolution of powers and functions, *see* devolution
    preempting the states, *see* federal pre-emption
    and spending, 6
Federal Lottery Act of 1895, 187
federal mandates, 6
federal pre-emption of the states, *ii, iii,* 22, 23, 87, 88, 95, 100, 126, 130, 183, 193, 205, 206
    see federalism, jurisdictional disputes
Federal Register, ii, 6, 212
federalism
    backlash, 40
    commercial, 1–14
    competitive, 23
    conflicting visions of, *iv,* 3, 47–80
        Clinton's vs. Reagan's, *i, iii,* 43, 45, 125

Index

       libertarian vs. states' rights, 8–10, 54–75
       textualism vs. constructionism, 8, 11, 47
  defined, 2, 3
       textualism, 4, 5–13
            conservative, or states' rights, 8
            libertarian, 9, 66–67
       broad constructionism, 3, 11, 47
       state sovereignty, 8
       traditional interpretation, 3, 51
  and the delicate balance of powers, *see* balance of powers, Founding Fathers
  Domestic Policy Council Working Group on, 2, 41
  executive orders on, 41, 87
       see also executive orders
  Framers' / Founders' vision of, 10, 11, 12, 13, 26, 47, 56, 83–84, 88, 99, 119, 147, 192, 201, 203
  framework for, iv, 13, 14, 48, 50, 81–118
  fundamental principles of, v
  the "knockout blow" to, 38
  policymaking criteria, i–ii
  reform, 121
       tools for, 119–143
  steps for reviving, 13–14
  top-down, 48
  see also balance of powers, devolution, enumerated powers
Federalism Act of 1998, 126
Federalism Enforcement Act of 1998, 126
Federalism Policymaking Criteria, i–ii, 41, 42, 43, 127, 128, 204, 205–206, 210–211
Federalist Papers, 18, 19, 21, 22, 23, 63
Federal Reserve Bank of Minneapolis, 135
Federalist Society, 5
Ferejohn, John, 26, 147
Field, Justice Stephan J., 60, 64, 65, 69, 73, 75, 183, 184
  and *Slaughter-House* dissent, 31
Fifth Amendment, 7, 63, 89, 141, 170, 189, 190
financial services industry, 1, 10, 12, 13, 83, 92, 102, 105, 116, 132, 141
Finch, James, 85
First English Evangelical Lutheran Church of Glendale v. County of Los Angeles (1987), 89
first principles, constitutional, ii, iv
  see also Constitution
Fiske, John, 17
Fletcher v. Rhode Island, 182

235

Forte, David, 35
Founding Fathers / Framers, *iii*, 2, 11, 12
    and Articles of Confederation, 2, 15
    and delicate balance of constitutional powers, 10–14, 23, 26, 27, 28, 35, 37, 38, 46, 47, 55, 57, 68, 76, 147, 192, 203
    and interstate commerce, 19, 51, 99, 146
    see also federalism, originalism
Four Horsemen, 36, 70
Fourteenth Amendment, 9, 28, 29, 30, 31, 33, 34, 35, 59, 63, 64, 65, 67, 69, 73, 89, 98, 173, 183, 185, 186, 187, 188, 189, 190, 191–192
framework for determining federalism / jurisdiction, 18, 21, 81–118
franchise service markets, 134
free market, free trade, 11, 13, 56, 78, 147
    and local autonomy, 84
    see also GATT, NAFTA, trade
free speech, 89
freedom of contract, 33, 74, 77, 179, 185, 187, 188, 190, 191, 194
    see also Contract Clause
Fuller, Justice Melville Weston, 36, 101, 186

G

Garcia v. San Antonio Metro. Transit Authority (1985), 38, 39, 49, 55, 56, 97, 98, 199, 200, 201
GATT, *see* General Agreement on Tariffs and Trade
Gavora, Carrie J., 91
Gaziano, Todd, vi
Gellhorn, Ernest, 32, 33, 34
General Agreement on Tariffs and Trade (GATT), 56, 57
General Welfare Clause, 192
    see also Constitution
Genessee Chief v. Fitzhugh (1852), 27, 183
Gibbons v. Ogden (1824), 25, 26, 58, 180
Gingrich, Representative Newt, 5
Graglia, Lino A., 58
Gray, C. Boyden, 40
Great Depression, 192
Gregory v. Ashcroft (1991), 45, 46, 55, 147, 200–201
Greve, Michael, v
Guarantee Clause, 20
Gun-Free School Zones Act of 1990, 201
guns, *see* handguns

Index

Gunther, Gerald, 17, 23

H

Hall, Kermit L., 28
Hamilton, Alexander, 18, 147
Hammer v. Dagenhart (1918), 35, 101, 190, 195
handguns, 201, 202
Harlan, Justice John Marshall, 186, 189
Hayworth, Representative J. D., 45, 130
health care policy, public health, 9, 12, 69, 73, 83, 91, 107, 110
    see also police powers
Hellerstein, Walter, 133
The Heritage Foundation, v, vi, 5, 6, 35, 55, 76, 122, 124, 141
Higgs, Robert, 50
highways, 105, 122, 196
Historical Regulatory Forum Test, 84, 90–95
Hodge, Scott A., 122
Holmes, Oliver Wendell, 187–188
Holmes, Kim R., 55
Horowitz, Michael, 94
House Government Reform and Oversight Committee
    Subcommittee on Regulatory Affairs, *iii*, 44
H. P. Hood & Sons, Inc. v. DuMond (1949), 146, 196
Hudec, Robert E., 57, 78, 84, 104
Hudson River, 25, 180
Hughes, Justice Charles Evans, 189
Hunt v. Washington Apple Advertising Commission (1977), 110, 199
Hunter, Lawrence A., 40

I

Illinois, 32, 115, 185, 191, 196
immigration procedures, 49, 121, 122
Indiana Economic Development Council, 135
indirect effects test, 37, 38, 39, 111
individual liberty, rights, i, 14, 22, 23, 53, 66, 76, 78, 121, 146,
    147, 179, 183, 189
industrial policy, 132, 133, 135, 136, 137
industries, 1, 4, 81, 91, 102, 103, 105, 132, 146, 185, 192
    airlines, aviation, 1, 13, 94, 95, 103, 105, 113
    broadcast and cellular, 102, 103, 105
    clothing and apparel, 105
    computer, 1, 105
    electricity, 1, 2, 7, 10, 12, 13, 91–92, 95, 103, 105, 108–
        109, 113, 137
    and environmental regulation, 101, 105

financial services and securities, 1, 2, 10, 12, 13, 92, 102, 105, 116, 140–141
high-tech, 119, 143
highway construction, 105
insurance, 10, 83, 93, 94, 105, 116, 187
Internet, 2, 7, 10, 12, 13, 102, 105, 114–116
interactive services, 1
mail order businesses, 105
shipping, 1, 20, 27, 95, 105, 183
telecommunications, 92, 102, 105, 137–139
telephone, 102
transportation, 1, 12, 13, 105, 190, 196
on the wireless electromagnetic spectrum, 102, 114
Inman, Robert P., 147
Institute for Justice, 9, 66
instrumentalities of commerce, 26, 111, 180
   see also Commerce Clause, interstate commerce
insurance, insurance industry 10, 83, 94, 105, 141, 187
   see also auto choice
interactive services, 1
   see computer industry
intergovernmental affairs, 126
international diplomacy, 121, 122
international trade
   see trade
Internet, 2, 7, 10, 12, 13, 102, 105, 114–116
Internet Protection Act of 1997, 114
Internet Tax Freedom Act, 7, 114
interpretation, *see* Constitution
interstate commerce, 4, 8, 9, 12, 16, 19, 21, 25, 30, 40, 49, 53, 60, 78, 81–118, 121, 122, 123, 132, 180, 181, 184, 185, 187, 189, 194, 195, 200, 201, 202
   barriers to, 95, 99, 104, 192
   and definitional discrepancies, 36, 81, 201
   direct vs. indirect test of, 186, 192, 195
   and free flow of, 23, 72, 77, 123, 145, 191
   and jurisdictional two-tier tests, 13, 84–118
      Constitutional Rights Test, 84, 87–90
      Historical Regulatory Forum Test, 84, 90–95
      Interstate Commerce Test, 100–106
      National Need Test, 84, 87–90
      Practical Interpretory Considerations, 98–118
      Stare Decisis Considerations, 84, 95–98
      Substantial Interstate Spillover Test, 84, 106–112
      Technological Complexity Test, 85, 112–118

Index

nature of, 14, 102
and negative externalities, 84, 85, 106–112
see also Commerce Clause
Interstate Commerce Commission, 189
Iowa, 200

J

Jackson, Judge Robert H., 196
Jefferson, Thomas, ii, 204
Johnson, John W., 38
judicial precedents, 85, 183
see also stare decisis
judicial review, 126, 147, 208
jurisdiction, 4, 12, 14, 81, 83, 90, 100, 106, 112, 149
and responsibility for, 91, 106, 122, 125, 137, 146
and two-tier tests of, 13–14, 84–118
jurisdictional disputes, iv, 8, 13, 22, 56, 117, 122
just compensation, just cause, 7, 77, 89, 170
J. W. Hampton, Jr. & Co. v. U.S. (1928), 129

K

Kaiser, Daniel, 94
Kansas, 190
Kassel v. Consolidated Freightways Corp. (1981), 110, 111, 200
Kitch, Edmund W., 92

L

labor protections, 193
laissez-faire, 64, 188
land use, management of public lands, 101, 105, 122
see also zoning
Leboeuf, Jacques, 8, 57, 106, 107
Leo, Leonard, v
Levy, Leonard W., 19
libertarians, 4, 10, 62, 73, 75
and conservatives, 62
and constitutional interpretation, 11
and textualism, 4, 9, 63–75, 76, 88, 96
liberty of contract
see freedom of contract, individual liberty
License Cases (1847), 27
licensing laws, 33, 61
Lochner v. New York (1905), 33, 34, 74, 188
Lockean natural law theory, 179
Lopez, see United States v. Lopez
lottery tickets, 187
Louisiana, 30, 183, 187, 198

Low-Level Radioactive Waste Amendments of 1985, 201
Low v. *Austin*, 180
Lowi, Theodore, 129
Lucas v. South Carolina Coastal Council (1992), 89

M
Macedo, Stephan, 66
Macey, Jonathan R., 117, 142
Mackinac Center, 133
Madison, James, 18, 19, 21, 50, 99
mail order businesses, 83, 105, 115
Maine v. Taylor (1986), 110
Maltz, Earl M., 54
mandates, federal, 6, 45, 124
    see also Unfunded Mandates Reform Act
Manne, Henry G., 29, 101
manufacturing
    as distinct from production, 36
    see also commerce vs. manufacturing distinction
maritime, *see* navigation, trade
Marshall, Chief Justice John, 25, 26, 28, 58, 180, 181
Maryland, 180
Massachusetts, 108–109, 180, 182, 201
"Matching Principle" theory, 117–118, 142
    see also environmental and natural resource concerns
McCarthy, David J., 109
McConnell, Michael, 54
McConnell, Senator Mitch, 93
McCulloch v. Maryland (1819), 25, 179, 180
McIntosh, Representative David, 44
McLaughlin, Andrew C., 17
McReynolds, Justice James, 36
meat packing industry, 190
medical care, 122
Meese, Edwin III, vi, 16
Merritt, Deborah Jones, 39, 40
Michelin Tire Corporation v. Wages (1976), 180
milk industry, milk or dairy subsidies, 107, 195, 196, 201
Miller, Dan, 94
Miller III, James, 41
Minge, Representative David, 135, 136
minimum wage, 194, 195
mining, 193
Miniter, Richard, 67
Mississippi, 198

Index

Missouri, 184
Moffit, Robert E., 5, 124
monetary policy, system, 60, 88, 121, 122, 141, 154
monopolies, state-created, 33, 92, 134, 183
Moran, Representative James, 126
Morley, Felix, 146
Mugler v. Kansas (1887), 73, 74
Muller v. Oregon (1908), 34, 188, 191
multilateral trade agreements, 117
    see also trade
municipalities, 107, 136
Munn v. Illinois (1887), 30, 32, 33, 185, 191

N

NAFTA, see North American Free Trade Agreement
National Association of Counties, iv
National Association of Regulatory Utility Commissioners, 131, 132
National Bellas Hess, Inc. v. Illinois Department of Revenue (1967), 115
National Conference of Commissioners on Uniform State Laws, 130, 131, 132
National Conference of Mayors, 137
National Conference of State Legislators, iv, 137
national defense, national security, 85, 86, 88, 121, 160
National Governors' Association, iv, 137
National Industrial Recovery Act, 192
National League of Cities, iv, 38, 198, 200
National League of Cities v. Usery (1976), 38, 39, 198–199
national standards, uniformity, 42, 54, 182, 183, 184, 195, 196
natural law, natural rights, 29, 63, 179
navigation, 183
Nebbia v. New York (1934), 191
Necessary and Proper Clause, 180
Negative Commerce Clause, 57, 58
    see Dormant Commerce Clause,
negative externalities, 106, 112, 117
    Negative Externalities Test, 106–112
Nelson, William E., 29, 30, 32
network externalities, 95, 117, 118
New Deal, i, 30, 34, 35, 48, 62, 70, 92, 123, 128, 191, 192, 193, 201
    and the Four Horsemen, 70
    jurisprudence, 35, 40, 49, 65, 198, 200
New Energy Co. of Indiana v. Limbach (1988), 61

New Federalism, 40, 41
New Hampshire, 181
New Jersey, 199, 200
New State Ice Co. v. Liebmann (1932), 33, 65, 191
New York
    and milk price fixing, 107, 191, 192, 196
    and restrictions of working hours, 34, 188
    and steamboat monopoly, 25, 180
    and taxes on ship passengers, 182
New York v. Miln (1837), 27, 181
New York v. United States (1992), 45, 46, 50, 201, 202
Ninth Amendment, 22, 63, 171
N.L.R.B. v. Jones & Laughlin Steel Co. (1937), 37, 49, 97, 194
Nollan v. California Coastal Commission, 89
non-discrimination, *see* protectionism
Norris v. Boston, 182
North American Free Trade Agreement (NAFTA), 56
North Carolina, 199
North Dakota, 115
Northern Securities Co. v. United States (1904), 186, 187

O

Oakerson, Ronald J., 40
O'Connell, Jeffrey, 94
O'Connor, Justice Sandra Day, 46, 50, 55, 201
O'Driscoll, Gerald, v
Office of Management and Budget, 126
Ogg, Frederic A., 18
Oklahoma, 191
original intent, originalism, originalists, iii, 4, 51, 52, 53, 63, 83–84, 97, 106
    see textualism

P

Packers and Stockyards Act of 1921, 190
Passenger Cases (1849), 27, 182
patents (and copyrights), 20, 49, 88
Peckham, Judge Rufus, 74, 75, 188
Peirce v. New Hampshire, 182
Pennsylvania, 110, 182
    and regulation of port of Philadelphia, 27
Philadelphia v. New Jersey (1978), 110, 199
Pierce, Richard J., Jr., 32, 33, 34, 101, 106, 108
Pike v. Bruce Church, Inc. (1970), 72, 110, 196, 198
Pilon, Roger, v, 50, 51, 57

Index

police powers, 9, 11–12, 30, 31, 32, 34, 66, 69, 75, 76, 90, 104, 107, 132, 181, 183, 184, 185, 186, 187, 190, 196, 199
    and definitions of, 73–75, 110
    and "reasonableness standard," 31, 32, 34, 73, 186
pollution, 81, 93, 105, 117, 141
ports, 18, 27, 182
    see also shipping, trade
Powell, Justice Lewis F., 39, 40
Power Marketing Administrations, 139
pre-emption, see federal pre-emption
Prentice, Ezra Parmalee, 26, 81
Printz v. United States (1997), 45, 46, 118, 202
prisons, 122
privatization, 121
Privileges and Immunities Clause, 20, 29, 31, 59–60, 63, 64, 69, 75, 89, 98, 183, 165
probate law, 131
product labeling, 123, 141
product liability laws, 83
production, see manufacturing
prohibition of retroactive laws, see ex post facto laws
property rights, 7, 30, 66, 68, 69, 77, 89, 90, 118, 141, 179, 189, 170
protectionism, 58, 59, 92, 95, 99, 100, 111–112, 122, 133, 136, 141, 180, 190, 199, 200
    and Articles of Confederation, 56
    see also state-based protectionism, police powers
public interest doctrine, public interest standard, 32, 33, 110, 134, 185, 191, 198
public land management, 141
public safety, legislating, 9, 12, 69, 83, 110
    see also police powers
Public Service Commission, 139
public utilities, 131, 132, 191
Public Utilities Regulatory Policies Act of 1978 (PURPA), 139
Public Utility Commission, 139
Public Utility Holding Company Act of 1935 (PUHCA), 139
Puerto Rico, 130

Q

Quill Corp. v. North Dakota (1992), 115

R

railroads, railroad industry, 95, 105, 189, 196
Ray, P. Orman, 18
Raymond Motor Transportation, Inc. v. Rice (1978), 111

243

Reagan, President Ronald, 2, 4, 40, 41, 88, 126
    and definition of federalism, 2, 41
    see also Executive Order 12612
reasonableness standard, 31, 34, 73, 186
reciprocity, 117
Reconstruction era, 28, 64
Reed, Lawrence W., 133, 134, 137
Regan, Donald H., 111
regulation, ii, iv, 6, 12, 14, 19, 21, 32, 33, 35, 43, 44, 53, 65, 70, 78, 90–91, 100, 101, 104, 106, 110, 115, 128, 138, 146, 162, 183, 184, 185, 190, 191, 193, 195, 196, 199, 202, 203, 206, 211
    environmental, 85, 110, 142–43
    health and safety, 69–71, 83, 91, 110, 183, 186
    without representation, see anti-delegation
    see also deregulation
regulatory agencies, 128
Regulatory Responsibility Matrices, 137–143
    Electricity, 140
    Financial Services, 140
    Telecommunications, 139
Rehnquist, Chief Justice William, 78, 89, 110, 111, 198
Republicans, 5, 8, 10
    and Fourteenth Amendment, 30
    and libertarian textualism, 63
    and the 105th Congress, 5, 10
    see also Contract With America
retroactive laws, 77
    see also ex post facto laws
Rhode Island, 181
roads and highways, 105, 122
Roberts, Justice Owen, 192
Rolnick, Arthur J., 135
Roosevelt, President Franklin Delano, 36, 38, 192, 194
    and court-packing efforts, 36, 193
Rubenfield, Daniel L., 147
rule of law, 51

S

sanctions, unilateral trade, 83, 85
    see also trade
sanitation, 93
    see also public health
satellite transmissions, 114
Scalia, Justice Antonin, 52, 53, 57, 60–61, 72, 84, 98

Index

Scheiber, Harry N., 74
Schmahmann, David, 85
Schoenbrod, David, 129, 130
schools and school zones, 122
Schuck, Peter H., 5
Seay, Douglas, 5, 55, 76, 124
Second Agricultural Adjustment Act (1938), 37
Second Bank of the United States, 179
securities regulation, 102–103, 141, 161
selective exclusiveness, *see Cooley* Doctrine of
separation of powers, 129, 147, 201
    see also Constitution, federalism
Seventeenth Amendment, 21, 39
Sherman Antitrust Act of 1890, 186, 186
shipping industry, 1, 20, 27, 95, 105
Shreveport Rate Case (1914), 187, 189–190
Schriver, Melinda L., 91
Siegan, Bernard H., 17, 29, 65, 101
Slaughter-House Cases (1873), 30, 31, 33, 64, 65, 183, 184, 185
slavery, 29, 73, 181, 182
Small Business Regulatory Enforcement Fairness Act of 1996, 127
Smith, Wesley, 55, 76, 124
social compact theory, 179
South Carolina, 89, 110, 181, 194
South Carolina State Highway Department v. *Barnwell Brothers* (1938), 110, 194
Southern Pacific Co. v. *Arizona* (1945), 110, 111, 196
speed limit, 5
Stafford v. *Wallace* (1922), 190
standards, constitutional
    see public interest standard, reasonableness standard
stare decisis, 60, 84, 95–98
state-based protectionism, 16, 19, 21, 26, 50, 57, 58, 99, 100, 122, 135, 180
    and cross-subsidization mechanisms, 132
    and discriminatory laws, 85, 87, 100, 111, 117
    and economic war between the states, 18, 108
    and hidden taxes, 132
    see also Commerce Clause, federalism
state government, 4, 66, 198
    activities, 4
    and "grassroots tyranny," 69, 71
    jurisdiction, 4, 100, 103
        and auto insurance, 83, 94
    and police powers of, 9, 11–12, 30, 31, 32, 66, 69, 90

and protectionism, 100
and Senate appointments, 21
state legislators, 131
states' rights, 5, 9, 11, 54, 56, 62, 66
    absolutism, 56, 66, 77
state sovereignty, i, iii, 4, 11, 12, 14, 21, 28, 52, 76, 77, 104, 115, 119, 145, 147, 198, 201, 149, 204
    textualist view of, 4, 8, 9, 54–63, 76
state supremacy, i
Stone, Justice Harlan Fiske, 194
stranded cost recovery, 108, 109
subsidization, state mechanisms of, 133, 134, 136, 137
substantial spillover effects, 106, 108, 109, 115, 117
Substantial Spillover Test, 84, 106–112
substantive due process, *see* due process
sugar trust, 186
Superfund, 141
supermajority veto power, 123
Supremacy Clause, 20, 21, 85, 86, 88, 106, 180
Supreme Court, 24, 28, 32, 36, 57, 64, 91, 106, 146, 147, 161, 180
    and balancing tests, 105, 109
    cases, *see* Appendix III
    and Commerce Clause interpretation, 25, 35, 57, 59, 60, 81, 97, 100, 106
    and the New Deal, 36, 37, 38, 49, 191
Sutherland, Justice George, 36, 61, 65, 70, 73, 75, 191, 193
    see also Four Horsemen
Swift & Co. v. United States (1905), 35, 187, 190
Swift v. Tyson (1842), 27

T

Taebel, Delbert A., 41
takings, 77
Takings Clause, 63, 69
Taney, Chief Justice Roger Brooke, 26, 27, 28, 181
tariffs and economic barriers, 17, 18
Tauzin, Representative W. J. (Billy), 114
tax incentives, 133, 134, 136
tax jurisdictions, number of, 68
taxation, taxes, 6, 20, 68, 71, 81, 83, 91, 101, 102, 108, 115, 180, 181, 152, 157, 160, 162
    federal excise, 137
taxi dispatches, 102
Taylor, Jerry, 130

Technological Complexity, 112
technologies, *see* industries
Telecommunications Act of 1996, 103–104
telecommunications industry, 102, 105, 137
    and Telecommunications Regulatory Responsibility Matrix, 138, 139
telephone industry, 102
Tenth Amendment, ii, 5, 21, 22, 124, 171, 190, 193, 198
Tennessee Valley Authority (TVA), 90, 91, 139
term limits, 124
tests of constitutionality and jurisdiction, 13, 84–118
    Historic Regulatory Forum, 84, 90–95
    National Need, 84, 87–90
    Practical Interpretory Considerations, 98–118
    Strict Textual Analysis, 85–98
textualism, textualists, 4, 5–12, 13, 47, 51–79, 98, 120, 179, 192
    and constitutional interpretation, 11, 53, 88, 96, 192
    and divide between conservatives and libertarians, 4, 5–12, 53, 62
    on synthesizing the schools of thought, 76–79
    Textual Literalism Test, 86
    see also state sovereignty textualism
Thierer, Adam D., 109, 114, 115, 141
Thomas, Justice Clarence, 35, 36, 38, 58, 72, 104, 106
Thompson, David H., 124
Thompson, Senator Fred, iii, 44, 45, 126
Thurlow v. Massachusetts, 182
Toft, Graham S., 135, 136
tort system, 94
trade, 16, 17, 51, 60, 82, 84, 85, 86, 88, 117, 121, 184, 190, 198, 149, 153
    and duties, 180
    and economic barriers to, 55, 56, 196, 197
    sanctions, 83
    as subsequent to manufacture, 35
    and taxes, tariffs, 81
    see also GATT, industries, NAFTA
trains, *see* railroads
transportation industry, 1, 12, 13, 95, 105, 132, 184, 190, 196
treaty negotiations, 16, 121, 151, 152, 162, 164, 167
trucks, trucking industry, 95, 105, 194, 200

U

Unfunded Mandates Reform Act of 1995, 6, 124, 126, 127, 128
uniform state laws, 130, 131, 132

union membership, 189, 194
United State Advisory Commission on Intergovernmental Relations, 40
United States Conference of Mayors, iv
United States v. Darby (1941), 37, 49, 97, 195, 196
United States v. E. C. Knight Co. (1895), 36, 101, 106, 186, 187, 190
United States v. Lopez (1995), 8, 45, 46, 55, 58, 78, 104, 106, 110, 111, 201–202
U.S. Virgin Islands, 130

V

Vaiana, Mary, 94
Van Devanter, Justice Willis, 36
Vermont, 107, 192
veto power, 21, 123
Viscusi, W. Kip, 141
voluntary associations, 71
"voting with their feet," 49, 54, 101
vouchers, 124

W

wage and hour regulation, 38, 192, 193, 194, 195
Waite, Chief Justice Morrison, 32, 185
Washington Legal Foundation, 51, 123
Washington State, 110, 194, 199
waste disposal, 199
water, water quality, 77, 105, 132, 141
Webster, Daniel, 25
Wechsler, Herbert, 39
welfare reform, 5, 12
Welton v. State of Missouri (1875), 60, 184
West Coast Hotel Co. v. Parrish (1937), 194
West Lynn Creamery, Inc. v. Healy (1994), 61, 108–109, 201
Weston v. Charleston (1829), 25, 181
wetlands protection, 141
White, Representative Richard, 114
Wickard v. Filburn (1942), 37, 38, 49, 97, 195–196
Willson v. Black Bird Creek Marsh Co. (1829), 25, 181
Willkie II, Wendell L., 87, 88
wireless and wireline telephone, 102, 103, 105, 112, 114
Wisconsin, 107
Woodruff v. Parham (1869), 180
Wolfe, Christopher, 77, 78
Wyden, Senator Ron, 114

Y
"yellow dog contracts," 188–189, 190
Z
zoning laws, 33, 61, 66, 70, 77, 101, 103, 122, 138